Mind Machines

The New Era of Brain-Computer Interfaces

J.F. Thornton

Disclaimer Notice

Educational and Informational Purposes Only

The content of *MIND MACHINES: The New Era of Brain-Computer Interfaces* is provided for educational and informational purposes. The scientific information, technological developments, ethical analyses, and future projections presented are based on current research, expert interviews, and the author's investigative reporting, and are intended to inform public understanding of brain-computer interface technology.

No Medical or Investment Advice

This book does not provide medical advice, treatment recommendations, or investment guidance. The information about brain-computer interfaces, neural implants, and related medical devices is presented for educational purposes only and should not be construed as medical advice or endorsement of any specific treatments, procedures, or companies.

Rapidly Evolving Field

Brain-computer interface technology is advancing rapidly. Information about specific devices, companies, research findings, and regulatory statuses may become outdated between the time of writing and publication. Readers should consult current sources and qualified professionals for the most up-to-date information about BCI technologies and their applications.

Ethical and Social Considerations

The ethical frameworks, social implications, and policy recommendations presented represent the author's analysis and synthesis of various expert perspectives. These should be considered as contributions to ongoing societal discussions rather than definitive conclusions about complex moral and social questions that continue to evolve.

No Guarantee of Future Outcomes

While the book presents scenarios and projections about the future development of brain-computer interfaces, these are speculative analyses based on current trends and expert opinions. The actual development of BCI technology may differ significantly from any predictions or scenarios presented.

Personal Responsibility and Professional Consultation

Readers considering participation in BCI research, clinical trials, or medical treatments involving neural interfaces are strongly encouraged to consult with qualified healthcare professionals, bioethicists, and legal advisors. Decisions about medical procedures, research participation, or technology adoption should be made in consultation with appropriate professionals and based on individual circumstances.

Technology Risks and Safety

Brain-computer interfaces involve complex technologies with potential risks that are not fully understood. The book's discussion of these technologies should not be interpreted as minimizing potential dangers or encouraging participation in experimental procedures without proper medical supervision and informed consent.

Privacy and Security Considerations

The book discusses emerging privacy and security issues related to neural data and brain-computer interfaces. Readers should be aware that the privacy landscape for neural technologies is rapidly evolving and should seek current information about data protection when considering BCI applications.

International and Regulatory Variations

BCI regulations, availability, and ethical frameworks vary significantly across countries and jurisdictions. Information about regulatory approvals, legal frameworks, and available treatments may not apply to all regions. Readers should consult local authorities and professionals for region-specific information.

Acknowledgement of Understanding

By reading this book, you acknowledge that:

- You understand this book is for educational and informational purposes only

- You will not rely on this book as a substitute for professional medical, legal, financial, or other expert advice
- You accept full responsibility for how you choose to use and apply the information contained within
- You recognize that brain-computer interface technology involves complex scientific, ethical, and social considerations that require consultation with qualified professionals
- Your use of this publication signifies that you have read, understood, and agreed to this disclaimer

Table of Contents

Introduction

Jan Scheuermann sits motionless in her wheelchair, her body rendered immobile by spinocerebellar degeneration, a cruel disease that has systematically severed the connections between her mind and muscles. But her eyes sparkle with anticipation as she stares at the robotic arm positioned beside her. Two small sensors, each no larger than a shirt button, have been implanted in her motor cortex, the brain region that once commanded her paralyzed limbs. Now they listen to the electrical whispers of neurons that still fire with intention, still dream of movement.

"Just think about reaching," says the researcher. "Imagine you're moving your own arm toward the chocolate."

Jan closes her eyes and concentrates. For a moment, nothing happens. Then, slowly, impossibly, the robotic arm begins to move. It extends forward with fluid grace, its mechanical fingers opening to grasp a piece of chocolate from the table. As Jan guides it back toward her mouth, thinking *up, closer, careful now* her face breaks into a radiant smile.

"Oh my God," she whispers as the robotic fingers place the chocolate gently between her lips. After nearly fifteen years of paralysis, Jan has fed herself again. Not with her biological hands, which remain motionless in her lap, but with synthetic limbs controlled by the pure force of intention. The boundary between mind and machine has dissolved, replaced by a new kind of embodiment that transcends the limitations of flesh and bone.

This moment, captured in a Pittsburgh research laboratory in 2012, represents more than a medical breakthrough. It represents humanity's first meaningful step across the neural frontier, the boundary between biological consciousness and artificial extension, between the mind as we have always known it and the mind as it might become.

The Promise

Jan's story is just the beginning. In laboratories around the world, researchers are developing brain-computer interfaces that promise to revolutionize not just medicine, but human capability itself. Paralyzed patients are learning to control computer cursors with their thoughts, achieving typing speeds that rival healthy individuals. Stroke victims are regaining the ability to speak through devices that decode their intended words directly from neural signals. The blind are beginning to see again through artificial retinas that bypass damaged eyes entirely.

But these remarkable applications barely hint at the transformative potential that lies ahead. Scientists are developing neural interfaces that could enhance memory, allowing us to recall information with photographic precision. Brain-to-brain communication systems could enable direct sharing of thoughts and experiences, making telepathy a technological reality rather than a fantasy. Cognitive augmentation tools could expand human intelligence beyond biological limitations, helping us solve problems that have puzzled our species for millennia.

Imagine students downloading new languages directly into their brains, mastering Mandarin or calculus in a matter of hours rather than years. Picture scientists sharing insights not through clumsy words and symbols, but through direct neural connection, accelerating discovery at unprecedented rates. Envision a world where depression and anxiety respond to precisely calibrated neural interventions, where age-related cognitive decline becomes optional rather than inevitable, where the accumulated wisdom of human civilization becomes directly accessible to any mind willing to connect.

These possibilities are not distant science fiction fantasies. The fundamental technologies already exist in primitive forms, tested successfully in animals and early human trials. The trajectory of development points toward increasingly sophisticated applications that will arrive not in centuries, but in decades, perhaps within the working lifetimes of today's college students.

The Peril

Yet with each advance across the neural frontier, we venture into territory fraught with unprecedented dangers. The same technologies that could liberate us from biological limitations could also enslave us to new forms of control and manipulation. The brain-computer interfaces designed to restore human capability could ultimately be used to monitor, modify, and control human consciousness itself.

Consider the implications of neural surveillance. If devices can decode our intentions to move robotic limbs, might they also decode our private thoughts, our secret desires, our political beliefs? Could authoritarian governments use neural interfaces to create the ultimate panopticon, monitoring dissent not just through external behavior but through direct access to internal mental states? The thought police of dystopian fiction may seem tame compared to systems that could literally police thoughts themselves.

Or consider the specter of cognitive inequality. If neural enhancement becomes available primarily to those who can afford it, we risk creating new forms of discrimination based not on race or class, but on cognitive capability itself. Enhanced individuals might dominate education, employment, and positions of power, relegating the unenhanced to second-class citizenship in a world optimized for augmented minds.

Perhaps most troubling is the question of authenticity and identity. If our memories can be modified, our personalities adjusted, and our decision-making processes augmented by artificial intelligence, what happens to the essential self? Are we still fully human if significant portions of our mental lives depend on technological systems? Do our enhanced achievements truly belong to us, or to the algorithms that made them possible?

These are not merely philosophical puzzles, they are practical challenges that will require concrete answers as neural technology advances. The decisions we make about brain-computer interfaces in the coming decades will shape not just individual lives, but the trajectory of human civilization itself.

The Inflection Point

We stand today at a unique moment in human history. For the first time since our species emerged from the African savanna, we possess the tools to consciously direct our own cognitive evolution. The random mutations and environmental pressures that shaped our minds over millions of years are giving way to deliberate technological interventions that could transform human consciousness within a single generation.

This transition from natural to directed evolution represents a phase change comparable to the agricultural revolution or the development of written language. Like those earlier transitions, it promises tremendous benefits but also unprecedented risks. Unlike those earlier transitions, it offers us the opportunity to shape our own transformation consciously and deliberately, if we choose to do so.

The window for conscious choice, however, may not remain open indefinitely. Neural technology is advancing rapidly, driven by competitive pressures, humanitarian needs, and the inexorable logic of scientific progress. As brain-computer interfaces become more powerful and widespread, the options for alternative development paths may narrow. The decisions we make today about research priorities, ethical frameworks, and regulatory approaches will echo through history.

We are perhaps the last generation to experience purely biological consciousness, and quite possibly the first to consciously direct the evolution of human cognition. This unique position comes with extraordinary responsibility. The choices we make about neural technology will influence not just our own lives, but the lives of our children, grandchildren, and descendants stretching far into the future.

The Journey Ahead

This book is an exploration of that choice, a journey across the neural frontier to examine both the extraordinary promise and the profound peril of brain-computer interfaces. It is a story told through the experiences of remarkable individuals like Jan Scheuermann, whose courage in volunteering for experimental treatments has opened new possibilities for millions of people facing paralysis, depression, blindness, and other conditions that limit human potential.

But it is also a story of scientists and engineers pushing the boundaries of what's possible, entrepreneurs transforming laboratory discoveries into commercial applications, ethicists grappling with unprecedented moral questions, and policymakers trying to govern technologies that evolve faster than regulations can adapt.

We will explore the scientific foundations that make neural interfaces possible, from the discovery of brain electricity to the development of machine learning algorithms that can decode human intentions. We will meet the visionaries whose bold ideas are reshaping our understanding of the mind-machine boundary, and the patients whose participation in clinical trials is turning science fiction into medical reality.

We will examine the technical challenges that researchers face in building reliable, safe, and effective brain-computer interfaces, from the fundamental problem of extracting meaningful signals from noisy neural data to the practical challenges of creating devices that can survive in the corrosive environment of the human brain for decades.

Perhaps most importantly, we will confront the ethical and social implications of neural enhancement head-on. What happens to human agency when our choices are influenced by algorithmic suggestions? How do we preserve privacy when our thoughts become digital data? What does it mean to be human when our minds are augmented by artificial intelligence?

These questions have no easy answers, but they demand our urgent attention. The neural revolution is not waiting for us to resolve these dilemmas, it is advancing regardless of whether we address them thoughtfully or ignore them until they become crises.

A Participatory Future

The future of brain-computer interfaces will not be determined solely by scientists in laboratories or executives in boardrooms. It will be shaped by the choices of ordinary people, patients deciding whether to participate in clinical trials, parents considering cognitive enhancement for their children, voters supporting research funding and regulatory frameworks, consumers choosing which neural technologies to adopt.

This distributed decision-making process offers both hope and concern. Hope, because it means that the development of neural technology can reflect democratic values and diverse perspectives rather than narrow technical or commercial interests. Concern, because it requires an informed public capable of engaging with complex technical and ethical issues.

The decisions ahead are too important to be left to experts alone, but too complex to be made without expert input. They require a new kind of public engagement that combines scientific literacy with ethical reflection, technical understanding with humanistic wisdom.

This book aims to contribute to that engagement by making the world of brain-computer interfaces accessible to readers who are not neuroscientists or engineers, but who will be affected by the choices made about neural technology. It seeks to bridge the gap between laboratory research and public understanding, between technical possibility and social implication, between what we can do and what we should do.

The Choice Before Us

As Jan Scheuermann demonstrated when she used thought alone to guide that robotic arm toward the chocolate, the neural frontier is not a distant destination, it is a boundary we are already crossing. Each new brain-computer interface, each successful clinical trial, each breakthrough in neural decoding takes us further into territory where the traditional boundaries between mind and machine, self and technology, human and posthuman begin to blur.

The question is not whether we will continue across that frontier, the momentum of scientific progress, commercial opportunity, and human need makes that inevitable. The question is how we will navigate that crossing. Will we stumble blindly into a posthuman future shaped primarily by technological capability and market forces? Or will we chart our course deliberately, guided by our deepest values and highest aspirations?

The choice is ours to make, but only if we choose to make it consciously and collectively. The neural revolution requires not just technical innovation, but wisdom about human nature and careful consideration of the kind of species we want to become.

Jan's smile as she tasted that piece of chocolate, the joy of a person rediscovering agency after years of paralysis, reminds us of what's at stake. At its best, neural technology represents the triumph of human ingenuity over biological limitation, the extension of compassion through scientific capability, the fulfillment of our species' deepest aspiration to transcend suffering and expand possibility.

But that chocolate also represents something more, the first taste of a future in which the boundaries we have always taken for granted between mind and matter, self and technology, human and posthuman are dissolving before our eyes. Whether that future enhances or diminishes our humanity will depend on the wisdom we bring to choices that are no longer theoretical, but immediate and urgent.

The neural frontier awaits. The question is not whether we will cross it, but who we will choose to become on the other side.

Part I: The Foundation

Chapter 1

Decoding the Electric Brain

The dead frog's leg twitched.

It was 1780, and Luigi Galvani was dissecting frogs in his laboratory at the University of Bologna when he made the observation that would forever change our understanding of life itself. As his metal scalpel touched the frog's spinal nerve while the animal lay on a brass plate, the leg convulsed as if the creature had suddenly returned to life. What Galvani witnessed was not resurrection, but revelation, the nervous system operated on electricity.

For centuries, philosophers and physicians had puzzled over the mechanism of thought and movement. How did the mind command the body? What invisible force carried intentions from brain to muscle? Some proposed flowing spirits, others mysterious vapors. None suspected that the answer crackling through every synapse was the same force that split the sky during thunderstorms.

Galvani called it "animal electricity," and though his understanding was incomplete, his discovery illuminated a profound truth: our thoughts, emotions, and movements all arise from electrical signals dancing through networks of neurons. Every memory you form, every decision you make, every word you speak begins as a cascade of electrical impulses racing through the three-pound universe inside your skull.

This electrical nature of the brain would prove to be the key that eventually unlocked the possibility of brain-computer interfaces. But the path from Galvani's twitching frog legs to today's thought-controlled robotic arms would span nearly two and a half centuries of painstaking discovery.

The Architecture of Thought

To understand how we learned to decode the electric brain, we must first understand what we discovered about its architecture. The human brain contains roughly 86 billion neurons, more than ten times the number of stars in our galaxy. Each neuron connects to thousands of others through synapses, creating a network of staggering complexity, approximately 100 trillion connections in total.

Yet for all this complexity, the basic operating principle of each neuron is elegantly simple. Like a biological battery, every neuron maintains an electrical charge across its membrane. In its resting state, the inside of the cell is negatively charged relative to the outside, typically about 70 millivolts difference. This may seem tiny compared to the 1.5 volts of an AA battery, but at the cellular scale, it represents an enormous electrical field.

When a neuron receives sufficient stimulation from its neighbors, something remarkable happens. Channels in the cell membrane suddenly open, allowing positively charged sodium ions to rush inside. This influx of positive charge causes the neuron's voltage to spike dramatically, shooting from -70 millivolts to +40 millivolts in less than a millisecond. This spike, called an action potential, races down the neuron's axon like a fuse burning toward an explosive.

The nineteenth-century physiologists who first recorded these action potentials were astounded by their consistency. Unlike the variable currents in early electrical circuits, neural spikes followed an all-or-nothing principle. Each action potential had the same magnitude and duration, regardless of how strongly the neuron was stimulated. The information wasn't encoded in the size of the spike, but in the timing and pattern of multiple spikes.

This discovery was crucial for the eventual development of brain-computer interfaces. It meant that the electrical language of the brain, while incredibly complex in its patterns, was digital in nature, composed of discrete, measurable events that could potentially be decoded by machines.

Listening to the Brain's Symphony

The next breakthrough came from an unexpected source, a German psychiatrist named Hans Berger who was obsessed with telepathy. In the 1920s, Berger believed that if thoughts were electrical, they might generate fields that could be detected outside the skull. While his motivation was misguided, he hoped to prove that human minds could communicate directly, his methodology was sound.

Berger placed metal electrodes on the scalps of his patients and connected them to a sensitive galvanometer borrowed from the physics department. What he recorded on July 6, 1924, changed neuroscience forever, regular, rhythmic waves of electrical activity emanating from the living human brain. He called it an electroencephalogram, or EEG.

The patterns Berger observed were mesmerizing. When his subjects were awake and alert, the recordings showed rapid, low-amplitude fluctuations, like the visual representation of static. But when they closed their eyes and relaxed, slower, more organized waves emerged, rolling across the paper at about 10 cycles per second. These became known as alpha waves, the brain's idle rhythm.

Berger's early EEG recordings were crude by today's standards, but they proved something profound, the brain's electrical activity could be monitored from outside the skull. The implications were staggering. For the first time in human history, scientists could observe the living brain in action without opening the skull or causing any harm to the patient.

The medical community initially greeted Berger's work with skepticism. How could such tiny electrical signals, mere microvolts in amplitude travel through the skull and scalp to be detected by external electrodes? The answer lay in the collective nature of neural activity. While individual neurons fire independently, groups of neurons often synchronize their activity, creating electrical fields strong enough to penetrate the brain's protective barriers.

By the 1930s, neurologists around the world were using EEG to diagnose epilepsy, brain tumors, and other neurological conditions. The brain's electrical patterns, once hidden and mysterious, had become a medical window into the mind's inner workings.

The Birth of Signal Processing

As EEG technology matured, researchers began to realize that different mental states produced characteristic electrical signatures. Deep sleep generated slow, high-amplitude delta waves. REM sleep brought rapid, chaotic patterns resembling wakefulness. Focused attention created beta waves, while meditation enhanced alpha rhythms.

But the real breakthrough came when researchers discovered that specific mental tasks generated distinctive patterns that could be reliably detected and classified. In the 1960s, researchers found that imagining movement of the left hand produced different EEG patterns than imagining movement of the right hand. Even more remarkably, these patterns appeared in the motor cortex even when no actual movement occurred, the brain's electrical activity reflected the intention to move, not just the movement itself.

This observation was revolutionary. It suggested that the brain's electrical signals contained information about a person's intentions, not just their actions. If scientists could decode these intention signals reliably, they might be able to create devices that responded to thought alone.

The challenge was enormous. Unlike the clean, predictable signals that engineers work with in electronic circuits, brain signals are buried in noise, constantly changing, and individually unique. Each person's brain generated slightly different patterns, even when performing identical tasks. The same person might produce different signals on different days, depending on their mood, attention level, or fatigue.

To make matters worse, the skull acted like a low-pass filter, attenuating high-frequency signals and blurring the spatial resolution of EEG recordings. Signals from deep brain structures were nearly impossible to detect from the scalp, and the exact location of signal sources could only be estimated using complex mathematical models.

Despite these challenges, researchers pressed forward, developing increasingly sophisticated methods for extracting meaningful information from the brain's electrical cacophony. They borrowed techniques from other fields such as signal processing methods developed for radar and telecommunications, statistical analysis tools from psychology, and pattern recognition algorithms from early artificial intelligence research.

The Rise of Invasive Recording

While EEG provided valuable insights into brain function, its limitations drove some researchers to take a more direct approach, placing electrodes directly on or in the brain tissue itself. This invasive recording, though requiring surgery and carrying significant risks, offered unprecedented access to neural signals.

In 1969, Eberhard Fetz at the University of Washington achieved a milestone that would echo through the decades of BCI research that followed. Working with macaque monkeys, he showed that individual neurons in the motor cortex could be trained to control external devices. By providing audio feedback, he taught monkeys to consciously increase or decrease the firing rate of single neurons to move a meter needle. For the first time, the gap between neural activity and external control had been bridged at the level of individual brain cells.

Fetz's experiments revealed something profound about the brain's plasticity. Neurons that normally fired in response to arm movements could learn new patterns when provided with appropriate feedback. The brain, it seemed, was remarkably adaptable, capable of learning to control not just biological limbs but artificial devices as well.

The implications were staggering. If individual neurons could learn to control external devices, perhaps networks of neurons could be trained to operate more complex systems. Perhaps, researchers dared to imagine, the paralyzed could regain control over their environment through direct neural interface.

But recording from individual neurons presented its own challenges. The electrodes had to be incredibly small, finer than human hair and positioned with microscopic precision. The brain's immune system often attacked the foreign objects, encasing them in scar tissue that gradually degraded signal quality. Many implants failed within months or years as the tissue reaction grew too severe.

Moreover, the brain existed in a constant state of motion, expanding and contracting with each heartbeat, shifting with changes in blood pressure, swelling and shrinking with inflammation. These tiny movements, imperceptible to the naked eye, could displace delicate electrodes enough to lose contact with their target neurons entirely.

Despite these obstacles, invasive recording revealed the richness of information encoded in neural signals. Researchers discovered that individual neurons in the motor cortex carried information not just about whether a movement would occur, but about the direction, speed, and force of intended movements. Groups of neurons working together created population vectors that could predict movement parameters with remarkable accuracy.

The Digital Revolution Meets Neuroscience

The development of practical brain-computer interfaces required more than just an understanding of neural signals, it demanded the computational power to process those signals in real time. The digital revolution of the 1970s and 1980s provided the missing piece of the puzzle.

Early computers had been room-sized behemoths, far too large and expensive for neuroscience laboratories. But as microprocessors became more powerful and affordable, researchers gained access to the computational tools needed to analyze neural signals in unprecedented detail. Digital signal processing, once the exclusive domain of aerospace and telecommunications engineers, became a standard tool in neuroscience laboratories.

The transformation was remarkable. Where earlier researchers had been limited to observing neural signals on oscilloscope screens or chart recorders, the new generation could apply sophisticated mathematical algorithms to extract patterns invisible to the human eye. Fast Fourier transforms revealed the frequency content of neural signals. Correlation analysis identified relationships between different brain regions. Machine learning algorithms began to automatically classify different types of neural activity.

Perhaps most importantly, digital computers made real-time processing possible. For the first time, researchers could analyze incoming neural signals and immediately translate them into control commands for external devices. The feedback loop between thought and action, broken by paralysis or neurological damage, could potentially be restored through artificial means.

The convergence of neuroscience and computer science created a new field of study. Researchers began to think of the brain not just as a biological organ, but as an information processing system that could potentially interface with artificial information processing systems. The boundary between mind and machine started to blur.

The Promise and the Challenge

As the twentieth century drew to a close, all the pieces seemed to be falling into place for practical brain-computer interfaces. Scientists understood the electrical basis of neural communication. They had developed techniques for recording neural signals both invasively and non-invasively. Digital computers provided the processing power needed to analyze these signals in real time. And most importantly, researchers had demonstrated that both individual neurons and neural networks could learn to control external devices.

Yet significant challenges remained. The brain's signals were still noisy and variable. Long-term stability of invasive electrodes remained elusive. The computational demands of real-time neural decoding pushed even the most powerful computers to their limits. And the biological and technological systems seemed to operate according to fundamentally different principles.

The brain was wet, warm, and salty, a challenging environment for electronic devices designed for the dry, clean conditions of computer circuits. Biological systems evolved through millions of years of natural selection, creating robust but complex solutions to computational problems. Artificial systems were engineered according to logical principles, creating efficient but fragile solutions.

Bridging this gap between biological and artificial systems would require innovations not just in neuroscience and engineering, but in materials science, computer science, and medicine. It would demand new kinds of electrodes that could survive in the brain's hostile environment, new algorithms that could adapt to the brain's ever-changing patterns, and new surgical techniques that could safely implant devices in the most precious organ in the human body.

But the potential rewards were extraordinary. For the millions of people living with paralysis, the prospect of controlling computers, wheelchairs, or robotic arms through thought alone offered hope for unprecedented independence. For researchers studying the brain, direct neural interfaces promised insights into the nature of consciousness, decision-making, and human cognition.

As the new millennium approached, the stage was set for the next chapter in the story of brain-computer interfaces. The fundamental principles had been established, the basic technologies had been developed, and a new generation of researchers was ready to turn the promise of mind-controlled machines into reality.

The electric brain that Galvani first glimpsed in his twitching frog legs was about to reveal its deepest secrets and humanity was about to take its first tentative steps toward a future where the boundary between mind and machine would become increasingly difficult to define.

In laboratories around the world, researchers were preparing for experiments that would push the boundaries of both neuroscience and technology. They would soon discover that the brain's electrical language, refined through millions of years of evolution, was more sophisticated and more adaptable than anyone had dared to imagine.

The age of brain-computer interfaces was about to begin.

Chapter 2

The First Connections

The bull charged across the arena with murderous intent, its massive head lowered, horns gleaming in the Spanish afternoon sun. The matador stood motionless in its path, cape abandoned, arms at his sides. Death seemed inevitable.

Then José Delgado pressed a button on his radio transmitter.

The bull skidded to a halt just feet from the Spanish neurophysiologist, its charge broken not by fear or fatigue, but by a thin wire electrode implanted deep in its brain. With a simple electronic signal, Delgado had reached across the gap between mind and machine, overriding millions of years of bovine evolution with the press of a button.

The year was 1963, and the demonstration at a ranch in Córdoba would become one of the most famous and controversial moments in the history of brain research. For the first time, the world witnessed direct, wireless control of a living brain. The implications were both thrilling and terrifying. If thoughts could be controlled from a distance, what did that mean for human freedom and dignity?

But Delgado's dramatic bull-stopping experiment was just one milestone in a decade that would see the birth of practical brain-computer interfaces. The 1960s marked humanity's first serious attempts to create functional connections between minds and machines, efforts that would lay the groundwork for every BCI breakthrough that followed.

The Mind Controller

José Manuel Rodríguez Delgado was not your typical neuroscientist. Born in Spain but working primarily at Yale University, he possessed a flair for the dramatic that matched his ambitious vision of technologically mediated mind control. While his colleagues were content to study the brain from the outside, Delgado wanted to reach inside and take direct command.

His tool was elegantly simple, thin metal wires, barely thicker than human hair, inserted through small holes drilled in the skull and positioned with millimeter precision in specific brain regions. These electrodes could both stimulate neurons with tiny electrical pulses and record their activity. Delgado called his implantable devices "stimoceivers", a portmanteau of stimulator and receiver that reflected their dual function.

The results of his experiments were unlike anything the scientific world had seen. Electrical stimulation of the hypothalamus could trigger immediate rage or profound calm. Activation of certain limbic structures caused laboratory animals to repeatedly perform complex behaviors, pressing levers, climbing poles, or engaging in elaborate courtship rituals. Most remarkably, stimulation of motor areas could cause precise, coordinated movements that appeared completely natural to observers.

In one famous experiment, Delgado implanted a mother monkey with electrodes in her motor cortex. When he activated the stimulator, she would immediately abandon her infant and walk to the opposite side of the cage, a behavior so contrary to maternal instincts that it shocked even experienced researchers. When the stimulation stopped, she would rush back to comfort her confused offspring, apparently unaware of what had just transpired.

But it was the bull experiment that captured the world's attention. Working with a breed known for its aggression, Delgado had implanted an electrode in the animal's caudate nucleus, a brain region involved in motor control and behavioral inhibition. The wireless stimulator he carried was primitive by today's standards, a bulky radio transmitter with vacuum tubes and a range of only a few hundred yards. Yet it was sufficient to demonstrate a principle that would echo through decades of BCI research, the brain could be controlled remotely through artificial interfaces.

The media response was explosive. Life magazine featured Delgado on its cover, depicting him as either humanity's savior or its most dangerous man. Popular science writers speculated about a future of mind-controlled soldiers and wirelessly managed citizens. Science fiction authors found new inspiration for dystopian futures where human agency became obsolete.

Yet Delgado himself was deeply thoughtful about the implications of his work. In his 1969 book "Physical Control of the Mind," he argued that understanding the brain's control mechanisms was essential for treating mental illness and enhancing human capabilities. But he also warned against the potential for abuse, calling for careful ethical oversight of neurotechnology development.

His work established several principles that remain central to modern BCI research. First, that precise control of neural activity was possible through carefully positioned electrodes. Second, that brain stimulation could modify not just simple reflexes but complex behaviors and emotional states. Third, wireless communication with implanted devices was technically feasible. And finally, that such power demanded serious consideration of ethical boundaries.

Restoring the Senses

While Delgado was exploring the brain's control centers, other researchers were pursuing a different vision of brain-machine interfaces, one focused not on controlling behavior but on restoring lost capabilities. The most promising target was the auditory system, where researchers were beginning to understand how the brain processes sound.

The human ear is an exquisite biological transducer, converting sound waves into electrical signals that the brain can interpret. Hair cells in the cochlea, the ear's spiral-shaped inner chamber detect different frequencies and transmit this information via the auditory nerve to the brainstem and ultimately to the auditory cortex. When these hair cells are damaged or destroyed, the result is sensorineural hearing loss, affecting millions of people worldwide.

In the 1960s, William House, an otologic surgeon in Los Angeles, proposed a radical solution to bypass the damaged hair cells entirely by stimulating the auditory nerve directly with electrical pulses. The concept seemed almost impossibly ambitious. How could crude electrical stimulation replicate the subtle, frequency-specific signals that healthy hair cells provided?

House's first cochlear implant was implanted in 1961 in a patient who had lost his hearing due to acoustic trauma. The device was primitive, a single electrode that delivered trains of electrical pulses directly to the auditory nerve. The patient couldn't understand speech or recognize melodies, but he could detect environmental sounds and even distinguish between different types of noise.

More importantly, he could hear.

The early results were modest but encouraging. Patients reported that the implants helped them with lip reading, allowing them to synchronize visual cues with auditory information. They could detect approaching cars, ringing telephones, and barking dogs, sounds that provided crucial safety information and social connection.

But House's most significant contribution wasn't the technology itself, it was the proof of principle. He demonstrated that the nervous system could accept and interpret artificial electrical signals. The brain, it seemed, was remarkably adaptable, capable of learning to extract meaning from patterns of stimulation that bore little resemblance to natural neural activity.

This plasticity would prove crucial for all future BCI development. Unlike digital computers, which require exact inputs to function properly, biological systems could work with approximations, gradually learning to interpret new types of signals through experience and adaptation.

The cochlear implant field progressed rapidly through the 1970s and 1980s. Researchers developed multi-channel devices that could stimulate different portions of the auditory nerve, providing crude frequency discrimination. Signal processing algorithms became increasingly sophisticated, extracting important acoustic features and converting them into patterns of electrical stimulation.

By the 1990s, cochlear implants had evolved from experimental curiosities to standard medical treatments. Children born deaf could learn to speak normally if implanted early enough. Adults who lost their hearing could return to telephone conversations and music appreciation. The technology had successfully bridged the gap between the acoustic world and the electrical language of the nervous system.

The cochlear implant's success provided a template for other sensory prostheses. If hearing could be restored through direct neural stimulation, perhaps vision could be as well. Researchers began developing retinal implants, devices that bypassed damaged photoreceptors by stimulating retinal ganglion cells directly. While progress was slower than with hearing, vision requires processing far more complex information, the basic principle remained the same.

The Pentagon's Interest

The military applications of brain-computer interfaces were obvious from the beginning. An agency tasked with maintaining America's technological edge could hardly ignore the potential of technologies that promised superhuman capabilities or new forms of weapons systems.

The Defense Advanced Research Projects Agency (DARPA) had been created in 1958 in response to the Soviet launch of Sputnik, with a mandate to ensure that America would never again be surprised by technological breakthroughs. When reports of Delgado's mind-control experiments began circulating in the early 1960s, DARPA program managers took notice.

The agency's initial interest focused on the darker applications of neurotechnology. Could enemy soldiers be incapacitated through remote brain stimulation? Could captured personnel be made to reveal secrets through precisely applied neural interventions? Could the performance of American troops be enhanced through technological augmentation of their cognitive abilities?

DARPA's classified neuroscience programs in the 1960s and 1970s explored all these possibilities. Working with researchers at universities and defense contractors, the agency investigated techniques for remote neural monitoring, chemical methods for memory enhancement and suppression, and electromagnetic approaches to influencing brain function.

Most of these early programs yielded disappointing results. The brain's complexity proved far greater than military planners had anticipated. The individual variability in neural responses made it impossible to develop standardized "weapons" that would work reliably across different targets. The ethical concerns raised by such research created political problems that hindered development.

But DARPA's investment in basic neuroscience research proved invaluable for the field's long-term development. Agency funding supported pioneering work in neural recording techniques, signal processing algorithms, and brain stimulation technologies. Academic researchers who might never have secured traditional grants found support for ambitious, high-risk projects that established the foundation for modern BCIs.

Perhaps more importantly, DARPA's involvement legitimized neurotechnology research as a serious scientific discipline. The agency's reputation for identifying transformative technologies attracted top researchers who might otherwise have pursued more conventional career paths. The interdisciplinary approach that DARPA encouraged bringing together neuroscientists, engineers, computer scientists, and clinicians became the standard model for BCI development.

By the 1970s, DARPA's focus had shifted from exotic mind-control weapons toward more practical applications. The agency began funding research into neural prosthetics for wounded veterans, communication systems for soldiers in high-noise environments, and cognitive enhancement technologies that could improve decision-making under stress.

This evolution reflected broader changes in how the scientific community viewed brain-computer interfaces. The early fantasies of total mind control gave way to more realistic goals of restoring function to the disabled and enhancing human capabilities within ethical boundaries.

Naming the Revolution

As the 1970s progressed, it became clear that the various efforts to connect minds and machines represented something new, a distinct field of research that deserved its own name and identity. The term that would eventually define this field came from an unexpected source, a computer scientist at UCLA who was studying how to help disabled individuals control computers more effectively.

Jacques Vidal had been working with paralyzed patients, exploring whether EEG signals could be used to operate simple computer programs. His approach was different from Delgado's invasive stimulation or House's sensory prosthetics. Instead of inserting devices into the brain, Vidal wanted to listen to neural signals from outside the skull and translate them into computer commands.

The technical challenges were enormous. EEG signals were weak, noisy, and highly variable. The skull and scalp severely attenuated neural signals and blurred their spatial resolution. The computational power available in the early 1970s was barely adequate for real-time signal processing. Yet Vidal was convinced that non-invasive brain-computer communication was possible.

In 1973, he published a paper that would prove historically significant not for its technical contributions, but for its terminology. Vidal coined the phrase "brain-computer interface" to describe his vision of direct communication pathways between the brain and external devices. The term was broader than previous concepts like "neural prosthetics" or "brain stimulation", it encompassed any technology that could establish information flow between neural tissue and artificial systems.

Vidal's BCI concept was revolutionary in its implications. Rather than simply replacing damaged neural pathways, as cochlear implants did, or controlling behavior through stimulation, as Delgado had done, BCIs would create entirely new channels of communication. The paralyzed could control computers without moving their hands. The blind could navigate using tactile feedback systems. The deaf could communicate through visual displays of speech.

Most importantly, BCIs could potentially augment normal human capabilities rather than simply restoring lost ones. Healthy individuals might gain access to information networks through direct neural interfaces. Cognitive abilities could be enhanced through artificial processing systems that worked in parallel with biological neural networks. The boundary between human and artificial intelligence could become increasingly blurred.

Vidal's early experiments were modest by today's standards. He recorded EEG signals from volunteers as they performed various mental tasks, then used simple pattern recognition algorithms to classify their brain states. When the system correctly identifies a specific mental state such as imagining movement of the left hand it would move a cursor on a computer screen.

The control was slow and unreliable. Users had to maintain specific mental states for several seconds before the computer would respond. The cursor movements were jerky and imprecise. Error rates were high, and the system required extensive training before users could achieve even basic control.

But it worked.

For the first time in human history, thought alone had been translated into computer action. The mind-machine barrier had been breached not through invasive surgery or pharmaceutical intervention, but through the careful analysis of naturally occurring neural signals.

From Laboratory Curiosity to Medical Necessity

The 1970s and early 1980s saw rapid progress in all aspects of brain-computer interface technology. Delgado's work with implanted stimulators evolved into more sophisticated deep brain stimulation systems for treating movement disorders. House's cochlear implants became commercially available and increasingly effective. Vidal's EEG-based computer control inspired researchers around the world to explore non-invasive BCIs.

But perhaps the most significant development was a shift in motivation. What had begun as scientific curiosity and military interest was becoming a medical imperative. The Vietnam War had produced thousands of young veterans with spinal cord injuries. Advances in emergency medicine were saving the lives of stroke and accident victims who in previous eras would have died. The population of people living with severe disabilities was growing, and they were demanding better solutions than traditional rehabilitation could provide.

This growing need coincided with rapid advances in computer technology. The microprocessors that made personal computers possible also enabled sophisticated real-time signal processing. Digital signal processing techniques, once available only to aerospace engineers, became accessible to neuroscience researchers. The computational tools needed for practical BCIs were finally becoming available.

Researchers began to envision a future where BCIs would be standard medical devices, as common and accepted as pacemakers or artificial joints. Paralyzed patients would control wheelchairs and robotic arms through thought alone. Stroke survivors would regain communication abilities through brain-controlled speech synthesizers. Amputees would operate prosthetic limbs with the same precision and intuition they once had with biological limbs.

These visions drove increasingly ambitious research programs. Academic laboratories began serious collaborations with medical device companies. The FDA started developing regulatory frameworks for implantable neural devices. Venture capitalists began investing in neurotechnology startups.

The transition from research curiosity to medical technology was accelerating. The fundamental principles had been established in the laboratories of pioneers like Delgado, House, and Vidal. The technical tools were rapidly improving. The clinical need was undeniable.

But the most challenging phase lay ahead. Translating laboratory demonstrations into reliable, safe, effective medical devices would require solving problems that the pioneers had barely begun to address. The human brain was far more complex than the animal models used in early experiments. Long-term stability of implanted devices remained questionable. The individual variability in neural responses posed challenges for standardized treatments.

Most importantly, the ethical and social implications of widespread BCI adoption were only beginning to be understood. The questions that Delgado had raised with his dramatic bull-stopping demonstration would become even more pressing as BCIs became more powerful and more common. How much control should technology have over the human mind? Who would have access to cognitive enhancement technologies? What were the risks of creating new forms of inequality between the enhanced and unenhanced?

As the 1980s began, brain-computer interfaces stood at a crossroads. The basic feasibility had been proven, the technical foundations had been laid, and the clinical need was clear. But transforming these early demonstrations into practical medical treatments would require a new generation of researchers, new levels of interdisciplinary collaboration, and new approaches to the complex challenges of interfacing minds with machines.

The age of laboratory curiosity was ending. The age of clinical translation was about to begin. And with it would come the first attempts to restore function to the human nervous system through direct technological intervention, attempts that would push the boundaries of medicine, technology, and human enhancement in ways that the early pioneers could barely have imagined.

The first connections between minds and machines had been established. Now the real work of building practical, safe, effective brain-computer interfaces could begin.

Chapter 3

Reading Minds, Moving Matter

The monkey sat motionless in her chair, electrodes surgically implanted in her brain, her arms gently restrained. On the computer screen before her, a cursor moved left, then right, then up toward a target circle. With each movement, she received a small reward, a drop of fruit juice but her hands never touched a joystick or keyboard.

Belle was controlling the cursor with her thoughts alone.

It was 1999, and in Miguel Nicolelis's laboratory at Duke University, something unprecedented was happening. For the first time in the history of life on Earth, a brain was directly controlling a machine in real-time, translating neural intentions into digital commands without any intermediate biological action. The cursor moved because Belle wanted it to move, and her wanting was sufficient to make it so.

But this was only the beginning. As Belle learned to control the cursor with increasing precision, Nicolelis and his team were secretly recording every neural signal, building a mathematical model of how her brain encoded movement intentions. When they felt ready, they would attempt something even more audacious, allowing Belle to control not just a cursor on a local computer screen, but a robotic arm hundreds of miles away.

The experiment that followed would shatter the traditional boundaries between mind and matter, proving that consciousness could reach across vast distances to manipulate the physical world. It would mark the beginning of an era in which the ancient dream of telekinesis, moving objects through thought alone would finally become scientific reality.

The 100-Neuron Symphony

Miguel Nicolelis had always been fascinated by orchestras. A Brazilian neuroscientist with an appreciation for classical music, he often compared the brain to a symphony, with individual neurons playing their parts in a larger, harmonious composition. But unlike a musical symphony, where each instrument's role was clearly defined, the brain's symphony seemed impossibly complex, billions of musicians playing simultaneously, their individual contributions lost in the overwhelming cacophony of neural activity.

The challenge facing BCI researchers in the 1990s was how to extract meaningful information from this neural orchestra. Previous researchers had focused on recording from single neurons, painstakingly isolating individual cells and studying their firing patterns. While this approach had revealed important principles about neural coding, it seemed inadequate for controlling complex devices in real-time.

Nicolelis proposed a radically different approach, instead of listening to individual musicians, he would record from entire sections of the neural orchestra simultaneously. He developed arrays of microelectrodes, dozens of fine wires bundled together that could monitor the activity of up to 100 neurons at once. This "ensemble recording" technique promised to capture the collective intelligence of neural populations rather than the limited information available from single cells.

The mathematical foundation for this approach came from work by Apostolos Georgopoulos, who had discovered that individual neurons in the motor cortex encoded the direction of intended movements. Each neuron had a "preferred direction", it fired most vigorously when the animal intended to move in a particular direction, and less vigorously for movements in other directions. By combining the signals from many neurons, each with its own directional preference, it was possible to calculate a "population vector" that accurately predicted the intended direction of movement.

Nicolelis extended this concept, developing algorithms that could extract not just movement direction but also movement velocity, force, and other parameters from the collective activity of neural ensembles. The key insight was that the brain used a distributed code: no single neuron contained complete information about movement intentions, but the population as a whole contained far more information than the sum of its parts.

The first tests of this approach were conducted with Belle, an owl monkey whose motor cortex had been implanted with an array of 96 microelectrodes. As Belle learned to control a computer cursor to earn juice rewards, the research team recorded the activity of dozens of neurons simultaneously. Machine learning algorithms analyzed these neural patterns in real-time, gradually learning to predict Belle's movement intentions with increasing accuracy.

The results exceeded all expectations. Within a few training sessions, Belle could control the cursor with remarkable precision, moving it smoothly to targets scattered across the screen. The system could predict her movement intentions up to 600 milliseconds before she actually moved her brain was already planning and encoding movements before her muscles received the command to act.

This temporal prediction was crucial for practical BCIs. It suggested that neural interfaces could potentially provide faster control than natural limbs, since the brain's movement intentions could be detected before the slower biological processes of muscle contraction and limb movement had begun.

But Nicolelis had an even more ambitious goal in mind. If Belle's neural signals could control a local cursor, could they control a robot on the other side of the world?

Transcontinental Telepathy

On a winter day in 2000, Belle sat in her familiar chair in Durham, North Carolina, controlling a cursor on the computer screen before her. Unknown to the monkey, however, her neural signals were being transmitted via the internet to a laboratory at MIT in Cambridge, Massachusetts, where they were controlling the movements of a robotic arm.

As Belle moved the cursor to touch targets on her screen, the robot arm 600 miles away mimicked her intended movements, reaching toward corresponding targets in three-dimensional space. For the first time in history, a brain in one location was directly controlling matter in another location, with the information transmitted not through sound, sight, or touch, but through the digital analysis of neural electrical activity.

The media response was immediate and intense. Headlines proclaimed the dawn of the "age of telepathy" and speculated about future soldiers controlling weapons from across the globe. Science fiction writers found their wildest imaginings suddenly within the realm of scientific possibility.

But for the researchers involved, the demonstration represented something more profound than technological showmanship. It proved that neural interfaces could operate over arbitrary distances, limited only by the speed of digital communication networks. More importantly, it demonstrated that the brain could learn to control devices that bore no resemblance to biological limbs.

The robotic arm that Belle controlled had different kinematics than her own arm, different joint angles, different degrees of freedom, different mechanical constraints. Yet her brain adapted to these differences, learning to generate the neural patterns that produced the desired robotic movements. This adaptability suggested that the human brain might be equally capable of learning to control artificial devices, regardless of their mechanical design.

The success of the transcontinental experiment opened new possibilities for BCI applications. Paralyzed patients might control not just local devices but robots anywhere in the world. A quadriplegic individual could potentially perform physical tasks in remote locations, regaining the ability to manipulate objects and interact with the physical world despite their biological limitations.

But perhaps the most significant implication was philosophical. If consciousness could directly control matter across vast distances, what were the boundaries of the self? Was Belle's body limited to her biological flesh, or did it extend to include the robotic arm that responded to her neural commands? The experiment raised fundamental questions about identity, embodiment, and the nature of conscious control that would only become more pressing as BCIs became more sophisticated.

The Leap to Human Trials

The success of Belle's experiment created enormous pressure to test similar technologies in human volunteers. The potential benefits for paralyzed individuals were obvious, and the technical feasibility had been demonstrated in multiple animal studies. But the leap from animal research to human trials represented a quantum jump in complexity, risk, and ethical responsibility.

The challenges were formidable. While Belle's electrode array could be replaced if it failed, human participants would live with their implants for years or decades. The brain's immune response to foreign objects was still poorly understood, and long-term biocompatibility remained questionable. Surgical implantation carried risks of infection, bleeding, and brain damage that were acceptable for research animals but demanded the highest standards of safety for human volunteers.

Moreover, human neural signals proved more complex and variable than those recorded from laboratory animals. Humans had larger, more sophisticated brains with greater individual variability in anatomy and function. Their movement intentions were influenced by emotions, attention, fatigue, and countless other factors that were difficult to control in experimental settings.

Despite these challenges, several research groups began the careful process of translating animal BCI research to human applications. The first human trials focused on individuals with the most severe disabilities, people with high-level spinal cord injuries who had lost all voluntary movement below the neck. For these individuals, the potential benefits of BCI technology far outweighed the experimental risks.

John Donoghue at Brown University led one of the first major human BCI trials, called BrainGate. Working with neurosurgeon Leigh Hochberg and a multidisciplinary team of engineers, neuroscientists, and clinicians, Donoghue adapted the electrode arrays and signal processing algorithms developed in animal studies for use in human participants.

The technical challenges were immense. Human skulls were thicker than those of laboratory animals, requiring more powerful surgical tools and longer procedures. The electrodes had to be positioned with millimeter precision in brain regions identified through sophisticated imaging techniques. The signal processing algorithms had to be optimized for human neural patterns, which differed significantly from those recorded in monkeys.

But the most difficult challenge was psychological. The human participants in these early trials were not naive laboratory animals, they were intelligent, articulate individuals who understood the experimental nature of the procedures and the uncertainty of the outcomes. They faced the possibility of surgical complications, device failures, and the emotional roller coaster of participating in cutting-edge research where success was far from guaranteed.

Profiles in Courage

Matthew Nagle was 25 years old when a knife attack severed his spinal cord, leaving him unable to move anything below his shoulders. An athlete and musician before his injury, Matt found himself dependent on others for even the most basic tasks, eating, drinking, turning pages in a book. When researchers at Brown University approached him about participating in the first BrainGate trial, he didn't hesitate.

"I knew it was experimental," Matt would later recall. "I knew there were risks. But I also knew that if I didn't try, nothing would ever change. Maybe I couldn't be helped, but maybe someone else could be."

The surgical procedure to implant Matt's BrainGate array took place in June 2004. Neurosurgeon Leigh Hochberg carefully removed a small section of skull over the motor cortex and inserted the 96-electrode array into the brain tissue. The surgery went smoothly, but the real test would come in the following weeks as researchers attempted to decode Matt's neural signals.

The first recording sessions were frustrating for everyone involved. Matt's neural signals were unlike anything the researchers had seen in animal studies. The patterns were more complex, more variable, and more difficult to interpret. The machine learning algorithms that had worked beautifully with Belle struggled to find consistent patterns in Matt's brain activity.

But gradually, progress emerged. Matt learned to modulate his neural activity by imagining movements of his paralyzed hand. The computer learned to recognize these imagined movement patterns and translate them into cursor movements. After weeks of training, Matt achieved his first moment of BCI control, moving a cursor across a computer screen through thought alone.

The emotional impact of that first successful control session was overwhelming. For Matt, it represented the first time since his injury that his intentions had directly controlled his environment. For the research team, it validated years of animal research and opened the door to practical clinical applications. For the broader scientific community, it marked the beginning of a new era in neurotechnology.

But Matt's success was just the beginning. In subsequent sessions, he learned to control more complex cursor movements, play simple computer games, and even control a robotic arm well enough to perform basic grasping tasks. The videos of Matt controlling a robotic hand to lift a cup or manipulate objects became iconic symbols of BCI technology's potential.

Other participants soon joined the BrainGate trial, each bringing their own unique neural signatures and challenges. Each person's brain encoded movement intentions slightly differently, requiring individualized calibration and training. Some participants achieved better control than others, reflecting the complex interplay between individual neural anatomy, electrode placement, and learning ability.

One of the most remarkable participants was Jan Scheuermann, a quadriplegic woman who joined a later BCI study at the University of Pittsburgh. Jan's control of a robotic arm reached unprecedented levels of precision, she could manipulate objects with smooth, natural-looking movements that seemed almost effortless. Videos of Jan feeding herself chocolate using a brain-controlled robotic arm went viral, inspiring millions and demonstrating the technology's potential for restoring independence to paralyzed individuals.

The Technical Gauntlet

While the media focused on the inspiring stories of BCI participants, the researchers grappled with an array of technical challenges that threatened the long-term viability of the technology. The problems fell into several categories, each representing a potential showstopper for clinical applications.

Signal degradation was perhaps the most serious issue. The brain's immune system recognized implanted electrodes as foreign objects and surrounded them with scar tissue. This "gliosis" created a barrier between the electrodes and the neurons they were meant to record, causing signal quality to deteriorate over time. Many implants that worked well initially became useless within months or years as the tissue response intensified.

The mechanical mismatch between rigid silicon electrodes and soft brain tissue exacerbated the problem. Every heartbeat, breath, and head movement caused tiny but significant motion between the electrodes and surrounding tissue. These micromotion induced chronic inflammation and accelerated the scarring process. Some electrodes broke entirely, their fine wires snapping under the constant mechanical stress.

Even when signals remained stable, they were often contaminated by noise from multiple sources. Electrical activity from nearby neurons, muscle contractions in the scalp, and electromagnetic interference from medical equipment all contributed to a noisy recording environment. Sophisticated signal processing techniques were required to extract the relevant neural information from this electrical cacophony.

The computational demands were equally challenging. Real-time decoding of neural signals required powerful processors running complex algorithms. Early BCI systems filled entire rooms with computer equipment, making them impractical for daily use. The dream of portable, wireless brain-computer interfaces would require dramatic advances in both algorithm efficiency and computing hardware.

Perhaps most frustratingly, BCI performance varied dramatically from day to day. A participant who achieved excellent cursor control on Monday might struggle to move the cursor at all on Tuesday. Changes in electrode impedance, neural signal drift, user fatigue, attention, and motivation all affected system performance in unpredictable ways. Developing robust BCIs that worked consistently over long periods remained an elusive goal.

The Psychological Journey

For the participants in these early BCI trials, the experience was as much psychological as technological. Learning to control external devices through neural signals required a fundamental rewiring of the brain's motor control circuits, circuits that had been shaped by millions of years of evolution to control biological limbs.

The process began with imagination. Participants were instructed to think about moving their paralyzed hands or arms, even though no actual movement would occur. For many, this was initially difficult and emotionally painful. Imagining movements that had been lost to injury could trigger grief, frustration, and despair.

But as training progressed, something remarkable happened. The imagined movements began to feel real again. Participants reported sensations of moving their phantom limbs, feeling their fingers curl around virtual objects, experiencing the weight and texture of things they manipulated through robotic arms. The brain, it seemed, was remarkably willing to accept artificial feedback as genuine sensory experience.

This neural plasticity was crucial for BCI success. Participants whose brains could adapt to the artificial control paradigm achieved much better performance than those who struggled with the psychological transition. The most successful users reported that controlling robotic devices eventually felt natural and intuitive, as if the machines had become extensions of their own bodies.

The social and emotional impacts were equally profound. For individuals who had lost independence due to paralysis, even limited BCI control represented a restoration of agency and autonomy. Being able to control a computer cursor, play a simple game, or manipulate a robotic arm provided psychological benefits that extended far beyond the specific tasks accomplished.

Family members and caregivers often experienced the emotional impact as intensely as the participants themselves. Watching a loved one regain some measure of control over their environment after years of complete dependence was deeply moving for everyone involved. The technology offered hope not just for individual participants but for families and communities affected by severe disability.

Ripple Effects

The success of these early human BCI trials created ripple effects throughout the neuroscience and medical communities. Funding agencies increased their investment in BCI research, recognizing the technology's potential for addressing unmet medical needs. Venture capitalists began investing in neurotechnology startups, hoping to capitalize on the commercial potential of brain-computer interfaces.

Medical device companies started serious development programs, working to translate academic research into commercially viable products. The regulatory pathway for neural implants became clearer as the FDA gained experience with BCI clinical trials. Insurance companies began considering coverage policies for BCI devices that could demonstrate clear clinical benefits.

Perhaps most importantly, the success of these trials attracted a new generation of researchers to the field. Young scientists and engineers were inspired by the possibility of developing technologies that could dramatically improve the lives of disabled individuals. The interdisciplinary nature of BCI research, combining neuroscience, engineering, computer science, and medicine appealed to technically minded individuals who wanted their work to have immediate social impact.

Academic programs in neural engineering began appearing at universities around the world. Professional societies organized conferences and workshops dedicated to BCI research. Scientific journals launched special issues focused on brain-computer interfaces. The field was rapidly maturing from a collection of individual research projects into a recognized scientific discipline.

The early human trials also revealed the enormous complexity of translating neural signals into useful control commands. While the basic feasibility had been proven, significant technical hurdles remained before BCIs could become practical medical devices. The challenges of signal stability, noise reduction, computational efficiency, and individual variability would require years of additional research to solve.

But the fundamental barrier had been breached. For the first time in human history, paralyzed individuals had regained the ability to control their environment through thought alone. The ancient dream of mind over matter had become scientific reality, opening possibilities that would have seemed like magic just decades earlier.

As the first generation of human BCI participants adapted to their new capabilities, researchers around the world were already working on the next phase of development. More sophisticated electrodes, better signal processing algorithms, and more advanced robotic systems were under development. The goal was no longer simply to prove that BCIs could work, but to make them work well enough to transform the lives of millions of people living with paralysis and other neurological conditions.

The age of practical brain-computer interfaces was beginning. The mind had learned to move matter directly, and there was no turning back. The implications for human enhancement, medical treatment, and the very nature of consciousness were only beginning to be understood. But one thing was clear, humanity had taken its first steps toward a future where the boundaries between mind and machine would become increasingly difficult to define.

Part II: The Pioneers

Chapter 4

The Visionaries

Elon Musk stood before a room full of journalists and investors, a small plastic disk the size of a coin resting in his palm. Inside the device, he claimed, were over 3,000 electrodes capable of reading and writing neural signals with unprecedented precision. He called it the Link, and he promised it would eventually allow humans to achieve "symbiosis with AI" and download skills directly into their brains.

"This is not a dystopian scenario," Musk declared with characteristic confidence. "This is a good outcome. We will enable someone with paralysis to use a smartphone with their mind faster than someone using thumbs."

The year was 2020, and Musk's neurotechnology company, Neuralink, was making claims that sounded like science fiction to many observers. Yet behind the bold promises and theatrical presentations lay a deeper vision of humanity's future, one where the merger of minds and machines would become not just possible, but necessary for human survival in an age of artificial intelligence.

Musk was not alone in his audacious vision. Around the world, a new generation of entrepreneurs, scientists, and philosophers were pushing the boundaries of what brain-computer interfaces could achieve. These visionaries brought different backgrounds, different motivations, and different approaches to the grand challenge of connecting minds to machines. But they shared a common belief that BCIs represented humanity's next evolutionary leap, a transformation as profound as the development of language or the invention of writing.

Their stories reveal not just the technical challenges of building better brain-computer interfaces, but the fundamental questions about what it means to be human in an age of technological enhancement.

The Entrepreneur's Gambit

Elon Musk's entry into neurotechnology seemed almost inevitable in retrospect. A serial entrepreneur who had revolutionized online payments, electric vehicles, and space travel, Musk had consistently chosen problems that others considered unsolvable or impractical. When he turned his attention to brain-computer interfaces in 2016, the field was ripe for the kind of ambitious, well-funded disruption that had become his trademark.

But Musk's interest in BCIs went deeper than technological opportunism. He genuinely believed that artificial intelligence posed an existential threat to humanity. As AI systems became more capable, he argued, humans would become increasingly irrelevant unless they could somehow merge with artificial intelligence. Brain-computer interfaces represented the only pathway to what he called "neural lace", a high-bandwidth connection between human brains and digital systems that would allow people to keep pace with AI development.

"If you can't beat them, join them," Musk explained at a 2017 presentation. "We're going to have the choice of either being left behind and being effectively useless or like a pet, or we can take the ride and have some chance of agency in the outcome."

This philosophical motivation shaped Neuralink's approach from the beginning. While most BCI researchers focused on medical applications, helping paralyzed patients control computers or prosthetic limbs, Musk aimed directly at human enhancement. Neuralink's ultimate goal was not to restore lost capabilities but to augment normal human cognition, allowing healthy individuals to interface directly with artificial intelligence systems.

The technical challenges were enormous. Existing BCI systems required large surgical procedures, produced unstable signals, and achieved data transfer rates measured in bits per second. Musk envisioned interfaces that would be minimally invasive, ultra-reliable, and capable of transmitting millions of bits per second between brains and computers. Achieving these goals would require breakthroughs in electrode design, surgical robotics, signal processing, and wireless communication.

Neuralink's solution was characteristically bold. The company developed flexible polymer threads, each thinner than human hair, capable of carrying multiple electrodes deep into brain tissue. A custom surgical robot would insert these threads with precision impossible for human surgeons, avoiding blood vessels and minimizing tissue damage. The entire system would be wireless, with the implant communicating through the skull to external devices.

The first public demonstrations were impressive but modest. In 2020, Neuralink showed a pig named Gertrude with an implanted device that could predict her movements and detect when she was eating. The following year, they demonstrated a macaque monkey playing the video game Pong using only neural signals. While these achievements were technically sophisticated, they largely replicated capabilities that academic researchers had demonstrated years earlier.

Critics argued that Neuralink's bold promises were far ahead of its actual achievements. The company's claims about bandwidth, safety, and timeline seemed implausible to many neuroscientists. The emphasis on media spectacle over peer-reviewed research raised questions about scientific rigor. Some worried that Neuralink's approach prioritized publicity over the careful, methodical progress needed for safe medical devices.

But Musk's influence extended far beyond his company's specific technical achievements. His high-profile advocacy brought unprecedented attention and investment to the BCI field. Young engineers and entrepreneurs who might never have considered neurotechnology suddenly saw brain-computer interfaces as an exciting frontier. Venture capital flowed into neurotechnology startups at levels that would have been unimaginable just a few years earlier.

Perhaps most importantly, Musk normalized the idea of elective neural enhancement. While previous BCI research had focused on medical necessity, helping disabled individuals regain lost capabilities, Neuralink explicitly targeted healthy individuals seeking cognitive augmentation. This shift in framing opened possibilities that the medical BCI community had barely begun to explore.

The Scientist's Dedication

While Musk captured headlines with bold predictions and flashy demonstrations, Leigh Hochberg was quietly revolutionizing the lives of paralyzed individuals through careful, methodical research. A neurologist and neuroscientist at Massachusetts General Hospital and Brown University, Hochberg had dedicated his career to translating BCI research from laboratory curiosities to practical medical treatments.

Hochberg's path to BCI research began in medical school, where he encountered patients with devastating neurological injuries. Unlike the dramatic spinal cord injuries featured in media coverage, many of Hochberg's patients suffered from strokes, ALS, or other conditions that gradually robbed them of their ability to communicate and control their environment. For these individuals, even modest technological assistance could mean the difference between isolation and connection, despair and hope.

"Every day I see patients who are cognitively intact, fully aware, but trapped in bodies that no longer respond to their commands," Hochberg explained in a 2019 interview. "If we can give them even a small window back to the world, the ability to type an email, control their environment, and communicate with loved ones, that's transformative."

This patient-centered philosophy shaped every aspect of Hochberg's approach to BCI research. Where other researchers focused on maximizing technical performance metrics, Hochberg emphasized real-world usability and clinical benefit. His BrainGate trials prioritized safety, reliability, and practical functionality over impressive but impractical demonstrations.

The results spoke for themselves. Under Hochberg's leadership, the BrainGate system achieved unprecedented levels of performance and stability. Participants could control computer cursors with speed and accuracy approaching that of healthy individuals using traditional interfaces. Some achieved typing speeds of over 40 words per minute using only their thoughts, faster than many people could type on smartphone keyboards.

But Hochberg's greatest contribution may have been his insistence on rigorous scientific methodology. While startups and media-savvy entrepreneurs made bold claims based on limited data, Hochberg's team published detailed, peer-reviewed studies that established the scientific foundation for clinical BCI development. Their work provided the evidence base that regulatory agencies needed to approve BCI devices for widespread use.

The human stories emerging from Hochberg's trials were as compelling as any technology demonstration. Dennis Degray, a participant with ALS, used the BrainGate system to communicate with his family during the final months of his life, typing messages with his thoughts when his voice had failed. Sanda Suvino, paralyzed by a stroke, achieved independent computer control that allowed her to reconnect with friends and pursue personal interests that had been inaccessible for years.

These individual success stories accumulated into a powerful argument for the clinical value of BCI technology. Hochberg's work demonstrated that brain-computer interfaces were not just fascinating research tools but practical medical interventions that could meaningfully improve the lives of disabled individuals.

The Rehabilitation Revolutionary

Randolph Nudo brought a different perspective to brain-computer interface development, one grounded in decades of research on neuroplasticity and stroke recovery. A neuroscientist at the University of Kansas Medical Center, Nudo had spent his career studying how the brain reorganizes itself after injury and how rehabilitation interventions can promote recovery.

His insight was profound yet simple, brain-computer interfaces should not just bypass damaged neural pathways but actively promote the recovery of those pathways. Rather than replacing lost function with artificial substitutes, BCIs could potentially stimulate the brain's natural healing mechanisms and restore biological function.

"We've learned that the adult brain is far more plastic than we once believed," Nudo explained. "Intensive, task-specific training can promote remarkable recovery even years after stroke. BCIs offer a new way to provide that intensive training, allowing patients to practice movements mentally even when their bodies can't respond."

Nudo's approach, which he called "restorative BCI," represented a fundamental shift in thinking about neural interfaces. Traditional BCIs focused on extracting motor signals from the brain and using them to control external devices. Nudo proposed closing the loop, using artificial stimulation to provide sensory feedback to the brain, creating a training environment where damaged neural circuits could gradually regain function.

The theoretical foundation was solid. Neuroscientists had long known that "neurons that fire together, wire together", repeated activation of neural pathways strengthens the connections between neurons. If BCI systems could artificially recreate the patterns of neural activity associated with successful movements, they might be able to strengthen weakened connections and promote recovery.

Early trials of Nudo's approach showed promising results. Stroke patients using restorative BCI systems not only achieved better control of external devices but also showed improvements in their biological movement abilities. Brain imaging revealed changes in neural connectivity that suggested genuine recovery rather than just adaptation to artificial control systems.

The implications were revolutionary. If BCIs could promote neural recovery rather than simply bypassing damaged circuits, they might transform rehabilitation medicine. Stroke patients, spinal cord injury survivors, and individuals with other neurological conditions might regain biological function that had been thought permanently lost.

But Nudo's vision extended beyond individual patient outcomes. He envisioned a future where BCIs would become standard tools in rehabilitation medicine, as common as physical therapy or occupational therapy. The technology would evolve from exotic experimental intervention to routine clinical practice, helping millions of people recover from neurological injuries and diseases.

The Consciousness Explorer

Antonio Damasio approached brain-computer interfaces from yet another angle, bringing the perspective of a philosopher-neuroscientist who had spent decades studying consciousness, emotions, and the nature of self. Based at the University of Southern California, Damasio saw BCIs as more than medical devices or technological marvels, they were windows into the fundamental mysteries of human consciousness.

"When we create an interface between brain and machine," Damasio observed, "we are not just connecting two different types of systems. We are exploring the boundary between mind and matter, between subjective experience and objective reality. These technologies force us to confront basic questions about what it means to be conscious."

Damasio's interest in BCIs was deeply philosophical. He had long argued that consciousness was not confined to the brain but emerged from the complex interactions between brain, body, and environment. BCIs offered a unique opportunity to test this theory by creating new types of embodiment, situations where consciousness could potentially extend into artificial systems.

His research focused on the subjective experiences of BCI users. When a paralyzed person controlled a robotic arm through neural signals, did they experience the robot as part of their body? When someone used a BCI to communicate, were they conscious of the artificial processing steps between thought and expression? These questions had profound implications for understanding the nature of consciousness and identity.

Damasio's investigations revealed the remarkable flexibility of human consciousness. BCI users often reported that controlled devices felt like natural extensions of their bodies. They experienced ownership of robotic limbs, presence in virtual environments, and agency over distant machines. The boundaries of the self, it seemed, were far more malleable than philosophers had traditionally assumed.

These findings had practical implications for BCI design. Systems that acknowledged and supported the psychological aspects of human-machine interaction achieved better performance than purely technical approaches. Users who felt a sense of embodiment with their BCIs learned faster, performed better, and reported greater satisfaction than those who experienced the technology as foreign or artificial.

But Damasio's work also raised troubling questions about the future of human identity. If consciousness could extend into artificial systems, what would happen as those systems became more sophisticated? Would humans gradually merge with artificial intelligence, losing their biological identity in the process? Or would consciousness resist such merging, maintaining human uniqueness even in an age of advanced BCIs?

The Cognitive Enhancer

Bryan Johnson represented perhaps the most radical vision of BCI development. The founder of Kernel, a neurotechnology company focused on cognitive enhancement, Johnson believed that brain-computer interfaces would eventually make human intelligence obsolete unless humans actively enhanced their own cognitive capabilities.

Johnson's background was in technology entrepreneurship rather than neuroscience. He had founded and sold multiple successful companies, accumulating the wealth and influence needed to pursue ambitious long-term projects. His entry into neurotechnology was motivated by a simple but profound realization, artificial intelligence was advancing exponentially, while human intelligence remained largely static.

"We are building AI systems that will soon surpass human capabilities in virtually every domain," Johnson argued. "If we don't enhance human intelligence, we will become irrelevant. BCIs are our only hope for keeping up."

Kernel's approach was uncompromisingly focused on enhancement rather than restoration. While most BCI companies targeted medical applications, Johnson explicitly sought to augment normal human cognition. His goal was nothing less than the creation of enhanced humans who could match or exceed artificial intelligence in reasoning, memory, and creativity.

The technical challenges were staggering. Enhancing normal cognition was far more difficult than restoring lost capabilities. The brain's healthy neural networks were already optimized by millions of years of evolution, improving them required understanding and modifying systems of enormous complexity and subtlety.

Kernel's initial approach focused on memory enhancement. The company developed implantable devices that could record neural patterns associated with memory formation and play them back to strengthen memory consolidation. Early experiments suggested that artificial stimulation could indeed enhance memory performance, though the effects were modest and limited to specific types of memories.

Johnson's vision extended far beyond memory enhancement. He envisioned BCIs that could accelerate learning, enhance creativity, improve decision-making, and expand the bandwidth of human communication. Ultimately, he hoped to create direct brain-to-brain interfaces that would allow humans to share thoughts and experiences directly, creating collective intelligence networks that could match or exceed artificial AI systems.

Critics argued that Johnson's goals were unrealistic and potentially dangerous. Enhancing normal brain function carried risks that were poorly understood. The long-term consequences of cognitive enhancement were unpredictable. There were serious questions about equity, safety, and the social implications of creating enhanced humans.

But Johnson's work highlighted an important reality, as artificial intelligence continued advancing, humans would face increasing pressure to enhance their own capabilities. BCIs might evolve from medical necessity to competitive advantage, with enhanced individuals gaining significant advantages in education, employment, and social interaction.

Convergent Visions, Divergent Paths

Despite their different backgrounds and approaches, these visionaries shared several common insights about the future of brain-computer interfaces. All recognized that BCIs represented more than incremental technological progress, they were potentially transformative technologies that could reshape human capabilities and society.

They also shared a sense of urgency. Whether motivated by the threat of AI superintelligence, the needs of disabled patients, or the mystery of consciousness itself, each believed that BCI development could not be left to gradual academic progress. The stakes were too high and the timeline too compressed for business as usual.

Yet their different philosophies led to markedly different approaches to BCI development. Musk prioritized bold engineering breakthroughs and aggressive timelines. Hochberg emphasized careful clinical validation and patient safety. Nudo focused on understanding and harnessing neuroplasticity. Damasio explored the philosophical implications of human-machine merger. Johnson pursued direct cognitive enhancement despite uncertain risks and benefits.

These different approaches reflected deeper disagreements about the proper role of technology in human life. Should BCIs primarily serve medical needs, restoring function to those who have lost it? Should they enhance normal human capabilities, creating new forms of augmented intelligence? Should they preserve human uniqueness or facilitate merger with artificial systems?

The answers to these questions would shape not just the technical development of BCIs but their social acceptance and regulatory approval. They would determine whether brain-computer interfaces became narrow medical devices or broad enhancement technologies. They would influence who would have access to neural augmentation and under what circumstances.

Perhaps most importantly, these visionaries were defining the terms of humanity's ongoing relationship with artificial intelligence. Their competing visions represented different possible futures, Musk's symbiosis with AI, Hochberg's compassionate restoration of human capabilities, Nudo's biological recovery through technological assistance, Damasio's expansion of consciousness into artificial systems, and Johnson's competitive enhancement of human intelligence.

As BCI technology continued advancing, these philosophical differences would become increasingly important. The technical challenges of building better brain-computer interfaces were difficult but ultimately solvable. The question of what kind of future those interfaces would create and whether that future would be desirable remained wide open.

The visionaries had articulated the possibilities. Now it would be up to society as a whole to choose which possibilities to pursue and which to avoid. The choices made in the coming decades would determine whether brain-computer interfaces became tools of liberation or instruments of control, whether they preserved human dignity or undermined human autonomy, whether they created a better future for all or advantages for only a privileged few.

The age of neural enhancement was beginning. The only question was what form it would take.

Chapter 5

The Patients Who Changed Everything

Matthew Nagle stared at the computer screen, his eyes focused with an intensity that seemed to make the air around him vibrate with concentration. His body was motionless, paralyzed from the neck down by a knife attack three years earlier but something extraordinary was happening. The cursor on the screen was moving, responding to his thoughts alone.

"I can't move my body," Matt said quietly, "but I can still move things with my mind. It's like I'm commanding this cursor to move, and it listens to me."

It was December 2004, and Matt had just become the first human being in history to control a computer through a brain implant. The moment was captured on video, preserved forever as evidence of a threshold crossed, a barrier broken, a new chapter in the story of human capability begun.

But behind that historic moment lay a more personal story, one of courage, hope, frustration, and determination. Matt was not just a research subject or a proof-of-concept demonstration. He was a 26-year-old man who had lost his independence, his career, and his sense of agency in a single violent moment. The BrainGate system represented more than technological achievement; it offered the possibility of reclaiming some measure of control over his life.

Matt's story, and those of the extraordinary individuals who followed him into the uncharted territory of human brain-computer interfaces, reveal the profound human dimensions of this revolutionary technology. These patients didn't just validate scientific theories or enable research publications. They transformed abstract possibilities into lived realities, showing the world what it meant to think a machine into action, to extend consciousness beyond the boundaries of the biological body, to become living bridges between mind and digital realm.

Their courage changed everything, not just for BCI technology, but for our understanding of human resilience, adaptation, and the malleable boundaries of the self.

The Pioneer's Path

Matt Nagle had been a star athlete at Weymouth High School, a young man whose life revolved around physical capability and competitive achievement. Football, basketball and hockey Matt excelled at sports that demanded split-second coordination between mind and muscle. His body was his instrument, responsive to his slightest intention, perfectly calibrated to translate thought into action.

That seamless integration between mind and body was severed on July 3, 2001, during what should have been a routine summer evening. Matt was attending a beach party in Marshfield, Massachusetts, when a fight broke out. In the chaos that followed, someone pulled a knife. The blade found its mark just below Matt's hairline, severing his spinal cord at the C3 level and instantly paralysing everything below his shoulders.

The transition from able-bodied athlete to quadriplegic was devastating. Matt could no longer feed himself, dress himself, or perform any of the countless physical tasks that define independent living. He required round-the-clock care, breathing assistance, and help with every aspect of personal hygiene. The young man who had once dominated athletic fields was now confined to a wheelchair, dependent on others for his most basic needs.

But Matt's mind remained sharp, his personality intact. Inside his paralyzed body lived the same intelligent, determined individual who had thrived on competition and challenge. When researchers from Brown University approached him about participating in an experimental brain-computer interface trial, Matt saw an opportunity to reclaim some measure of agency.

"I knew it was risky," Matt would later explain. "Brain surgery is never safe. But I was already living with the consequences of one terrible moment. If there was a chance this could help me, or help someone else like me, I had to try."

The surgical procedure to implant Matt's BrainGate array took place on June 22, 2004. Neurosurgeon Leigh Hochberg carefully drilled a small hole in Matt's skull, directly over the motor cortex region that had once controlled his right hand. The 96-electrode array, a silicon chip smaller than a baby aspirin, was inserted four millimeters into the brain tissue, positioned to record from the neural population that still generated movement intentions despite the severed spinal cord.

The surgery was successful, but the real test would come in the following weeks as researchers attempted to decode the neural signals captured by the implant. Unlike the animal studies that had preceded this work, Matt was a conscious, intelligent participant who could provide feedback about his intentions and experiences. He could think about specific movements, describe his mental strategies, and actively collaborate in the training process.

The first recording sessions were frustrating for everyone involved. Matt's neural signals were unlike anything the researchers had seen in their animal studies. The patterns were more complex, more variable, influenced by factors like attention, mood, and fatigue that were difficult to control. The machine learning algorithms struggled to find consistent relationships between Matt's intentions and his neural activity.

But gradually, progress emerged. Matt learned to modulate his neural signals by imagining movements of his paralyzed right hand. He would visualize squeezing his fingers, rotating his wrist, or reaching toward targets, and the computer would learn to recognize these imagined movement patterns. After weeks of patient training, the moment of breakthrough finally arrived.

The cursor moved.

Matt's excitement was palpable as he achieved his first successful BCI control. The cursor responded to his mental commands, moving left when he imagined moving his hand left, moving right when he imagined the opposite motion. For the first time since his injury, his intentions had directly controlled his environment without any intermediate biological action.

"It's amazing," Matt said during one of his early training sessions. "I'm thinking 'left' and it goes left. I'm thinking 'right' and it goes right. It's like the cursor knows what I want it to do."

As Matt's skill improved, the research team added new challenges. He learned to control two-dimensional cursor movements, guiding the pointer to targets scattered across the computer screen. He mastered click-and-drag operations, moving virtual objects from one location to another. He even played simple video games, including Pong, using only his thoughts to control the paddle.

But perhaps the most meaningful accomplishment was communication. Matt learned to use an on-screen keyboard, slowly spelling out words and sentences by moving the cursor to individual letters. His typing was laborious, just a few words per minute but it represented something profound, direct communication between his mind and the digital world.

The videos of Matt controlling the computer cursor became iconic symbols of BCI technology's potential. Media outlets around the world featured stories about the paralyzed man who could move objects with his thoughts. The images were powerful, Matt sitting motionless in his wheelchair while a cursor danced across the screen in response to his mental commands.

But the technology had limitations that the media coverage often overlooked. The BrainGate system worked only when Matt was connected to room-sized computer equipment via cables that emerged from his skull. The control was slow and sometimes unreliable. Signal quality gradually degraded over time as scar tissue formed around the implant. After 96 days, the system stopped working entirely.

Despite these limitations, Matt's participation in the BrainGate trial established a crucial proof-of-principle for human BCIs. His success demonstrated that people with spinal cord injuries retained the neural signals needed for BCI control. His detailed feedback helped researchers understand the subjective experience of brain-computer interaction. His courage in undergoing experimental surgery opened the door for other participants to follow.

Matt died in 2007, three years after his groundbreaking BCI trial, from complications related to his spinal cord injury. He was 26 years old. His death was a profound loss for his family and friends, and a reminder of the urgent medical need that drives BCI research. But his legacy lived on in every subsequent BCI breakthrough, every paralyzed person who regained computer control, every advancement in neural interface technology.

The Virtuoso of Mind Control

Jan Scheuermann's introduction to brain-computer interfaces came 13 years after her diagnosis with spinocerebellar degeneration, a progressive genetic disorder that had gradually robbed her of the ability to move. Unlike Matt Nagle's sudden injury, Jan's loss of function had been slow and inexorable, a decade-long retreat from physical capability that left her mind sharp but her body increasingly unresponsive.

By 2012, when Jan enrolled in the University of Pittsburgh's BCI trial, she was quadriplegic and ventilator-dependent, able to move only her eyes and facial muscles. Yet her personality remained vibrant, she was witty, optimistic, and intellectually curious about the technology that might restore some measure of control to her life.

"I've always been a very independent person," Jan explained before her surgery. "I was a pilot, I loved working with my hands, I enjoyed cooking and crafts. This disease took all of that away. If there's a chance to get some of it back, even in a different form, I want to try."

The surgical procedure to implant Jan's BCI arrays was more extensive than Matt's had been. Researchers placed two 96-electrode grids on the surface of her motor cortex, positioned to record from the brain regions that controlled both arms. The dual arrays promised richer neural information and potentially better control than single-implant systems.

Jan's training proceeded faster than anyone expected. Within hours of her first recording session, she was controlling a computer cursor with remarkable precision. Within days, she was manipulating objects in three-dimensional virtual environments. Within weeks, she was controlling a robotic arm with fluid, natural-looking movements that amazed even experienced BCI researchers.

The breakthrough moment came when Jan used the robotic arm to feed herself chocolate. The video of this achievement, a paralyzed woman guiding a mechanical hand to lift a piece of candy to her lips became one of the most watched BCI demonstrations in history. The symbolism was powerful: technology had restored not just function but dignity, not just capability but pleasure.

"I was in charge of that arm," Jan said after the successful feeding demonstration. "I made it move where I wanted it to go. It's been so many years since I've been able to move anything. This gives me hope."

Jan's control of the robotic arm reached unprecedented levels of sophistication. She could reach toward objects with smooth, coordinated movements that looked entirely natural. She could grasp items with appropriate force, neither crushing delicate objects nor dropping heavy ones. She could manipulate complex objects, rotating them to examine different angles or positioning them precisely in space.

The research team documented Jan's achievements in extraordinary detail. Her neural signals were recorded during hundreds of reaching movements, creating a rich database of human motor intention signals. Her subjective reports provided insights into the phenomenology of robotic control, what it felt like to command an artificial limb through pure thought.

"It doesn't feel artificial," Jan reported during one training session. "When I want the hand to move, it moves. When I want to grasp something, it grasps. It feels like the robotic arm is part of me."

This sense of embodiment was crucial for BCI success. Users who experienced controlled devices as extensions of their own bodies achieved better performance than those who remained cognitively detached from the artificial systems. Jan's natural ability to incorporate the robotic arm into her body schema made her one of the most skilled BCI users ever documented.

Jan's achievements extended beyond robotic control. She mastered multiple BCI applications, computer cursor control, virtual reality navigation, communication interfaces, and environmental control systems. Her versatility demonstrated that skilled BCI users could adapt their neural control strategies to different tasks and technologies.

Perhaps most importantly, Jan became an eloquent advocate for BCI research and development. Her public presentations combined technical sophistication with personal warmth, helping audiences understand both the potential and limitations of current technology. She emphasized that BCIs were not miracle cures but valuable tools that could meaningfully improve the lives of disabled individuals.

"This technology won't make me walk again," Jan explained in a 2013 interview. "But it gives me back some control over my environment. I can interact with computers, manipulate objects, and express my intentions in ways that weren't possible before. For someone in my situation, that's transformative."

Jan participated in BCI research for several years, contributing to dozens of scientific publications and helping train a new generation of BCI researchers. Her electrodes remained functional longer than most early implants, providing researchers with unprecedented longitudinal data about human neural control signals.

When Jan's implant arrays were finally removed in 2016, she had logged over 200 hours of BCI control across multiple years. Her data contributed to algorithm improvements that benefited subsequent BCI users. Her advocacy helped build public support for continued BCI research funding. Her courage inspired other potential participants to enroll in clinical trials.

Jan passed away in 2019, seven years after her BCI implantation. Her death marked the end of an era in BCI research; she had been one of the longest-participating and most accomplished users in the field's history. But her contributions lived on in every improvement to BCI technology, every new participant who achieved successful control, every advance toward practical neural interfaces.

The Coffee Moment

Erik Sorto had been paralyzed for 13 years when he first grasped a cup of coffee with his mind. The moment was captured on video of Erik sitting in his wheelchair, electrodes implanted in his brain, watching intently as a robotic arm responded to his neural commands. The mechanical hand reached toward the cup, grasped it gently, and lifted it to Erik's lips for his first independent drink in over a decade.

"It was just a sip of coffee," Erik would later reflect. "But it was the first time since my accident that I controlled something myself. I decided when to reach for the cup, how to grasp it, when to bring it to my mouth. For those few seconds, I felt like myself again."

Erik's path to that coffee moment had been long and difficult. At age 21, he had been shot in the back during a gang-related incident in Los Angeles, suffering a complete spinal cord injury at the T4 level. The injury left him paralyzed from the chest down, ending his dreams of a career in architecture and forcing him to redefine his sense of identity and possibility.

Unlike some BCI participants who enrolled immediately after their injuries, Erik had lived with paralysis for more than a decade before joining the BCI research program at Caltech. He had adapted to his disability, learned to navigate the world in a wheelchair, and built a new life around his limitations. The BCI trial represented not desperate hope but informed optimism, a chance to regain some capabilities while maintaining realistic expectations.

Erik's BCI implantation was part of an innovative research program led by Richard Andersen, a neuroscientist who had spent decades studying the brain regions involved in movement planning. Rather than recording from the primary motor cortex, as most previous studies had done, Andersen's team targeted the posterior parietal cortex, the brain areas involved in the intention to move rather than the execution of movement.

The distinction was crucial. Primary motor cortex generated the detailed commands that controlled muscle contractions. Posterior parietal cortex encoded higher-level intentions, the goal of reaching for an object rather than the specific muscle activations required to achieve that goal. Andersen hypothesized that recording from intention areas might produce more intuitive and reliable BCI control.

The hypothesis proved correct. Erik's initial BCI training progressed remarkably smoothly. Instead of learning to modulate neural signals through trial and error, as many previous participants had done, Erik found that simply thinking about desired movements produced appropriate neural patterns. The system seemed to read his intentions directly rather than requiring him to develop artificial control strategies.

"It felt natural from the beginning," Erik explained. "I would think about reaching for something, and the robotic arm would reach. I would think about grasping, and the hand would close. It was like the robot understood what I wanted to do."

This naturalness was reflected in the quality of Erik's robotic control. His movements were smooth and coordinated, lacking the jerky, artificial appearance of many earlier BCI demonstrations. He could perform complex manipulation tasks such as grasping objects of different shapes and sizes, pouring liquids, and manipulating tools with precision that approached normal human performance.

The coffee demonstration became a symbol of BCI achievement precisely because it appeared so natural. Erik didn't struggle with the robotic arm or require multiple attempts to complete the task. He simply reached for the cup, grasped it, and brought it to his mouth in a fluid sequence of movements that looked entirely normal despite being controlled by neural signals transmitted through artificial electronics.

But Erik's achievements extended beyond robotic control. He became one of the first BCI users to achieve high-speed typing through neural signals alone, reaching speeds of over 35 words per minute using an on-screen keyboard. This performance approached the typing speeds of healthy individuals using smartphones, suggesting that BCIs might eventually provide communication capabilities that were genuinely competitive with conventional interfaces.

Erik's success helped establish the viability of recording from movement intention areas rather than movement execution areas. His data contributed to the development of more intuitive BCI control algorithms that required less user training and adaptation. His public appearances helped build support for continued BCI research and development.

Perhaps most importantly, Erik demonstrated that BCI technology could provide meaningful benefit to people who had adapted to their disabilities rather than just those in acute medical crisis. His participation showed that BCIs might eventually serve not just as medical devices but as general-purpose tools for enhancing human-computer interaction.

The Architect's Vision

Rodrigo Hübner Mendes had been an architect before the diving accident that changed his life. Working in Brazil, he had designed buildings and spaces that enhanced human activity and interaction. When a spinal cord injury left him quadriplegic, Rodrigo found himself thinking about design from a radically different perspective, not just as someone who created accessible spaces, but as someone who needed them.

Rodrigo's approach to BCI research reflected his architectural background. He was interested not just in whether the technology worked, but in how it integrated into daily life. What did it mean for a home to be controlled by neural signals? How could brain-computer interfaces be designed to enhance rather than complicate the experience of disability?

"As an architect, I learned to think about how people interact with their environments," Rodrigo explained. "When I started working with BCIs, I brought that same perspective. It's not enough for the technology to work in the laboratory. It has to work in the real world, in real homes, with real families."

Rodrigo's BCI research took place in Brazil, where he worked with a team of neuroscientists and engineers to develop culturally appropriate neural interface technologies. The cultural dimension was important, BCI systems developed in American or European laboratories might not translate effectively to different social and economic contexts.

One of Rodrigo's most significant contributions was his work on environmental control systems. Rather than focusing on robotic manipulation or computer cursor control, he explored how BCIs could help paralyzed individuals manage their living spaces. His neural signals controlled lighting, temperature, television, music, and other aspects of his home environment.

The environmental control applications had immediate practical benefits. Rodrigo could adjust his surroundings without requiring caregiver assistance, increasing his independence and privacy. He could respond to changing conditions, turning on lights when it got dark, adjusting temperature when he felt cold without having to ask for help or wait for others to notice his needs.

But the psychological benefits were equally important. Environmental control restored a sense of agency over personal space that many paralyzed individuals lose. Rodrigo could create the atmosphere he preferred for different activities, bright lights for reading, dim lights for relaxation, specific music for different moods. The BCI system allowed him to shape his environment according to his preferences and needs.

Rodrigo's work also explored the social dimensions of BCI use. How did family members react to neural interface technology? What were the practical challenges of living with someone who used BCIs? How could the technology be designed to enhance rather than complicate family relationships?

These questions proved crucial for long-term BCI adoption. The most sophisticated neural interface technology would fail if it created social friction or imposed unreasonable burdens on family members and caregivers. Rodrigo's research helped identify design principles that made BCIs more socially acceptable and practically viable.

"Technology should bring families together, not divide them," Rodrigo observed. "When BCIs work well, they reduce the burden on caregivers and increase opportunities for normal interaction. When they work poorly, they create new problems and tensions."

Rodrigo became an international advocate for accessible BCI development, speaking at conferences around the world about the importance of including disabled individuals in the design process. His architectural background gave him a unique perspective on universal design principles that could make neural interfaces more usable for diverse populations.

The Ripple Effects

The courage and achievements of these pioneering BCI participants created ripple effects that extended far beyond their individual experiences. Their families, caregivers, and communities were transformed by witnessing the restoration of capabilities that had seemed permanently lost.

Matt Nagle's mother, Barbara, became an advocate for spinal cord injury research, speaking at conferences and fundraising events about the potential of BCI technology. She emphasized that her son's participation in the BrainGate trial had been motivated not just by personal benefit but by hope that others might be helped.

"Matt knew he was taking a risk," Barbara explained. "But he also knew that if he didn't try, nothing would change for people like him. He wanted his experience to pave the way for better treatments."

Jan Scheuermann's family documented her BCI journey in videos and blog posts that provided unprecedented insight into the daily reality of living with neural interfaces. Her husband and daughter described both the excitement of her achievements and the challenges of managing experimental medical technology.

"Jan was always optimistic about the research," her husband recalled. "Even when the system didn't work perfectly, she focused on what it might become rather than what it couldn't do yet. She saw herself as part of something bigger."

Erik Sorto's success inspired other members of the spinal cord injury community to consider participating in BCI trials. His public presentations emphasized the importance of realistic expectations, BCIs were valuable tools, not miracle cures but they could provide meaningful improvements in quality of life.

"I don't want people to think BCIs will solve all their problems," Erik said in a 2018 interview. "But they might solve some problems, and that's worthwhile. Being able to control my environment, communicate more easily, interact with technology, these things matter."

The families of BCI participants often became unofficial ambassadors for the technology, sharing their experiences with other families facing similar challenges. Their perspectives were crucial for understanding the broader social impact of neural interfaces and identifying design improvements that would benefit future users.

Perhaps most importantly, these pioneering participants demonstrated that BCIs could be integrated into meaningful, dignified lives. They were not passive research subjects but active collaborators who shaped the development of the technology they used. Their feedback influenced algorithm improvements, hardware designs, and user interface developments that benefited all subsequent BCI users.

The Psychological Transformation

The experience of controlling external devices through neural signals created profound psychological changes in BCI participants. Many reported that successful BCI control restored a sense of agency and competence that had been absent since their injuries.

"Before the BCI, I felt like a passenger in my own life," one participant explained. "Things happened to me, but I couldn't make things happen. The BCI changed that. Suddenly I could cause things to occur in the world again."

This restoration of agency had effects that extended beyond the specific capabilities provided by the BCI system. Participants often reported improvements in mood, motivation, and overall psychological well-being. The knowledge that they could control at least some aspects of their environment seemed to enhance their sense of possibility and hope.

The learning process itself was often transformative. Mastering BCI control required patience, persistence, and problem-solving skills that many participants hadn't exercised since their injuries. The intellectual challenge of learning to modulate neural signals provided cognitive stimulation and a sense of accomplishment.

"Training with the BCI was like learning a new skill," Jan Scheuermann observed. "I had to figure out what mental strategies worked best, how to stay focused during long sessions, how to adapt when the system didn't respond as expected. It made me feel mentally sharp again."

The social dimensions were equally important. BCI achievements provided participants with compelling stories to share, restoring their ability to surprise and impress others. Family members and friends who had grown accustomed to viewing the participant primarily as someone who needed care suddenly saw them as someone who could achieve remarkable things.

But the psychological impact wasn't uniformly positive. Some participants struggled with the limitations of current BCI technology, experiencing frustration when systems didn't work reliably or disappointment when capabilities didn't match expectations. The experimental nature of the research meant that participants often faced equipment failures, protocol changes, and uncertain timelines.

"There were definitely difficult moments," one participant recalled. "Days when nothing worked right, when I felt like I was wasting everyone's time, when the technology seemed more like a cruel tease than a genuine help. But those moments were balanced by the times when everything clicked and I could do things I hadn't done in years."

The experience of living with experimental neural interfaces also created unique perspectives on the relationship between mind and body. Participants often reported that BCI control felt both familiar and strange, familiar because they were using their own intentions to create the control, strange because those intentions were being translated through artificial systems.

"It's hard to describe what it feels like to control a robot with your mind," Erik Sorto explained. "In one sense, it feels completely natural, I think about what I want to do, and it happens. In another sense, it's obviously artificial, there are computers translating my thoughts into machine commands. Somehow both things are true at the same time."

The Legacy of Courage

The pioneering BCI participants changed everything, but not in the ways that might have been expected. Their most important contribution wasn't proving that the technology worked, that had already been demonstrated in animal studies. Instead, they proved that the technology mattered.

They showed that BCIs could provide genuine benefits to real people living with real disabilities. They demonstrated that the human brain was capable of the plasticity and adaptation required for successful neural interface control. They revealed the psychological and social dimensions of BCI use that would be crucial for successful clinical translation.

Perhaps most importantly, they proved that people with severe disabilities were capable of being true partners in advanced neurotechnology research. Their intelligence, dedication, and courage were essential elements of every breakthrough achieved. They were not passive recipients of technological charity but active collaborators in the development of tools that might transform the lives of millions.

Their legacy lives on in every subsequent BCI advancement. The algorithms that decode neural signals were refined using their data. The hardware designs that improve signal stability were informed by their experiences. The user interfaces that make BCIs more intuitive incorporate lessons learned from their feedback.

But their deepest legacy may be the change they created in how society views disability and human potential. They demonstrated that severe physical limitations need not constrain the reach of human consciousness. They showed that with appropriate technology, minds could transcend the boundaries of damaged bodies to interact with the world in new and powerful ways.

The patients who changed everything did so not through superhuman achievements but through profoundly human ones, through courage in the face of uncertainty, persistence in the face of frustration, and hope in the face of limitation. They proved that the most important component of any brain-computer interface is not the computer or the interface but the remarkable human brain that uses it.

Their example continues to inspire new participants, researchers, and advocates who are working to make neural interfaces more capable, more accessible, and more beneficial for everyone who needs them. The age of practical brain-computer interfaces began not with technological breakthroughs but with the courage of individuals who were willing to think machines into motion, one neural signal at a time.

Part III: The Science Behind the Magic

Chapter 6

Signal and Noise

"The brain is not a computer, and thoughts are not digital signals. They are analog, noisy, and constantly shifting like trying to hear a whispered conversation at a crowded party while the music keeps changing." - Dr. Krishna Shenoy, Stanford University

The Cocktail Party Problem of the Mind

In the basement laboratory of Stanford University's Neural Prosthetics Systems Lab, a thin bundle of wires no thicker than a human hair carries the hopes of paralyzed patients worldwide. These microelectrodes, each smaller than an eyelash, sit nestled in the motor cortex of a research volunteer, eavesdropping on conversations between neurons that have been trying to move an arm for years, an arm that no longer responds.

The signals they detect are simultaneously the most complex and most fragile information ever recorded. Each neuron fires in brief electrical bursts lasting mere milliseconds, generating voltages a million times smaller than those powering a hearing aid. Yet within this barely perceptible chatter lies something extraordinary, the neural code for human intention.

Dr. Krishna Shenoy, who has spent two decades trying to crack this code, describes the challenge with a simple analogy, "Imagine you're at a cocktail party where hundreds of people are having simultaneous conversations in dozens of languages, the music keeps changing volume, and you're trying to understand what just one person is whispering while standing outside the building."

This is the fundamental challenge of brain-computer interfaces, extracting meaningful signals from neural noise. It's a problem that sits at the intersection of neuroscience, engineering, and mathematics, requiring solutions that didn't exist when the first researchers began recording from individual brain cells in the 1950s. The story of how scientists learned to separate signals from noise in the human brain is also the story of how artificial intelligence came to understand the mind.

The Electric Symphony

To understand the magnitude of the signal processing challenge, consider what happens in the motor cortex when someone decides to reach for a coffee cup. This decision activates roughly 100,000 neurons across several cubic millimeters of brain tissue. Each neuron connects to approximately 10,000 others, creating a network more complex than the internet. The electrical activity from this neural storm generates what neuroscientists call "local field potentials", the combined electrical signature of thousands of cells working together.

But here's the challenge, current BCI technology can only "hear" a tiny fraction of this symphony. The most advanced implants, like those used in the BrainGate trials, contain 96 microelectrodes arranged in a grid smaller than a baby aspirin. Each electrode can reliably detect signals from only 1 to 4 neurons. In essence, researchers are trying to understand a 100,000-piece orchestra by listening to fewer than 400 instruments.

"It's like trying to understand a Beethoven symphony by listening to just the triangle and maybe a few violins," explains Dr. Leigh Hochberg, who leads the BrainGate clinical trials. "Remarkably, it turns out that even this limited information can be incredibly rich."

The richness comes from a fundamental property of the motor cortex discovered in the 1960s by researchers like Edward Evarts at the National Institutes of Health. Individual neurons in this brain region fire more rapidly when a person intends to move in a particular direction. A neuron might fire 20 times per second when someone thinks about moving their arm to the right, but only 5 times per second when thinking about moving left.

This "directional tuning" became the foundation for all modern BCIs. If researchers could record from enough directionally-tuned neurons simultaneously, they could theoretically decode movement intentions in real time. The concept was elegant in its simplicity but the execution proved devilishly complex.

The Machine Learning Revolution

The breakthrough came not from neuroscience but from artificial intelligence. In the early 2000s, as computer scientists developed increasingly sophisticated algorithms for pattern recognition, BCI researchers realized they had been thinking about the problem backwards. Instead of trying to understand what each individual neuron was saying, they could use machine learning to find patterns in the collective activity of many neurons simultaneously.

Dr. David Warland, a computational neuroscientist at UC Berkeley, was among the first to apply these techniques to neural data. "We stopped asking 'what does this neuron mean?' and started asking 'what patterns in this population of neurons correspond to specific intentions?'" he recalls. "It was a fundamental shift from trying to decode individual neural words to understanding the grammar of neural sentences."

The most successful algorithms turned out to be surprisingly simple. The Kalman filter, developed in the 1960s for tracking satellites and missiles, proved remarkably effective at tracking the intended movements encoded in neural signals. The filter works by maintaining a mathematical model of what the brain is trying to do and continuously updating that model based on incoming neural data.

When Erik Sorto thinks about reaching for a glass of water, his brain generates a complex pattern of neural activity. A Kalman filter trained on thousands of similar thoughts can recognize this pattern and predict, with remarkable accuracy, where Erik intends to move. The filter doesn't understand individual neurons any better than a weather prediction algorithm understands individual water molecules but it doesn't need to. It simply finds statistical relationships between neural patterns and intended movements.

The results have been transformative. In 2012, participants in the BrainGate trial achieved something that seemed like science fiction just a decade earlier: they controlled robotic arms with their thoughts alone, performing complex tasks like drinking coffee or playing piano. The neural signals that paralyzed patients' brains had been generating for years, signals that never reached their limbs were finally being heard and understood.

The Drift Problem

But even as BCI technology achieved these remarkable successes, a fundamental problem emerged that threatened to limit the clinical viability of brain implants, signal drift. The electrical signatures that researchers so carefully decode gradually change over time, rendering even the best-trained algorithms useless within months or years.

The problem begins at the cellular level. Brain tissue treats implanted electrodes as foreign objects, triggering an immune response that gradually encases the devices in scar tissue. As the scar tissue thickens, it insulates the electrodes from nearby neurons, weakening the recorded signals. Simultaneously, the mechanical properties of the brain tissue change around the implant, causing the electrodes to shift position slightly, altering which neurons they record from.

Dr. Cynthia Chestek of the University of Michigan has spent years studying this phenomenon. "It's like trying to use a radio that's constantly retuning itself," she explains. "The stations you were listening to yesterday might be completely different today, even though you haven't touched the dial."

The implications for BCI users are profound. Jan Scheuermann, one of the most successful BrainGate participants, initially achieved remarkable control over a robotic arm, manipulating objects with precision that amazed researchers. But over the 13 months of her trial, her performance gradually declined as her brain signals changed. By the end of the study, she required constant recalibration of the system to maintain even basic functionality.

Traditional approaches to this problem focus on developing "adaptive" algorithms that can continuously retrain themselves as signals change. These systems work reasonably well in laboratory settings, but they require constant attention from engineers and neuroscientists, hardly practical for patients who want to use BCIs in their daily lives.

The Wireless Revolution

Perhaps no single technology has the potential to transform BCI usability more than the elimination of wired connections. Every participant in current BCI trials must have cables physically connected to their skull, creating infection risks and severely limiting mobility. The cables also serve as a constant reminder of the experimental nature of the technology, hardly the seamless integration that patients desire.

The engineering challenges of wireless BCIs are formidable. Neural signals are incredibly weak and easily overwhelmed by electromagnetic interference from everything from cell phones to microwave ovens. The implanted systems must amplify these signals by factors of thousands while consuming minimal power; there's no practical way to frequently charge or replace batteries in an implanted device.

Several companies are now developing solutions. Neuralink has demonstrated wireless transmission of neural signals in pigs and monkeys, though the technology hasn't yet been tested in humans. Blackrock Neurotech, which manufactures the arrays used in BrainGate trials, is developing wireless versions of their systems. Kernel, founded by entrepreneur Bryan Johnson, is pursuing entirely different approaches using optical rather than electrical recording methods.

The most promising near-term solution may come from Paradromics, a company founded by Dr. Matt Angle that's developing extremely high-bandwidth neural interfaces. Their approach uses thousands of microwires, each thinner than a human hair, to record from far more neurons simultaneously than current systems. The increased information density should make the systems more robust to the inevitable loss of individual recording sites over time.

"If you're only listening to 100 neurons and you lose 20 of them, that's a 20% degradation in performance," explains Angle. "But if you're listening to 10,000 neurons and lose 20, it's barely noticeable."

Beyond the Motor Cortex

While most current BCIs focus on motor control, researchers are increasingly exploring signals from other brain regions. The posterior parietal cortex, which integrates sensory information and helps plan movements, may provide more stable signals than the motor cortex. The premotor cortex, active during movement planning, might allow BCIs to detect intentions even earlier in the neural decision-making process.

Dr. Richard Andersen at Caltech has pioneered the study of intention signals in the posterior parietal cortex. His research suggests that this brain region encodes not just what movements a person intends to make, but also why they want to make them, the goals and motivations behind motor actions.

"If someone is reaching for a cup, their motor cortex primarily encodes the mechanics of that reach, the direction, velocity, and force required," Andersen explains. "But the parietal cortex encodes something richer: 'I want to drink coffee.' That higher-level intention signal might be more stable and useful for BCIs."

This research is leading toward BCIs that could understand not just movement commands but the broader context of what users are trying to accomplish. Such systems might automatically adjust their behavior based on environmental cues or learned user preferences, requiring less conscious control from the user.

The Decoding Bottleneck

Despite decades of advances in recording technology and signal processing algorithms, a fundamental bottleneck remains in translating neural activity into useful commands. Current BCIs can reliably decode simple intentions, move left, move right, click, don't click but they struggle with the nuanced control that characterizes natural movement.

Consider the seemingly simple act of grasping a wine glass. A healthy person automatically adjusts their grip strength based on visual and tactile feedback, applying just enough force to lift the glass without crushing it. They modulate their movement speed based on the weight of the glass and the fullness of the wine. They make countless tiny adjustments throughout the movement based on sensory information.

Current BCIs lack access to most of this information. They can decode the intention to reach and grasp, but they cannot access the rich sensory feedback that normally guides such movements. The result is robotic control that, while remarkable for paralyzed users, remains far from the fluid grace of natural movement.

Dr. Sliman Bensmaia at the University of Chicago is working to address this limitation by developing BCIs that can both record motor intentions and stimulate sensory areas of the brain. His research participants can not only control robotic hands with their thoughts but also feel what those hands touch through direct neural stimulation.

"Motor control and sensation are intimately linked in the healthy nervous system," Bensmaia explains. "To restore truly natural control, we need to close the sensory loop."

The Promise of Optogenetics

While most BCI research focuses on recording electrical signals from neurons, a revolutionary new approach promises to transform both the recording and stimulation sides of the interface. Optogenetics, developed over the past two decades, allows researchers to control specific neurons using light rather than electricity.

The technique works by introducing light-sensitive proteins called opsins into neurons. When exposed to specific wavelengths of light, these proteins cause neurons to fire or stop firing on command. This precision is impossible to achieve with electrical stimulation, which affects all nearby neurons regardless of their type or function.

Dr. Ed Boyden at MIT, one of the pioneers of optogenetics, envisions BCIs that use light to both read from and write to the brain with single-cell precision. Such systems could potentially solve many of the current limitations of electrical BCIs, including the problem of signal drift and the challenge of providing realistic sensory feedback.

"Imagine a BCI that could activate exactly the right neurons to create the sensation of touching silk, or the precise motor neurons needed to play a violin," Boyden speculates. "That level of precision might be possible with optogenetics."

However, optogenetic BCIs face their own challenges. Introducing light-sensitive proteins into human neurons requires genetic modification, raising safety concerns that have yet to be fully addressed. The light sources needed for optogenetic control must be implanted directly into brain tissue, creating additional engineering challenges.

The Noise That Matters

As BCI technology advances, researchers are discovering that some neural "noise" may actually contain important information. The brain's electrical activity includes rhythmic oscillations at different frequencies, delta waves during deep sleep, alpha waves during relaxed wakefulness, gamma waves during intense concentration. These oscillations were traditionally considered background noise to be filtered out, but recent research suggests they play crucial roles in neural computation.

Dr. Rajesh Rao at the University of Washington has developed BCIs that decode these oscillatory patterns rather than individual neuron spikes. His approach, called "spectral power BCIs," analyzes how the strength of different frequency bands changes over time. Users can learn to voluntarily modulate these brain rhythms to control external devices.

"It's like learning to control your breathing or heart rate," Rao explains. "With practice, people can consciously change their brain's electrical rhythms in ways that BCIs can reliably detect."

Spectral power BCIs offer several advantages over spike-based systems. They require less invasive recording methods, even EEG electrodes placed on the scalp can detect some oscillatory patterns. They may also be more stable over time, as brain rhythms appear less susceptible to the tissue changes that affect individual neuron recordings.

The Integration Challenge

As BCI technology becomes more sophisticated, a new challenge emerges, integrating multiple types of neural signals to create more natural and intuitive interfaces. Modern research systems might simultaneously record spikes from individual neurons, local field potentials from small brain regions, and oscillatory patterns from large-scale brain networks.

Each type of signal provides different information and operates on different timescales. Individual spikes reflect the decisions of single neurons happening over milliseconds. Local field potentials capture the coordination between nearby groups of neurons over tens of milliseconds. Oscillatory patterns reflect the synchronization of large brain networks over seconds or minutes.

Dr. Bin He at Carnegie Mellon University is developing "multimodal" BCIs that combine information from multiple signal types and brain regions. His systems use advanced machine learning techniques to find patterns across these diverse data streams, potentially providing richer and more reliable control signals.

"The brain doesn't operate in isolation, different regions work together to produce coherent behavior," He explains. "Our BCIs need to mirror this integration if they're going to provide truly natural control."

Looking Forward: The Convergence of Technologies

The future of BCI signal processing lies at the convergence of several rapidly advancing fields. Advances in artificial intelligence, particularly in deep learning and neural networks, are providing new tools for decoding complex neural patterns. Developments in materials science are enabling new types of biocompatible electrodes that could reduce scarring and improve signal stability. Progress in wireless communication is making untethered BCIs increasingly feasible.

Perhaps most importantly, the growing understanding of neural computation itself is revealing new opportunities for more sophisticated interfaces. As neuroscientists uncover the computational principles underlying brain function, engineers can design BCIs that work with these principles rather than against them.

The ultimate goal remains the same as when José Delgado first demonstrated remote control of a bull's behavior in 1963, to create seamless communication between minds and machines. But the path to that goal now appears clearer than ever before. By learning to separate signals from noise in the electrical symphony of the brain, researchers are writing the first chapters of a new form of human-machine communication. One that could transform not just how we interact with technology, but how we understand consciousness itself.

In the sterile quiet of research laboratories around the world, the faint electrical whispers of human thoughts are finally being heard. The challenge now is learning to listen carefully enough to understand what they're trying to say.

Chapter 7

Beyond Paralysis

Dr. Helen Mayberg had seen the pattern too many times before. Another patient with treatment-resistant depression, sitting across from her desk, shoulders slumped in defeat. Traditional medications had failed. Psychotherapy had reached its limits. Electroconvulsive therapy had provided only temporary relief. But in 2003, Mayberg had something new to offer, something that would have seemed like science fiction just a decade earlier.

"We're going to place electrodes in your brain," she explained to the patient, a 60-year-old woman who had been battling severe depression for over two decades. "And then we're going to stimulate a specific region called Area 25."

The woman looked up with the first spark of hope Mayberg had seen in her eyes in months. Within weeks of the deep brain stimulation procedure, that spark would become a flame, and then a steady light that had been absent for years.

This was the moment that brain-computer interfaces truly began to expand beyond their original mission of helping paralyzed patients move robotic limbs. The realization that electrical signals could not only read the brain's intentions but also write new patterns into its circuits opened up possibilities that researchers were only beginning to explore.

The Depressed Brain's Electrical Signature

Depression, Mayberg discovered, wasn't just a chemical imbalance, it was an electrical one too. Using brain imaging, she had identified a hyperactive region deep in the limbic system, Area 25, that seemed to act like a stuck accelerator pedal in depressed brains. Traditional antidepressants worked by flooding the entire brain with chemicals, hoping to hit the right targets. But what if you could deliver electrical therapy with surgical precision?

The concept built on decades of research into deep brain stimulation for Parkinson's disease, where electrodes placed in the subthalamic nucleus could dramatically reduce tremors and rigidity. But targeting mood disorders required a more nuanced approach. Unlike the motor symptoms of Parkinson's, depression involved complex networks of emotion, memory, and cognition spread throughout the brain.

"We're not just flipping a switch," Mayberg explains, sitting in her laboratory at Mount Sinai Hospital in New York. Behind her, monitors display real-time brain scans from her latest clinical trial. "We're conducting an orchestra of neural activity, trying to restore harmony to circuits that have fallen out of tune."

Area 25, officially known as the subgenual anterior cingulate cortex, sits at the intersection of multiple brain networks. It connects to the prefrontal cortex, which governs executive function and decision-making, the amygdala, which processes fear and emotional memories, the hypothalamus, which controls stress hormones and the brainstem regions that regulate sleep, appetite, and energy. In healthy brains, Area 25 acts as a traffic controller, modulating the flow of information between these critical systems. In depression, it becomes hyperactive, creating a cascade of dysfunction that manifests as the familiar symptoms, persistent sadness, loss of pleasure, disrupted sleep, poor concentration, and feelings of hopelessness.

The surgical procedure itself is remarkably precise. Using MRI guidance, neurosurgeons thread hair-thin electrodes through small holes in the skull, navigating between blood vessels and critical structures to reach the target region. The electrodes are connected to a pacemaker-like device implanted in the chest, which can be programmed to deliver specific patterns of electrical stimulation.

The results from Mayberg's early trials were nothing short of remarkable. In her first study of six patients, four showed significant improvement within months of implantation. Patients who had been trapped in decades-long depressions began to respond within hours of stimulation. Sarah, a 45-year-old teacher who hadn't experienced joy in fifteen years, described the moment her stimulator was activated, "It was like someone had been slowly turning down the volume on my life for years, and suddenly they turned it back up. Colors seemed brighter. Food had taste again. I remembered what it felt like to laugh."

But the road wasn't always smooth. Michael, a 52-year-old accountant, experienced what he described as "emotional whiplash" during the first weeks after implantation. As his brain adapted to the stimulation, he cycled rapidly between periods of elation and confusion. "I'd forgotten what normal felt like," he recalls. "My brain had to relearn how to process emotions without the constant weight of depression."

The mechanism by which deep brain stimulation works remains partially mysterious. Unlike lesioning procedures that destroy tissue, DBS appears to modulate neural activity in complex ways. High-frequency stimulation can either increase or decrease activity in target regions, depending on the specific parameters used and the existing state of the neural circuits. Some researchers believe it works by imposing artificial rhythms on dysregulated brain networks, like a conductor bringing an orchestra back into time.

Brain imaging studies of Mayberg's patients revealed fascinating changes. Not only did Activity 25 normalize its activity levels, but the stimulation appeared to restore healthy communication patterns throughout the depression network. The prefrontal cortex showed increased activity during cognitive tasks, the amygdala became less hyperreactive to negative stimuli, and the default mode network, the brain's "screensaver" that becomes overactive in depression returned to more normal patterns.

The Science of Stimulation Parameters

The success of deep brain stimulation depends critically on finding the right electrical parameters for each individual patient. Frequency, amplitude, pulse width, and electrode configuration all affect how the brain responds to stimulation. Too little current and nothing happens, too much and patients can experience side effects ranging from tingling sensations to personality changes.

Dr. Cameron McIntyre at Case Western Reserve University has spent years developing computer models to optimize these parameters. His team creates detailed three-dimensional models of each patient's brain, using MRI and CT scans to map the exact anatomy around the implanted electrodes. They then use these models to predict how different stimulation settings will affect surrounding neural tissue.

"Every brain is unique," McIntyre explains, pointing to a computer screen showing a colorful representation of electrical fields spreading through brain tissue. "The same stimulation parameters that work perfectly for one patient might be completely ineffective or even harmful for another. We're trying to create a GPS system for the brain, allowing us to navigate to the exact neural targets we want to influence."

His models have revealed why some patients respond better to certain frequencies than others. Low-frequency stimulation (around 20-60 Hz) tends to decrease neural activity, while high-frequency stimulation (130 Hz and above) can either increase or decrease activity depending on the characteristics of the target neurons. The shape and orientation of the electrodes also matter, contacts placed along white matter tracts can influence signals traveling between distant brain regions, while those in gray matter primarily affect local neural activity.

Closed-Loop Psychiatry

But Mayberg's approach was just the beginning. The next generation of neural interfaces for mental health doesn't just deliver constant stimulation, they learn and adapt in real-time, creating the first truly "smart" psychiatric devices.

Dr. Edward Chang at the University of California, San Francisco, leads one of the most ambitious projects in this emerging field. His team has developed a system they call "precision psychiatry", a brain implant that can detect the onset of depressive episodes and automatically deliver targeted stimulation to counteract them.

"Think of it like a pacemaker for the brain," Chang explains during a visit to his laboratory. "Your heart has natural rhythms, and when they go wrong, a pacemaker steps in to restore normal function. We're doing the same thing with mood circuits."

The system relies on machine learning algorithms that have been trained to recognize the electrical signatures of different emotional states. Tiny electrodes implanted in multiple brain regions continuously monitor neural activity, looking for the telltale patterns that precede a depressive episode, changes in theta wave activity in the hippocampus, altered gamma rhythms in the prefrontal cortex, disrupted communication between the amygdala and anterior cingulate cortex.

The technology builds on decades of research into the brain's electrical patterns during different emotional states. Scientists have long known that specific brainwave patterns correlate with mood states. Alpha waves (8-12 Hz) are associated with relaxed awareness, while beta waves (13-30 Hz) accompany focused attention. Gamma waves (30-100 Hz) appear during moments of heightened consciousness and binding of sensory information. In depression, these normal patterns become disrupted, alpha activity decreases in the left frontal cortex, theta activity increases in the anterior cingulate, and gamma synchronization between brain regions breaks down.

Chang's first patient, a woman he refers to only as "Patient A" to protect her privacy, had suffered from severe, treatment-resistant depression for over a decade. She had tried seventeen different medications, multiple forms of psychotherapy, electroconvulsive therapy, and transcranial magnetic stimulation. Nothing provided lasting relief. Traditional medications had failed, and she had attempted suicide multiple times.

The implantation surgery took seven hours. Chang's team placed arrays of microelectrodes in five different brain regions: the orbitofrontal cortex, the anterior cingulate cortex, the amygdala, the hippocampus, and the ventral striatum. Each location was chosen based on its role in the depression circuitry and its accessibility through minimally invasive surgical approaches.

For the first month after surgery, the electrodes simply recorded. Patient A went about her daily life while the system learned her brain's unique patterns. Machine learning algorithms analyzed thousands of hours of neural data, identifying the specific combinations of brainwave patterns that preceded her depressive episodes.

"The most remarkable thing," Chang notes, "is that we can see the depression trying to return in her brain activity, the same patterns that used to spiral into weeks-long episodes. But now the system catches it and corrects it automatically, often before she's even consciously aware anything is wrong."

Within days of activating the therapeutic stimulation, Patient A's depression scores began to improve for the first time in years. Her Beck Depression Inventory score dropped from 33 (severe depression) to 14 (mild depression) over the course of six weeks. More importantly, she reported subjective improvements in mood, energy, and motivation.

"I can feel when the system kicks in," she describes. "It's like having a guardian angel in my brain. I'll start to feel that familiar heaviness creeping in, and then suddenly it lifts. I can think clearly again, make decisions, engage with people. It's given me my life back."

The closed-loop system adapts continuously. As Patient A's brain changes through natural plasticity, seasonal variations, or life stressors the algorithms adjust their detection criteria and stimulation parameters. The system has learned to distinguish between normal sadness (such as grief over a loss) and pathological depression, providing intervention only when needed.

Other research teams are developing similar approaches for different psychiatric conditions. Dr. Maryam Shanechi at the University of Southern California has created closed-loop systems for anxiety disorders, detecting the neural signatures of panic attacks and delivering calming stimulation to the amygdala and prefrontal cortex. Dr. Kafui Dzirasa at Duke University is working on bipolar disorder, developing algorithms that can detect the early signs of both manic and depressive episodes.

The Challenge of Psychiatric Heterogeneity

One of the greatest challenges in developing brain-computer interfaces for mental health is the enormous variability between patients. Unlike paralysis, where the goal is clearly defined, restore movement, psychiatric conditions present much more complex targets. Depression affects different people in dramatically different ways, involving varying combinations of mood, cognitive, and physical symptoms.

Dr. Conor Liston at Weill Cornell Medicine has been mapping this heterogeneity using advanced neuroimaging techniques. His team has identified four distinct "biotypes" of depression, each characterized by different patterns of brain connectivity. Some patients show primarily limbic dysfunction, with overactive emotional centers. Others have prefrontal deficits, with impaired cognitive control and decision-making. Still others show disrupted connectivity between brain networks.

"We're realizing that depression isn't one disease, it's probably at least four or five different diseases that happen to share some common symptoms," Liston explains. "This has huge implications for how we design brain stimulation treatments. The optimal target for one biotype might be completely wrong for another."

His research has shown that patients with different biotypes respond differently to various treatments. Those with limbic dysfunction respond well to stimulation of Area 25 or the nucleus accumbens. Patients with prefrontal deficits benefit more from stimulation of the dorsolateral prefrontal cortex or anterior cingulate. Those with connectivity problems might need more complex, multi-site stimulation protocols.

This precision psychiatry approach is beginning to influence clinical practice. Dr. Andrea Crowell at Emory University has developed a screening protocol that uses brief neuroimaging sessions to classify new patients into biotypes before selecting stimulation targets. Early results suggest this approach more than doubles the success rate compared to traditional one-size-fits-all protocols.

Predicting and Preventing Seizures

While psychiatric applications represent one frontier of BCI expansion, epilepsy has provided perhaps the most dramatic demonstrations of how brain interfaces can move beyond simple recording to active intervention. For the 65 million people worldwide living with epilepsy, seizures are unpredictable lightning strikes of electrical chaos that can strike without warning, disrupting lives and sometimes proving fatal.

Dr. Brian Litt at the University of Pennsylvania has spent two decades working to change that unpredictability. His NeuroVista system represents one of the most sophisticated attempts to create an early warning system for seizures, using machine learning algorithms trained on each patient's unique seizure patterns.

"Every person's brain is different," Litt explains, reviewing data from his latest clinical trial. "The electrical signature that precedes a seizure in one patient might be completely different in another. But once we learn those patterns, we can start predicting seizures hours or even days in advance."

The challenge of seizure prediction has frustrated researchers for decades. Early attempts focused on looking for universal warning signs, changes in heart rate, specific brainwave patterns, or behavioral indicators. But seizures proved to be highly individual phenomena. What worked for one patient failed completely for another.

Litt's breakthrough came from recognizing that seizure prediction needed to be personalized. His system implants electrodes in the brain regions where a patient's seizures originate, then records continuously for weeks or months to learn that individual's unique pre-seizure patterns. Machine learning algorithms analyze the data, looking for subtle changes in neural activity that precede seizures.

The mathematics involved are staggering. The system processes thousands of data points per second from multiple electrodes, looking for patterns in frequency bands ranging from 0.5 Hz to 500 Hz. It tracks not just the amplitude of different brainwave frequencies, but also their phase relationships, synchronization between different brain regions, and higher-order statistical properties of the signals.

"We're looking for needles in haystacks," Litt explains. "Most of the time, the brain's electrical activity looks completely random. But in the hours before a seizure, there are often subtle changes, maybe a slight increase in gamma activity in one region, or a change in the phase coupling between theta and gamma rhythms. Our algorithms are trained to spot these incredibly subtle patterns."

The implications are profound. Jessica, a 28-year-old graduate student in chemistry, had been forced to abandon her career after unpredictable seizures made laboratory work too dangerous. Her seizures came without warning, sometimes she would have multiple seizures in a day, other times she would go weeks without any. Traditional anti-seizure medications left her feeling foggy and unable to concentrate, but reducing the dosage brought back the seizures.

The decision to get a seizure prediction implant wasn't easy. The surgery involved placing depth electrodes in her temporal lobe, carrying risks of bleeding, infection, and brain damage. But after years of unpredictable seizures had essentially put her life on hold, Jessica decided the potential benefits outweighed the risks.

After receiving the NeuroVista implant, Jessica's life transformed again. The system learned to predict her seizures with remarkable accuracy, 93% in her case, giving her enough warning to take preventive medication, move to a safe location, or alert caregivers. The warnings came through a small device she carried, similar to a glucose monitor used by diabetics. A blue light meant low seizure risk, yellow indicated elevated risk, and red warned of high seizure probability within the next few hours.

"I got my life back," Jessica says. "I can travel, I can work in the lab again, I can drive. The seizures still happen sometimes, but they don't control my life anymore. I can plan activities with confidence, knowing I'll get enough warning if a seizure is coming."

The psychological impact was as important as the practical benefits. Years of unpredictable seizures had left Jessica anxious and hypervigilant, constantly scanning her body for warning signs that never came. The seizure prediction system freed her from this constant worry. When the device showed blue, she could relax completely. When it showed yellow or red, she could take appropriate precautions without panic.

But prediction was only the first step. The next generation of epilepsy devices actively intervenes to prevent seizures from occurring. The RNS (Responsive Neurostimulation) system, developed by NeuroPace, continuously monitors brain activity and delivers targeted electrical pulses when it detects the early signs of seizure activity.

Dr. Martha Morrell, NeuroPace's chief medical officer, describes the system as "a smoke detector for the brain that also has a built-in fire extinguisher." Clinical trials have shown that the system can reduce seizure frequency by more than 70% in patients who haven't responded to medications.

The technology works by detecting the characteristic high-frequency electrical activity that marks the beginning of a seizure and immediately delivering a brief pulse of electrical stimulation to disrupt the spreading abnormal activity. It's a delicate balance, too little stimulation and the seizure continues, too much and you risk triggering the very activity you're trying to prevent.

David, a 34-year-old teacher from Phoenix, had lived with epilepsy since he was sixteen. Despite trying multiple medications, he continued to have several seizures per month, forcing him to limit his activities and live with constant uncertainty. The decision to try the RNS system came after a particularly severe seizure left him hospitalized with a concussion.

The implantation surgery placed two strips of electrodes over the regions of his brain where seizures originated, connected to a matchbox-sized device implanted in his skull. For the first few months, the system only recorded, learning the electrical patterns that preceded his seizures. Then the therapeutic stimulation was activated.

The results exceeded everyone's expectations. David's seizures dropped from fifteen per month to fewer than three. Those that did occur were often shorter and less severe than before. Brain monitoring showed that many seizures were actually being detected and stopped before they could spread and cause symptoms.

"The device has given me freedom I haven't had in twenty years," David reflects. "I can take on new responsibilities at work, plan vacations, even consider starting a family. The seizures that do break through are just a reminder of what my life used to be like every single day."

The Neuroscience of Seizure Control

The success of responsive neurostimulation has revealed new insights into how seizures develop and spread through the brain. Dr. Gregory Worrell at the Mayo Clinic has used high-resolution brain monitoring to map the precise pathways that seizures follow as they propagate from their origin points to other brain regions.

"We used to think of seizures as electrical storms that spread randomly through the brain," Worrell explains. "But we're learning that they actually follow very specific pathways, like rivers flowing through established channels. If we can interrupt the flow at key chokepoints, we can prevent the seizure from spreading."

His research has identified what he calls "seizure highways", specific white matter tracts that seizures commonly use to spread between brain regions. By targeting stimulation at these critical junctions, the RNS system can often stop seizures with minimal disruption to normal brain function.

The technology continues to evolve. Newer versions of the RNS system can deliver more sophisticated stimulation patterns, including burst stimulation, frequency-matched stimulation, and even optogenetic approaches that use light to control genetically modified neurons.

Researchers are also exploring multi-site systems that can coordinate stimulation across multiple brain regions simultaneously.

Memory's Electrical Architecture

Perhaps no application of brain-computer interfaces holds more promise or presents greater challenges than the quest to restore memory in patients with Alzheimer's disease and other forms of dementia. As populations age worldwide, the number of people living with memory disorders continues to climb, creating an urgent need for new therapeutic approaches.

Dr. Theodore Berger at the University of Southern California has devoted his career to understanding how memories form and how technology might help when that process breaks down. His approach involves creating what he calls a "memory prosthesis", a device that can record, store, and play back the electrical patterns associated with memory formation.

"Memory isn't stored in one place in the brain," Berger explains, standing in front of a wall-sized display showing the intricate connections of the hippocampus. "It's a process, a pattern of electrical activity that flows through specific circuits. If we can understand that pattern, we can potentially restore it when disease disrupts it."

The hippocampus, a seahorse-shaped structure deep in the temporal lobe, plays a crucial role in converting short-term memories into long-term storage. Information flows from the neocortex into the hippocampus through a series of processing stages, each encoded by specific patterns of neural activity. In Alzheimer's disease, the accumulation of amyloid plaques and tau tangles disrupts these circuits, preventing new memories from forming and gradually erasing older ones.

Berger's team has spent years mapping the electrical codes that the hippocampus uses to process memories. Using arrays of microelectrodes, they record from hundreds of neurons simultaneously as subjects perform memory tasks, looking for the mathematical relationships that govern how information flows from short-term to long-term memory storage.

The breakthrough came when they realized they could create artificial versions of these memory codes. By analyzing successful memory formation trials, they identified the specific patterns of electrical activity that corresponded to information being successfully encoded. They then developed algorithms that could generate similar patterns artificially.

In rats and monkeys, they demonstrated that electrical stimulation patterns derived from successful memory formation could improve performance on memory tasks. The animals essentially received artificial memories that helped them remember information they had learned. In one dramatic experiment, monkeys who had learned a complex visual task, then had their performance impaired by drugs, recovered normal function when the memory prosthesis was activated.

The first human trials began in 2015, focusing on patients who already had electrodes implanted for epilepsy monitoring. The results were encouraging: patients showed improvements in memory formation of up to 37% when the memory prosthesis was activated.

Robert, a 67-year-old retired engineer with early Alzheimer's disease, was among the first to receive an experimental memory enhancement system. Before the implant, he had been unable to form new memories for more than a few minutes. Simple tasks like remembering where he put his keys or following a conversation became impossible.

The implantation surgery required extraordinary precision. Surgeons used MRI guidance to place arrays of microelectrodes in the CA3 and CA1 regions of Robert's hippocampus, areas critical for memory formation but also some of the first to be affected by Alzheimer's pathology. The procedure took twelve hours, with Robert awake for portions to ensure the electrodes were placed correctly.

For the first month after surgery, the system simply recorded Robert's brain activity during memory tasks. He would look at pictures, try to remember word lists, and listen to stories while hundreds of electrodes captured the electrical patterns in his hippocampus. Machine learning algorithms analyzed this data, learning the specific neural codes his brain used for successful memory formation.

"The first day we turned on the system, Robert was able to remember a list of words for over an hour, something he hadn't been able to do in two years," recalls Dr. Dong Song, who leads the clinical trials. "His wife broke down crying. It was the first real conversation they'd had in months."

The memory prosthesis worked by detecting when Robert's brain was trying to form a memory and providing electrical stimulation that mimicked the patterns associated with successful encoding. The system could distinguish between different types of memories, spatial, verbal, and visual and apply the appropriate stimulation pattern for each.

The improvements weren't limited to the laboratory. Robert began to show benefits in daily life. He could remember conversations with his family, follow the plots of television shows, and even recall where he had placed objects. His wife, Margaret, described the transformation as "getting my husband back, piece by piece."

"It's like having a computer helping my brain work properly again," Robert explains during a follow-up interview. "I can feel when the system kicks in. There's a moment when things just become clearer, more vivid. I can hold onto thoughts that would have slipped away before."

But the technology also revealed the complexity of human memory. The memory prosthesis worked best for simple, explicit memories, facts, names, and events. It was less effective for procedural memories, skills, habits and emotional memories, which involve different neural circuits. Robert could remember what he had for breakfast, but he still struggled with complex tasks like managing his finances or remembering to take medications.

The Molecular Basis of Memory Enhancement

Dr. Itzhak Fried at UCLA has taken a different approach to memory enhancement, focusing on the role of individual neurons in memory formation. His research has identified specific cells "concept cells" or "grandmother cells" that respond to particular people, places, or concepts. By stimulating these cells at the right moments, he can enhance the formation of specific memories.

"We've found neurons that respond to specific concepts," Fried explains, showing recordings from a patient's brain. "This cell fires when the patient sees pictures of Jennifer Aniston, but not other actresses. This one responds to the Eiffel Tower, but not other landmarks. By stimulating these cells during learning, we can make memories more vivid and lasting."

His experiments have shown that targeted stimulation of concept cells can improve memory performance by up to 50%. The enhancement is specific, stimulating cells that respond to faces improves face recognition, while stimulating place cells enhances spatial memory.

The discovery of concept cells has profound implications for understanding consciousness and identity. These neurons seem to encode our personal knowledge and experiences, forming the neural basis of our individual perspective on the world. As memory prostheses become more sophisticated, they raise questions about the nature of authentic experience and personal identity.

Sensory Resurrection: The Return of Sight and Sound

Beyond mood, seizures, and memory, brain-computer interfaces are beginning to restore the most fundamental human experiences, sight and sound. For the 39 million people worldwide who are blind and the 466 million with disabling hearing loss, neural interfaces offer the possibility of reconnecting with the sensory world.

The cochlear implant, first developed in the 1960s, was actually one of the earliest successful brain-computer interfaces, though it wasn't recognized as such at the time. By converting sound waves into electrical patterns that stimulate the auditory nerve, cochlear implants have restored hearing to over 700,000 people worldwide.

The success of cochlear implants provides a roadmap for other sensory restoration efforts. The auditory system has several advantages that make it relatively amenable to artificial stimulation. The cochlea's frequency organization is well understood, with different regions responding to different pitches. The auditory nerve maintains this organization, allowing precise frequency mapping. Most importantly, the brain's auditory cortex is remarkably plastic, capable of learning to interpret artificial electrical patterns as meaningful sounds.

Dr. Blake Wilson, the engineer who developed many of the signal processing strategies used in modern cochlear implants, describes the evolution of the technology, "The first implants could only provide crude awareness of environmental sounds, the difference between speech and music, a car horn versus silence. But as we learned more about how to encode information electrically, the devices became sophisticated enough to support telephone conversations, music appreciation, and even learning new languages."

Modern cochlear implants use sophisticated algorithms to analyze incoming sounds and convert them into patterns of electrical pulses delivered to up to 22 different locations along the cochlea. The processing happens in real-time, with delays of less than 10 milliseconds between sound input and electrical stimulation.

Maria Santos, a 34-year-old music teacher from São Paulo, lost her hearing suddenly at age 29 due to meningitis. The infection destroyed the hair cells in her cochlea, leaving her completely deaf. Traditional hearing aids were useless, there were no functioning hair cells left to amplify.

"The silence was devastating," Maria recalls. "Music has been my life, my career, my passion. Suddenly I was cut off from everything that mattered to me. I fell into a deep depression, couldn't work, and barely left my apartment."

The cochlear implant surgery was straightforward, a two-hour outpatient procedure. The surgeon made a small incision behind Maria's ear and drilled a channel through the temporal bone to access the cochlea. The implant's electrode array was threaded into the cochlea's spiral chamber, and the internal receiver was placed under the skin behind the ear.

The moment of activation, four weeks later, was overwhelming. "The first sound I heard was the audiologist's voice saying 'Can you hear me?' But it didn't sound like a voice, it was more like a robot, all electronic and mechanical. I started crying because I was so disappointed."

But Maria's brain began to adapt quickly. Within weeks, the robotic sounds started to resolve into speech. Within months, she could understand conversations without lip reading. After a year, she returned to teaching, though she had to learn new techniques for working with students.

"Music was the last thing to come back," she explains. "At first, it sounded terrible, like noise, not music at all. But gradually, my brain learned to make sense of the electrical signals. Now I can enjoy music again, though it's different from how I remember it sounding. It's like learning a new language of sound."

The latest generation of cochlear implants includes features that would have seemed impossible in the early devices. Some can connect directly to smartphones, allowing users to stream phone calls, music, and other audio directly to their implants. Others include noise reduction algorithms that can filter out background noise in restaurants and other challenging listening environments.

The Visual Challenge

But visual restoration has proven far more challenging than auditory restoration. The eye's retina contains over 100 million photoreceptors of multiple types, each encoding different aspects of visual information, brightness, color, motion, and contrast. The retina also performs significant processing before sending signals to the brain, extracting features like edges and movement patterns. Early attempts at artificial vision produced crude patterns of light and dark that were barely functional.

Dr. Daniel Palanker at Stanford University has developed a new approach that promises to change that. His photovoltaic retinal implant uses thousands of tiny solar cells to convert light directly into electrical stimulation, mimicking the natural function of photoreceptors with unprecedented precision.

"Instead of trying to replace the eye's complexity with electronics, we're working with the brain's natural ability to interpret electrical patterns," Palanker explains. "The visual cortex is remarkably adaptable, it can learn to see through almost any input, as long as that input contains useful information about the visual world."

Palanker's system consists of a thin film containing 378 photovoltaic pixels, each just 70 micrometers in diameter. The film is surgically implanted under the retina, where it converts light into electrical currents that stimulate the remaining retinal neurons. Unlike other retinal implants that require external electronics and battery packs, the photovoltaic system is powered entirely by light.

The system works with special glasses that project pulsed infrared light onto the implanted chip. The infrared light is invisible to normal vision but carries visual information captured by a camera mounted on the glasses. Image processing algorithms convert the camera input into patterns of infrared light that the implant can convert back into neural stimulation.

Maria Gonzalez, a 58-year-old artist who lost her sight to macular degeneration, was among the first to receive Palanker's implant. The transformation was gradual but profound. First came the ability to distinguish light from dark, then basic shapes, and finally detailed images.

The initial experience was disorienting. "I could see something, but I couldn't make sense of it," Maria describes. "It was like trying to understand a language I'd never heard before. Everything was fragmented and pixelated."

But her brain began to learn the new visual language. The process was aided by rehabilitation training, where Maria practiced identifying objects, reading large text, and navigating obstacles. Her visual cortex, starved of input for years, began to reorganize itself around the artificial signals from the implant.

"I can see my grandchildren's faces again," Maria says, tears streaming down her cheeks. "Not perfectly, it's like looking through static sometimes but I can see their smiles, their expressions. I thought that was gone forever."

The technology is rapidly improving. The latest generation of retinal implants can deliver high-resolution images sufficient for reading large print and navigating independently. Future versions promise even greater capabilities, potentially exceeding normal human vision in some respects.

Dr. Sheila Nirenberg at Cornell University is developing a different approach that focuses on recreating the retina's natural code. Rather than simply converting light into electrical pulses, her system mimics the complex patterns of neural activity that the retina normally sends to the brain.

"The retina doesn't just detect light, it processes visual information in sophisticated ways," Nirenberg explains. "It extracts edges, detects motion, and adjusts for different lighting conditions. If we can recreate these processing functions artificially, we should be able to provide much more natural vision."

Her approach uses algorithms that mimic different types of retinal ganglion cells, the neurons that send information from the retina to the brain. Some cells respond to edges, others to motion, still others to changes in brightness. By stimulating these different cell types with their preferred patterns, the system can provide richer visual information.

Early trials of Nirenberg's approach have shown promising results. Patients report that artificial vision seems more natural and easier to interpret than with previous systems. Objects appear more three-dimensional, motion is smoother, and the overall visual experience is less fatiguing.

Cortical Visual Prostheses

While retinal implants work by stimulating the eye's remaining neural circuitry, cortical visual prostheses bypass the eyes entirely, delivering electrical stimulation directly to the visual cortex. This approach holds promise for people who have lost their sight due to damage to the eyes or optic nerves, rather than retinal diseases.

Dr. William Dobelle pioneered cortical visual prostheses in the 1970s, demonstrating that electrical stimulation of the visual cortex could produce phosphenes, spots of light that patients could see and interpret.

His early systems were crude, producing only simple patterns of light and dark, but they proved that artificial vision was possible through direct brain stimulation.

Modern cortical implants use high-resolution electrode arrays that can stimulate hundreds of locations in the visual cortex simultaneously. The Orion Visual Cortical Prosthesis System, developed by Second Sight, consists of 60 electrodes implanted on the surface of the visual cortex, connected to external electronics that process camera input and convert it into stimulation patterns.

Jason Esterhuizen, a 30-year-old chef from South Africa, was blinded at age 22 in a car accident that severed both optic nerves. Traditional retinal implants couldn't help him because his eyes were intact but disconnected from his brain. He became one of the first recipients of the Orion system.

The surgery required removing a portion of the skull over the visual cortex and carefully placing the electrode array on the brain's surface. The procedure was risky, any damage to the visual cortex could cause seizures or other neurological problems. But for Jason, who had lost not just his sight but his career and independence, the potential benefits outweighed the risks.

The first activation session was both thrilling and frustrating. When individual electrodes were stimulated, Jason saw bright spots of light, phosphenes in specific locations in his visual field. By stimulating different combinations of electrodes, researchers could create simple patterns: lines, squares, and basic shapes.

"It wasn't like normal vision at all," Jason recalls. "The phosphenes were very bright, almost painful at first. And they didn't look like real objects, more like points of light on a dark background. But after eight years of complete darkness, even those simple patterns felt like a miracle."

Training with the cortical implant required months of intensive rehabilitation. Jason had to learn to interpret the artificial phosphene patterns as meaningful visual information. Simple tasks like distinguishing between a cup and a plate required concentration and practice. But gradually, his brain adapted to the new form of visual input.

"The breakthrough moment came when I was able to find a white door in a dark room," Jason remembers. "It sounds simple, but it meant I could navigate independently for the first time since my accident. I could see the outline of the doorway as a pattern of phosphenes and walk toward it without bumping into walls."

The system's limitations became apparent as Jason gained more experience with it. The resolution was low, only 60 points of light compared to the millions of photoreceptors in a normal retina. Colors were impossible; everything appeared as variations of brightness. Fine details like facial expressions or text were beyond the system's capabilities.

But within these constraints, Jason achieved remarkable functionality. He learned to identify common objects, navigate familiar environments, and even perform simple cooking tasks. The visual information was crude, but it was enough to restore a measure of independence.

"I can't see faces clearly, but I can tell when someone is standing in front of me," he explains. "I can't read normal text, but I can see the shape of letters if they're large enough. It's not perfect vision, but it's vision. After years of blindness, that means everything."

Rewiring Addiction: The Brain's Reward Circuits

One of the most surprising applications of brain-computer interfaces has emerged in the treatment of addiction. Traditional approaches to addiction treatment have focused on behavioral therapy and medications that block or substitute for addictive substances. But a growing body of research suggests that addiction fundamentally rewires the brain's reward circuits, creating electrical patterns that drive compulsive behavior.

Dr. Ali Rezai at West Virginia University has pioneered the use of deep brain stimulation to treat severe addiction. His approach targets the nucleus accumbens, a brain region central to reward processing and motivation.

"Addiction isn't a moral failing or a lack of willpower," Rezai emphasizes. "It's a disease of brain circuits. When someone is addicted, their reward system becomes hijacked, creating overwhelming urges that are incredibly difficult to resist through willpower alone."

The nucleus accumbens, sometimes called the brain's "pleasure center," plays a crucial role in motivation and reward-seeking behavior. It receives dopamine signals from the ventral tegmental area and integrates information from the prefrontal cortex, amygdala, and hippocampus. In healthy brains, this system helps us pursue beneficial activities, food when hungry, social connection when lonely and rest when tired.

But addictive substances hijack this natural reward system. Alcohol, cocaine, opioids, and other drugs trigger massive dopamine releases in the nucleus accumbens, far greater than any natural reward. Over time, the brain adapts to these artificial spikes by reducing its sensitivity to dopamine and decreasing natural dopamine production. The result is a system that craves the drug while finding little pleasure in anything else.

Brain imaging studies of people with addiction show characteristic changes in the reward circuits. The nucleus accumbens shows heightened activity when exposed to drug cues but reduced activity during other potentially rewarding experiences. The prefrontal cortex, which normally provides executive control over impulses, shows decreased activity and connectivity. The anterior cingulate cortex, involved in decision-making and impulse control, becomes hyperactive when trying to resist cravings but often fails to override the reward system's demands.

The results from Rezai's trials have been striking. Patients with severe alcohol addiction who had failed multiple treatment attempts showed dramatic improvements when the stimulation system was activated. Craving scores dropped by an average of 60%, and many patients were able to maintain sobriety for the first time in years.

Tommy Rodriguez, a 42-year-old construction worker who had struggled with alcohol addiction for over two decades, became one of Rezai's first patients. His addiction had cost him his marriage, his relationship with his children, and multiple jobs. He had been through rehab seven times, tried Alcoholics Anonymous, and experimented with various medications. Nothing provided lasting sobriety.

"I could go maybe two or three weeks without drinking, but then something would happen, stress at work, an argument with my ex-wife, just seeing a beer commercial on TV and the cravings would come back stronger than ever," Tommy explains. "It felt like there was this voice in my head constantly telling me I needed alcohol, and no matter what I did, I couldn't make it stop."

The decision to try deep brain stimulation wasn't easy. The surgery carried risks, and Tommy worried about having electrodes permanently implanted in his brain. But after his most recent relapse had landed him in the emergency room with alcohol poisoning, he felt he had run out of options.

The implantation procedure took four hours. Using MRI guidance, surgeons placed electrodes bilaterally in Tommy's nucleus accumbens, connecting them to a pacemaker-like device implanted in his chest. The surgery was performed under local anesthesia so Tommy could provide feedback as the electrodes were positioned.

"The strangest thing was that I could feel when they tested the electrodes," Tommy recalls. "There was this sudden sense of... not euphoria exactly, but like a weight lifting off my shoulders. The constant noise in my head, that voice demanding alcohol just got quieter."

For the first month after surgery, the system was turned off while Tommy recovered. During this period, his cravings returned to their previous intensity. But when the stimulation was activated, the change was dramatic and almost immediate.

Tommy describes the experience: "It wasn't like someone flipped a switch and suddenly I didn't want to drink. But the constant noise in my head, that voice always telling me I needed alcohol, it just got quieter. For the first time in years, I could think about something else. I could walk past a bar without my heart racing. I could have a conversation without part of my brain constantly calculating when I could get my next drink."

The mechanism appears to work by normalizing the dopamine signaling in reward circuits that have been disrupted by chronic substance use. Brain imaging studies show that patients receiving deep brain stimulation for addiction develop more normal patterns of activity in areas associated with decision-making and impulse control. The prefrontal cortex shows increased activity during cognitive tasks, while the nucleus accumbens becomes less hyperreactive to addiction-related cues.

But the treatment isn't a magic bullet. Tommy still attends therapy sessions and participates in a support group. The brain stimulation has made it possible for him to engage meaningfully with these traditional treatments by reducing the intensity of his cravings to manageable levels.

"The stimulation gives me a fighting chance," he explains. "Before, the cravings were so overwhelming that all the therapy in the world couldn't help. Now, when I get stressed or triggered, I can actually use the coping strategies I've learned. I can pause, think, make a choice instead of just reacting automatically."

Tommy has been sober for over two years since receiving the implant—his longest period of sobriety since his early twenties. He's rebuilding relationships with his children, has maintained steady employment, and recently started dating someone new.

The Complexity of Addiction Treatment

Dr. Anna Rose Childress at the University of Pennsylvania has been studying the brain mechanisms of addiction for over three decades. Her research has revealed the complexity of addiction's effects on neural circuits, suggesting that successful treatment may require multiple intervention points.

"Addiction affects not just the reward system, but multiple brain networks," Childress explains, reviewing brain scans from her latest studies. "There's the reward/motivation circuit, the habit/memory circuit, the stress/emotion circuit, and the cognitive control circuit. Different people show different patterns of dysfunction across these networks."

Her research has identified several distinct subtypes of addiction, each characterized by different neural profiles. Some patients show primarily reward system dysfunction, their brains have become insensitive to natural rewards while remaining hyperreactive to drug cues. Others show mainly cognitive control deficits; their reward sensitivity is relatively intact, but their prefrontal cortex cannot effectively regulate their impulses. Still others show stress-driven addiction, their emotional regulation systems are so disrupted that drugs become their primary means of managing anxiety and depression.

"This suggests we need personalized approaches to brain stimulation for addiction," Childress notes. "Patients with reward system dysfunction might benefit from nucleus accumbens stimulation. Those with cognitive control problems might need prefrontal cortex stimulation. Stress-driven addicts might respond better to stimulation of emotional regulation circuits."

Her team is developing a screening protocol that uses brain imaging and psychological assessments to classify patients into different subtypes before selecting stimulation targets. Early results suggest this personalized approach significantly improves treatment outcomes.

Beyond Stimulation: Optogenetic Approaches

While electrical stimulation has dominated the field of therapeutic brain interfaces, researchers are beginning to explore more precise approaches using light-sensitive proteins called opsins. Optogenetics, developed by Dr. Karl Deisseroth at Stanford, allows researchers to control specific types of neurons using pulses of light.

Dr. Kay Tye at the Salk Institute has been using optogenetic approaches to study and potentially treat anxiety and depression. Her team has identified specific neural circuits that become dysfunctional in these conditions and developed light-based interventions to restore normal function.

"The beauty of optogenetics is its precision," Tye explains. "Instead of affecting all neurons in a region with electrical stimulation, we can target specific cell types, dopamine neurons, GABA neurons, glutamate neurons and even specific connections between brain regions."

Her research has revealed the intricate circuit dysfunctions underlying anxiety disorders. In mouse models of anxiety, she found that neurons connecting the basolateral amygdala to the central amygdala become hyperactive, creating excessive fear responses. By using optogenetics to selectively inhibit this pathway, she could reduce anxiety-like behaviors without affecting other aspects of emotion or cognition.

"We can essentially perform brain surgery with light," Tye describes. "If we identify a specific connection that's malfunctioning, we can turn it up or down with precise timing and selectivity that's impossible with traditional electrical stimulation."

The clinical translation of optogenetics faces significant challenges. Delivering light-sensitive proteins to human brain cells requires gene therapy approaches that are still experimental. But early trials for inherited blindness using optogenetics to restore light sensitivity to retinal cells have shown promising results, suggesting the approach may eventually reach other neurological conditions.

The Social Brain: Treating Autism Spectrum Disorders

One of the most intriguing frontiers in brain-computer interfaces involves the social brain, the neural networks that govern our ability to understand others, form relationships, and navigate complex social situations. For individuals with autism spectrum disorders, difficulties in these areas can significantly impact quality of life and independence.

Dr. Kevin Pelphrey at the University of Virginia has spent years mapping the neural circuits involved in social cognition. His research has identified specific patterns of brain connectivity that differ between individuals with and without autism, providing potential targets for therapeutic intervention.

"Social cognition involves multiple brain networks working in coordination," Pelphrey explains. "There's the face processing network, the theory of mind network, the empathy network, and the social reward network. In autism, we often see disrupted connectivity within and between these networks."

His studies using brain imaging have revealed that individuals with autism show reduced activity in the superior temporal sulcus when viewing social scenes, decreased connectivity between the amygdala and prefrontal cortex during emotional processing, and altered patterns of activity in the mirror neuron system that normally helps us understand others' actions and intentions.

These findings have led to experimental trials of brain stimulation approaches for autism. Dr. Estate Sokhadze at the University of South Carolina has conducted studies using transcranial magnetic stimulation (TMS) to enhance activity in social brain networks. His results suggest that targeted stimulation can improve social communication skills and reduce repetitive behaviors in some individuals with autism.

"We're not trying to 'cure' autism," Sokhadze emphasizes. "We're trying to enhance specific skills that can improve quality of life and independence. If we can help someone better understand facial expressions or engage more comfortably in social situations, that can make a huge difference in their daily life."

Sarah Chen, a 19-year-old college student with high-functioning autism, participated in one of Sokhadze's TMS studies. She had always struggled with understanding social cues and forming friendships, despite being academically gifted.

"I could memorize every fact about molecular biology, but I couldn't tell if someone was joking or being serious," Sarah explains. "Social situations felt like trying to navigate without a map. Everyone else seemed to know rules that no one had taught me."

After six weeks of TMS treatment targeting her social brain networks, Sarah began to notice changes. She found it easier to interpret facial expressions, felt more comfortable making eye contact, and started recognizing emotional undertones in conversations that had previously been invisible to her.

"It's like someone adjusted the settings on my social radar," she describes. "I can pick up on subtleties that I missed before. Conversations that used to feel overwhelming now seem manageable. I've made more friends this semester than in all my previous years of school combined."

Eating Disorders and Body Image

Brain-computer interfaces are also showing promise for treating eating disorders, conditions that have historically been among the most challenging to treat with traditional approaches. Dr. Walter Kaye at UC San Diego has identified specific patterns of brain activity that characterize anorexia nervosa and bulimia, providing potential targets for intervention.

"Eating disorders involve dysfunction in multiple brain circuits," Kaye explains. "There's altered reward processing around food, heightened anxiety and perfectionism, distorted body image perception, and compulsive behaviors. Traditional treatments address the psychological aspects, but they often struggle to change the underlying neural patterns."

His research has shown that individuals with anorexia have altered activity in the insula, a brain region involved in body awareness and interoceptive signals like hunger and fullness. They also show disrupted connectivity in reward circuits, making food less inherently rewarding, and heightened activity in cognitive control regions, reflecting the excessive self-control that characterizes the disorder.

Dr. Jamie Feusner at UCLA has begun exploring brain stimulation approaches for body dysmorphic disorder, a condition closely related to eating disorders. His preliminary studies using TMS to target visual processing regions have shown promise in reducing distorted body image perceptions.

The Expanding Frontier

As brain-computer interfaces move beyond paralysis, they're revealing the fundamental electrical nature of many conditions previously thought to be purely chemical or psychological. Depression, epilepsy, memory loss, sensory impairment, and addiction all have distinctive electrical signatures that can potentially be detected, predicted, and corrected.

Dr. Kay Tye at the Salk Institute is pushing these boundaries even further, developing what she calls "optogenetics-inspired" approaches that can target specific types of neurons with unprecedented precision. Her team has identified neural circuits associated with anxiety, social behavior, and motivation, opening up possibilities for treating conditions like autism, social phobia, and eating disorders.

"We're just beginning to understand how rich and complex the brain's electrical language really is," Tye reflects. "Every emotion, every memory, every aspect of personality has its own electrical signature. As we learn to read and write this language more fluently, the possibilities become almost limitless."

The implications extend far beyond individual patients. If brain-computer interfaces can effectively treat depression, they might prevent the millions of suicides that occur worldwide each year. If they can predict and prevent seizures, they could restore independence to people with epilepsy. If they can enhance memory, they might delay or prevent the devastating progression of dementia.

But with these possibilities come new challenges. Unlike the clear medical need presented by paralysis, many of these applications exist in a gray area between treatment and enhancement. When does treating depression become mood manipulation? When does memory assistance become cognitive cheating? When does sensory restoration become superhuman perception?

Dr. Judy Illes, a neuroethicist at the University of British Columbia, has spent years grappling with these questions. "The line between therapy and enhancement isn't always clear," she notes. "A cochlear implant that restores normal hearing is clearly therapeutic. But what about one that allows you to hear frequencies beyond the normal human range? We need to have these conversations now, before the technology outpaces our ethical frameworks."

The regulatory landscape is also evolving to address these new applications. The FDA has established specific pathways for reviewing brain stimulation devices, but the rapid pace of technological development often outstrips the regulatory process. International differences in approval standards create additional complexity, with some countries moving faster than others to embrace new neurotechnologies.

Patient advocacy groups play an increasingly important role in shaping the development and deployment of these technologies. Organizations like the International Association of BCI Research and the Society for Neuroscience provide forums for researchers, patients, and ethicists to discuss the implications of emerging neurotechnologies.

The economics of brain-computer interfaces also present challenges. While the devices themselves are becoming more sophisticated, they remain expensive to develop, manufacture, and implant. Insurance coverage varies widely, and many promising treatments remain accessible only to those who can afford them or qualify for research studies.

Dr. Rajesh Rao at the University of Washington leads efforts to make brain-computer interfaces more affordable and accessible. His team has developed low-cost versions of brain stimulation devices that could potentially be deployed in resource-limited settings.

"Technology is only as good as its accessibility," Rao argues. "If we develop amazing brain interfaces that only wealthy patients in developed countries can access, we're not really solving the global burden of neurological disease. We need to think from the beginning about how to make these technologies available to everyone who needs them."

As brain-computer interfaces continue to expand beyond paralysis, they're not just changing individual lives, they're beginning to reshape our understanding of what it means to be human. The brain's electrical nature, once a curiosity studied by a few researchers, is becoming the foundation for a new form of medicine that treats the mind as directly as we've traditionally treated the body.

The patients who've volunteered for these early trials from those with treatment-resistant depression to severe addiction are pioneers in every sense of the word. Their courage in embracing experimental technologies is not just helping them reclaim their own lives; it's lighting the path toward a future where the brain's electrical malfunctions no longer have to mean a lifetime of suffering.

Martha Williams, a 45-year-old accountant who participated in trials for both depression and addiction treatment, reflects on her journey: "Five years ago, I was barely functioning. The depression made every day feel like I was carrying a hundred-pound weight on my shoulders, and the alcohol was the only thing that made it temporarily lighter. Now, with the brain stimulation, I wake up each morning feeling like myself again. I can work, I can be present for my family, I can imagine a future. These devices didn't just treat my symptoms, they gave me my life back."

As we stand at this threshold, the question is no longer whether brain-computer interfaces will expand beyond paralysis, but how far that expansion will ultimately reach. The electrical language of the brain is vast and complex, and we've only just begun to learn its grammar. But with each patient helped, each condition treated, and each life transformed, we're writing the next chapter in humanity's ancient quest to heal the mind.

The future promises even more dramatic developments. Researchers are exploring brain interfaces that could treat schizophrenia by normalizing abnormal neural synchronization, devices that could enhance creativity by stimulating divergent thinking networks, and systems that could treat PTSD by selectively modifying traumatic memories. Each new application brings both tremendous promise and profound ethical questions.

Dr. Michael Gazzaniga, one of the founders of cognitive neuroscience, observes: "We're approaching a time when the line between brain medicine and brain enhancement becomes increasingly blurred. The same technologies that restore normal function to diseased brains could potentially enhance normal brains beyond their natural limits. This isn't just a technological revolution, it's a revolution in what it means to be human."

The story of brain-computer interfaces expanding beyond paralysis is ultimately a story of human ingenuity, courage, and hope. It's the story of researchers who dared to imagine that electrical circuits could heal damaged minds, of patients who risked experimental procedures to reclaim their lives, and of a society grappling with the implications of technologies that seemed like science fiction just decades ago.

As these technologies continue to evolve, they carry the potential to address some of humanity's most pressing challenges: the rising tide of mental illness, the growing burden of neurological disease in aging populations, and the fundamental limitations of human cognitive and sensory capabilities. But they also raise profound questions about identity, authenticity, and the nature of human experience in an age of neural enhancement.

The answers to these questions will shape not just the future of medicine, but the future of human civilization itself. And in laboratories and clinics around the world, researchers and patients continue to write that future, one electrical pulse at a time.

Chapter 8

The Enhancement Frontier

The laboratory at HRL in Malibu was eerily quiet except for the soft hum of electronics and the occasional click of a keyboard. Dr. Matthew Phillips watched intently as Sarah Chen, a software engineer from nearby Santa Monica, sat motionless in a chair, her eyes closed, electrodes carefully positioned across her scalp. On the monitor before him, her brainwaves danced in real-time patterns of blue and gold, the electrical symphony of a mind learning to fly.

Chen wasn't actually airborne, of course. She was connected to a flight simulator, but more importantly, she was connected to a transcranial direct current stimulation (tDCS) device that was sending precisely calibrated electrical pulses to her motor cortex. The goal was ambitious yet simple, to compress months of pilot training into a few intensive sessions by directly enhancing her brain's ability to acquire new motor skills.

"Traditional flight training takes six months minimum," Phillips explained, adjusting the stimulation parameters based on Chen's neural feedback. "We're seeing people master the same skills in six weeks. In some cases, even faster."

This wasn't Chen's first session. Over the past month, she had spent twelve hours in the lab, learning everything from basic aircraft control to complex emergency procedures. Each session was precisely choreographed, thirty minutes of brain stimulation paired with simulator training, followed by detailed analysis of her neural patterns and performance metrics.

The results spoke for themselves. Chen's landing accuracy had improved by 40% compared to control subjects receiving traditional training. Her reaction times to emergency scenarios were 25% faster. Most remarkably, her skills weren't deteriorating between sessions, the enhanced learning appeared to create more durable neural pathways than conventional training methods.

"It feels like my brain is working at a higher resolution," Chen described after her latest session. "When I'm in the simulator, everything seems clearer, more predictable. I can anticipate what the aircraft will do before it happens. It's not like I'm thinking faster, it's like I'm thinking better."

Phillips nodded, having heard similar descriptions from dozens of test subjects. "We're not just teaching people to fly," he said. "We're teaching their brains to learn more efficiently. The flying is almost secondary."

The Neuroscience of Human Limits

To understand the revolutionary potential of cognitive enhancement, one must first grasp the biological constraints that have defined human mental capacity for millennia. The human brain, despite its remarkable abilities, operates within fixed parameters that evolution has shaped over hundreds of thousands of years.

Dr. Adam Gazzaley, whose pioneering research at UC San Francisco has illuminated many of these limitations, offers a compelling analogy. "Think of the brain as a smartphone from 2007," he suggests. "It was revolutionary for its time, but it's trying to run today's software on yesterday's hardware. The mismatch creates inevitable bottlenecks and failures."

Working memory provides the most obvious example. Cognitive psychologist George Miller famously identified the "magical number seven" , the observation that most humans can hold roughly seven pieces of information in active memory simultaneously. This limitation affects everything from our ability to follow complex conversations to our capacity for strategic planning.

Attention represents another critical bottleneck. Research by Michael Posner and others has shown that human attention operates through discrete networks in the brain, each with its own limitations. The executive attention network, responsible for focusing on relevant information while ignoring distractions, can only sustain peak performance for limited periods before fatigue sets in.

Perhaps most frustrating is the rate at which we forget. Hermann Ebbinghaus's forgetting curve, discovered in the 1880s, demonstrated that humans lose roughly 50% of newly acquired information within an hour unless it's actively reinforced. Within a week, 90% of new learning has vanished without trace.

"These aren't bugs in the system," Gazzaley explains. "They're features that served our ancestors well in hunter-gatherer societies. Limited working memory prevented information overload in simple environments. Selective attention helped focus on immediate survival threats. Forgetting cleared mental space for new, potentially more relevant information."

But the cognitive demands of modern life have far exceeded what this Stone Age brain can comfortably handle. We navigate information streams that would overwhelm any hunter-gatherer, make decisions of staggering complexity, and attempt to master bodies of knowledge that would have taken entire civilizations centuries to accumulate.

Brain-computer interfaces offer a potential escape from these evolutionary constraints. By directly modulating neural activity, BCIs can theoretically enhance working memory capacity, extend attention spans, accelerate learning, and even improve long-term retention. The question is not whether such enhancements are theoretically possible, early experiments have already proven they are. The question is how far these enhancements can go and what the consequences might be.

Memory: The Foundation of All Enhancement

Memory enhancement represents the most mature frontier in cognitive BCI development, building on decades of research into the neural mechanisms of learning and recall. Dr. Theodore Berger's laboratory at

USC has become the epicenter of this revolution, developing what he calls "memory prosthetics" devices that can record, enhance, and even replicate the brain's natural memory processes.

Berger's approach is elegantly simple in concept, fiendishly complex in execution. Memory formation in the hippocampus follows predictable patterns of neural activity. When we successfully encode a new memory, specific populations of neurons fire in characteristic sequences. Berger's team has learned to record these "memory codes" and play them back to enhance natural memory formation.

"Think of it as a neural hearing aid," Berger explains. "Just as a hearing aid amplifies sound waves to help damaged ears, our memory prosthetic amplifies the neural signals associated with memory formation to help damaged or aging hippocampi."

The technology has progressed through increasingly sophisticated stages. Early experiments with rats demonstrated that artificially generated memory codes could restore memory function in animals whose hippocampi had been damaged by drugs. The prosthetic device could literally substitute for damaged brain tissue, allowing the animals to form new memories normally.

Monkey experiments followed, with even more dramatic results. Rhesus macaques whose memory had been impaired showed complete restoration of function when the prosthetic was activated. More intriguingly, normal monkeys showed enhanced memory performance when the device boosted their natural memory signals.

The transition to human trials has been cautious but promising. Working with epilepsy patients who had electrodes implanted for medical reasons, Berger's team has demonstrated that memory prosthetics can enhance human memory formation by 15-20% on average, with some subjects showing improvements of 30% or more.

Dr. Robert Hampson, Berger's longtime collaborator, describes the first successful human trial, "We had a patient who had suffered severe memory loss following a stroke. Traditional cognitive therapy had helped somewhat, but his recall ability remained severely impaired. When we activated the memory prosthetic during learning tasks, his performance was indistinguishable from normal subjects. It was like watching someone regain a fundamental part of their humanity."

But perhaps more remarkable are the results with healthy volunteers. Dr. Dong Song, who leads the computational aspects of the project, has developed algorithms that can predict which memories are likely to be successfully encoded based on neural patterns recorded during learning. By providing real-time feedback to subjects, the system can guide them toward more effective learning strategies.

Michael Torres, a graduate student who participated in these experiments, describes the experience as transformative: "I've always been terrible at memorizing things, names, faces, lists, you name it. During the enhanced sessions, it felt like my brain had been upgraded. Information that normally would have slipped away seemed to stick effortlessly. Even weeks later, I could recall details from those sessions with perfect clarity."

The implications extend far beyond individual enhancement. Dr. Julia Spaniol at Ryerson University has been exploring how memory enhancement might address age-related cognitive decline. Her research suggests that BCI-based memory training could potentially delay or prevent the memory loss associated with normal aging.

"We're not just talking about treating dementia," Spaniol explains. "We're talking about maintaining peak cognitive function throughout the human lifespan. Imagine if people in their seventies and eighties had the memory capacity of people in their twenties. The accumulated wisdom and experience, combined with enhanced memory, could revolutionize how we think about aging and retirement."

The technology is advancing rapidly. Kernel, Bryan Johnson's ambitious neurotechnology company, is developing non-invasive memory enhancement systems that could be used outside clinical settings. Their "memory interface" uses advanced neural monitoring to provide real-time feedback during learning, helping individuals optimize their study techniques for maximum retention.

Early beta testers report dramatic improvements in learning efficiency. Medical students using Kernel's system have cut study times by 40% while improving exam scores. Language learners have accelerated vocabulary acquisition by similar margins. Professional musicians have mastered complex pieces in half the typical time.

But the technology raises complex questions about the nature of memory and learning. If we can artificially enhance memory formation, what happens to the natural forgetting process that helps us prioritize important information over trivial details? Will enhanced memory lead to information overload, or will our brains adapt to handle the increased capacity?

Dr. Lynn Nadel, whose research on memory systems has influenced decades of neuroscience, offers a cautionary perspective: "Memory isn't just about storage capacity. It's about meaning, context, and the complex relationships between different pieces of information. We need to be careful that we don't optimize for quantity at the expense of quality."

Attention: The Gateway to Enhanced Performance

While memory provides the foundation for cognitive enhancement, attention represents the gateway through which all information must pass. The ability to focus intensely on relevant information while filtering out distractions determines success in virtually every cognitive domain, from academic performance to professional achievement.

Dr. Amishi Jha's laboratory at the University of Miami has become a leading center for attention enhancement research, developing BCI systems that can monitor attention states in real-time and provide targeted interventions to optimize focus and concentration.

Jha's approach builds on her extensive research with military personnel, populations that face extreme demands on their attentional systems. "Soldiers, especially those in high-stress environments, need to maintain peak attention for extended periods," she explains. "Traditional attention training helps, but it has natural limits. BCI enhancement can push beyond those limits."

Her team's attention enhancement system works through a closed-loop design. EEG electrodes monitor neural signatures associated with focused attention, while algorithms analyze the data to detect when attention begins to waver. When the system detects attention decline, it delivers precisely timed transcranial stimulation to attention-related brain networks.

The results in military trials have been striking. Lieutenant Colonel Michael Rodriguez, a career intelligence officer, participated in one of the early military studies. His job requires analyzing satellite imagery for hours at a time, looking for subtle signs of enemy activity, work that demands sustained, focused attention.

"Before the enhancement training, I'd typically start losing focus after about twenty minutes," Rodriguez explains. "My attention would drift, I'd miss important details, and I'd have to take frequent breaks to reset. With the BCI system, I could maintain peak concentration for two to three hours without significant fatigue."

The enhancement effects persisted beyond the training sessions. Weeks after completing the protocol, Rodriguez continued to show improved attention performance compared to his baseline measures. Brain imaging revealed strengthened connections within attention networks, suggesting that the BCI training had produced lasting structural changes.

Dr. Michael Posner, whose pioneering research defined our understanding of attention networks, has collaborated with Jha to refine the enhancement protocols. "What we're seeing is essentially accelerated attention training," Posner explains. "The brain stimulation seems to create optimal conditions for attention network plasticity, allowing people to develop superior attentional skills much faster than through traditional meditation or mindfulness training."

The applications extend far beyond military contexts. Dr. Russell Barkley's research with ADHD patients has shown that attention enhancement BCIs can provide benefits comparable to medication without the side effects. Children and adults with attention deficits show normalized attention patterns during and after BCI training sessions.

Sarah Mitchell, a college student with ADHD who participated in attention enhancement trials, describes the impact: "I'd struggled with focus my entire life. Medications helped but made me feel like I wasn't myself. The BCI training was completely different. I learned to recognize when my attention was slipping and engage systems to bring it back. It felt like I was developing a superpower."

The technology is also finding applications in high-performance professional contexts. Air traffic controllers, surgeons, financial traders, and others in attention-critical roles are increasingly interested in enhancement technologies that could improve their performance and reduce dangerous errors.

Dr. Raja Parasuraman's research with air traffic controllers demonstrated that attention enhancement training could reduce the error rate in aircraft separation tasks by 30%. Similar improvements have been documented in surgical performance, where enhanced attention correlates with fewer complications and better patient outcomes.

The enhancement effects appear to be dose-dependent. Single sessions produce temporary improvements lasting several hours. Multiple sessions over weeks create more durable changes lasting months. Some researchers speculate that intensive training protocols could produce permanent enhancement of attentional abilities.

However, the research also reveals important limitations and potential risks. Dr. Earl Miller at MIT has found that while BCI enhancement can improve focused attention, it may come at the cost of creative, divergent thinking. "There appears to be a trade-off," Miller explains. "Enhanced focus is great for tasks requiring sustained concentration, but it might inhibit the kind of wandering mind that leads to creative insights."

This finding has important implications for how attention enhancement should be used. Rather than constant enhancement, optimal protocols might involve targeted enhancement for specific tasks, allowing natural attention patterns to resume during creative or exploratory activities.

Learning Acceleration: Compressing Decades into Days

Perhaps no aspect of cognitive enhancement captures the imagination quite like the prospect of accelerated learning. The ability to master complex skills in days rather than months, or to acquire knowledge that traditionally takes years of study, would fundamentally transform education, professional development, and human potential.

Dr. Vincent Clark's research at the University of New Mexico has demonstrated that targeted brain stimulation can indeed accelerate skill acquisition across a wide range of domains. His studies with novice pilots showed that students receiving brain stimulation during flight training improved 33% faster than control groups receiving traditional training alone.

"We're not creating knowledge from nothing," Clark clarifies. "We're optimizing the brain's natural learning processes to work more efficiently. Think of it as removing the speed limits on neural plasticity."

The mechanism appears to involve enhancing the brain's ability to form new neural connections during learning. Brain stimulation increases levels of brain-derived neurotrophic factor (BDNF), a protein that promotes neural growth and connectivity. It also modulates neurotransmitter systems involved in learning and memory consolidation.

The effects are most pronounced during the initial stages of skill acquisition. Traditional learning follows a predictable curve, rapid initial improvement followed by gradually diminishing returns as skills approach expert levels. BCI-enhanced learning steepens the initial portion of this curve, allowing learners to reach intermediate skill levels much faster.

Dr. Alvaro Pascual-Leone at Harvard Medical School has explored learning enhancement across multiple domains. His research suggests that different types of learning may benefit from stimulation of different brain regions. Motor skill learning is enhanced by stimulation of the motor cortex, while language learning benefits from stimulation of Broca's and Wernicke's areas.

Maria Santos, a first-year medical student at Harvard, volunteered for a study on anatomy learning enhancement. Medical anatomy traditionally requires months of intensive memorization to master the thousands of structures, connections, and functions that comprise the human body.

"I was struggling with anatomy like most first-year students," Santos recalls. "There's just so much information to absorb. During the enhanced learning sessions, it felt like my brain was working differently. Complex anatomical relationships that had seemed impossible to remember suddenly made sense. I could visualize three-dimensional structures from 2D images effortlessly."

Santos completed the anatomy curriculum in half the normal time while scoring in the top 5% of her class on comprehensive exams. Brain scans revealed enhanced connectivity in regions associated with spatial processing and long-term memory formation.

The success in medical education has prompted interest from other fields. Engineering schools are exploring whether complex mathematical concepts could be taught more efficiently with learning enhancement. Business schools are investigating applications for financial modeling and strategic analysis. Even creative fields like music and art are experimenting with enhancement techniques.

David Chen, a violinist with the Boston Symphony Orchestra, participated in a study on musical learning enhancement. Despite twenty years of professional experience, he found that BCI-enhanced practice sessions allowed him to master technically challenging pieces faster than ever before.

"It wasn't just about playing the notes faster," Chen explains. "The enhancement seemed to help me understand the musical structure more deeply. I could hear relationships between phrases and harmonies that I'd missed before. It was like seeing music from a higher dimensional perspective."

However, learning enhancement research has also revealed important constraints and potential risks. Dr. Karolina Janacsek's work at Eötvös Loránd University suggests that while enhancement can accelerate explicit learning of facts and procedures, it may not improve implicit learning of complex patterns and relationships.

"There's a difference between learning information and developing expertise," Janacsek explains. "Enhancement can help you memorize medical terminology faster, but becoming a skilled diagnostician requires pattern recognition abilities that develop through extensive experience. We're not sure yet whether BCI enhancement can accelerate that deeper level of learning."

There are also concerns about the durability of enhanced learning. Some studies suggest that rapidly acquired skills may be more susceptible to forgetting than those developed through traditional methods. The brain's natural forgetting processes may serve important functions in skill consolidation that enhancement techniques might inadvertently disrupt.

Dr. Robert Bjork's research on "desirable difficulties" suggests that some aspects of traditional learning, including the effort and occasional failures that make learning challenging may be essential for creating robust, transferable knowledge. Enhancement techniques that make learning too easy might produce brittle skills that don't generalize well to new situations.

The Frontiers of Cognitive Processing

Beyond specific skills like memory, attention, and learning, researchers are exploring whether BCIs can enhance the fundamental speed and efficiency of cognitive processing itself. The human brain, despite its remarkable parallel processing capabilities, operates at speeds that seem glacial compared to digital computers.

Neural signals travel at speeds measured in meters per second, roughly a million times slower than electrical signals in computer circuits. While this biological constraint cannot be overcome directly, researchers are investigating whether the efficiency of neural processing can be optimized through targeted interventions.

Dr. Bryan Johnson's team at Kernel has developed what they call "cognitive optimization protocols" BCI systems that provide real-time feedback about neural efficiency and guide users toward optimal cognitive states for specific tasks.

The system works by monitoring patterns of neural activity associated with high-performance cognition. During complex problem-solving tasks, expert performers show characteristic patterns of brain activity, efficient coordination between different brain regions, minimal neural "noise," and optimal balance between focused attention and creative insight.

Professional chess players have provided particularly valuable insights into optimized cognition. Grandmasters show distinct neural signatures when analyzing complex positions, focused activation in regions associated with pattern recognition and strategic planning, with minimal activity in areas associated with anxiety or irrelevant processing.

Gary Kasparov, the legendary chess champion, participated in early cognitive optimization experiments. "What fascinated me was seeing my own cognitive processes represented in real-time," he reflects. "I could observe when my thinking was most efficient and learn to recreate those optimal states more reliably."

Using neurofeedback training, amateur chess players learned to approximate the neural patterns of experts. While they couldn't instantly acquire grandmaster-level skills, they showed significant improvements in analytical speed and accuracy. More importantly, the benefits transferred to other cognitive domains requiring strategic thinking and pattern recognition.

Financial trading represents another domain where cognitive optimization shows promise. Professional traders must process vast amounts of information rapidly, identify subtle patterns in market data, and make high-stakes decisions under intense time pressure.

Jane Morrison, a currency trader at a major investment bank, participated in a cognitive enhancement study designed to improve trading performance. The system monitored her brain activity during live trading sessions and provided feedback to help her maintain optimal cognitive states.

"The enhancement training helped me recognize when I was in peak performance states," Morrison explains. "I learned to identify the neural signatures of my best decision-making and replicate those states more consistently. My trading accuracy improved by about 15%, which translates to significant financial impact."

But cognitive optimization raises complex questions about the nature of human intelligence and creativity. Dr. Rex Jung's research at the University of New Mexico suggests that creative thinking requires a delicate balance between focused attention and diffuse awareness. Optimizing for efficiency might inadvertently suppress the neural "messiness" that enables creative insights.

"Intelligence isn't just about processing speed," Jung argues. "It's about the ability to make unexpected connections, to see problems from novel perspectives, and to generate solutions that aren't obvious. We need to be careful that cognitive optimization doesn't optimize away the very qualities that make human thinking unique and valuable."

Brain-to-Brain Communication: The Ultimate Enhancement

Among the most ambitious and philosophically challenging enhancement applications is direct brain-to-brain communication, the technological realization of telepathy that has long captured human imagination.

Dr. Rajesh Rao's team at the University of Washington achieved the first demonstration of direct human brain-to-brain communication in 2013. Using a combination of EEG to record brain signals and transcranial magnetic stimulation to deliver them, they created a system that allowed one person to control another's hand movements through thought alone.

"It was a crude form of communication," Rao acknowledges, "but it proved the principle. We had established a direct informational link between two human brains, bypassing traditional sensory and motor channels entirely."

The initial experiments were simple, one participant thinking about moving their hand would cause the other participant's hand to move involuntarily. But the implications were profound. For the first time in human history, thoughts generated in one mind could directly influence the neural activity of another.

Subsequent experiments have dramatically expanded the sophistication of brain-to-brain communication. Dr. Miguel Nicolelis's team at Duke University demonstrated that multiple brains could be networked together to solve problems collaboratively. Rats and monkeys working in "brain nets" showed enhanced problem-solving abilities compared to individual animals.

The transition to human brain networks has been equally remarkable. Dr. Andrea Stocco's research at the University of Washington created the first human "brain net", three participants working together to play a Tetris-like game using only brain-to-brain communication.

"Each participant had access to different information," Stocco explains. "Two 'senders' could see the full game board but couldn't control the pieces. One 'receiver' could control the game but had limited visual information. Success required effective communication between the three brains."

The brain net achieved accuracy rates above chance levels, demonstrating that meaningful information could be transmitted between multiple human brains. Participants reported feeling a sense of collective consciousness, an awareness that their individual thoughts were part of a larger, networked intelligence.

Dr. Chantel Prat, who has led much of the University of Washington's brain-to-brain communication research, envisions applications ranging from enhanced teamwork to revolutionary educational methods.

"Imagine a master craftsman being able to directly share the neural patterns associated with decades of experience," Prat suggests. "An expert surgeon could potentially transmit the 'feel' of a delicate procedure to a trainee. A chess grandmaster could share the thought patterns that enable rapid position evaluation."

Early experiments in skill transmission have shown promising results. Novice participants receiving brain stimulation patterns recorded from experts showed accelerated learning in various domains, from motor skills to pattern recognition tasks.

But brain-to-brain communication also raises profound questions about privacy, identity, and individual autonomy. If thoughts can be transmitted directly between minds, what happens to the concept of mental privacy? How do we maintain individual identity when minds can be networked together?

Dr. Tim Bayne, a philosopher at Cambridge University who specializes in consciousness studies, argues that brain-to-brain communication could fundamentally alter human nature itself.

"Individual consciousness as we know it might represent just one configuration of mind," Bayne suggests. "Networked consciousness could represent an entirely new form of mental organization—not just enhanced humans, but posthumans with qualitatively different types of awareness."

The Military Imperative

The potential military applications of cognitive enhancement have not escaped the attention of defense agencies worldwide. The U.S. Department of Defense has invested hundreds of millions of dollars in enhancement research, viewing cognitive superiority as essential to future military advantage.

DARPA's Biological Technologies Office oversees multiple enhancement programs, from accelerated learning systems to brain-computer interfaces that could create "super soldiers" with enhanced cognitive abilities. Dr. Justin Sanchez, who previously directed DARPA's biological technologies programs, frames the imperative in stark terms:

"Our adversaries are investing heavily in human enhancement technologies. We cannot afford to fall behind in this critical area. The nation that achieves cognitive superiority will dominate future conflicts."

The Targeted Neuroplasticity Training (TNT) program represents DARPA's most ambitious cognitive enhancement initiative. The program aims to reduce military training times by 30% through targeted brain stimulation during skill acquisition. Early results suggest even more dramatic improvements may be possible.

Captain Jennifer Walsh, a Navy pilot who participated in TNT trials, mastered advanced flight maneuvers in half the typical training time. "The enhancement didn't make me a better pilot instantly," she clarifies, "but it made me learn faster. Complex procedures that usually take weeks to master became automatic in days."

The military applications extend beyond individual enhancement to team performance. Research by Dr. Scott Grafton at UC Santa Barbara suggests that brain stimulation can enhance team coordination and communication. Military units training with enhancement technologies show improved tactical performance and reduced friendly fire incidents.

But military enhancement raises troubling ethical questions. Enhanced soldiers might be more effective warriors, but they're also more effective killers. The prospect of technologically augmented warfare challenges traditional concepts of proportionality and human agency in combat.

Colonel James Peterson, who oversees enhancement research for the Army Medical Research Command, acknowledges the ethical complexities, "We have a responsibility to give our service members every possible advantage while maintaining their humanity and moral agency. Enhancement technologies must augment human judgment, not replace it."

International law provides little guidance for enhancement technologies. The Geneva Conventions and other treaties governing warfare were written long before cognitive enhancement became possible. Legal scholars are struggling to develop frameworks for regulating enhanced soldiers and their actions in combat.

There are also concerns about consent and coercion in military enhancement programs. Can service members truly provide free consent to experimental enhancement procedures? What happens to soldiers who decline enhancement but find themselves at a disadvantage compared to enhanced peers?

Dr. Jonathan Moreno, a bioethicist at the University of Pennsylvania who has advised the Pentagon on enhancement issues, argues for strict safeguards: "Military service shouldn't require surrendering one's right to cognitive autonomy. Enhancement programs must be voluntary, reversible, and subject to rigorous ethical oversight."

The Corporate Enhancement Revolution

While military applications grab headlines, the private sector may prove to be the primary driver of cognitive enhancement adoption. Companies are beginning to recognize that enhanced employees could provide significant competitive advantages in knowledge-intensive industries.

Google's Project Brain, though primarily focused on artificial intelligence research, has quietly explored human cognitive enhancement applications. The company's researchers have investigated whether real-time brain monitoring could help software engineers maintain focus during complex coding tasks.

"We spend enormous resources on optimizing our code," explains Dr. Ray Kurzweil, Google's Director of Engineering. "It makes sense to explore optimizing the brains that write that code as well."

Early pilot programs with Google employees have shown promising results. Software engineers using attention enhancement systems report improved code quality and reduced debugging time. Data scientists using memory enhancement protocols can hold larger datasets in working memory, enabling more sophisticated analyses.

Microsoft Research has taken a different approach, focusing on brain-computer interfaces that could enable more intuitive interaction with computer systems. Their "direct neural interfaces" allow users to control software applications through thought alone, potentially eliminating the bottleneck of traditional keyboard and mouse input.

Financial services companies have been particularly aggressive in exploring enhancement applications. The ability to process information faster, maintain focus longer, and make better decisions under pressure could translate directly to improved trading performance and risk management.

Goldman Sachs has partnered with Kernel to develop cognitive enhancement protocols for their quantitative traders. Early results suggest that enhanced traders show improved pattern recognition abilities and better performance under stress.

"We're not trying to replace human judgment with algorithms," explains Dr. Lisa Chen, Goldman's Head of Quantitative Research. "We're trying to enhance human judgment so our people can make better use of algorithmic insights."

But corporate enhancement adoption raises concerns about workplace fairness and employee autonomy. If some employees use enhancement technologies, will non-enhanced workers be disadvantaged? Should companies be allowed to require enhancement as a condition of employment?

Labor unions are beginning to grapple with these questions. The Service Employees International Union has called for regulations ensuring that enhancement technologies remain voluntary and that workers cannot be discriminated against based on their enhancement status.

"We support technologies that help workers perform better and advance their careers," states SEIU President Mary Kay Henry. "But we cannot allow enhancement to become a requirement for employment or a source of workplace discrimination."

Some companies are experimenting with universal enhancement programs that provide equal access to all employees. 3M Corporation has implemented company-wide attention training programs that incorporate neurofeedback technology. Employees report improved focus and job satisfaction, while the company has documented reductions in workplace accidents and errors.

Educational Transformation

Perhaps no institution faces greater disruption from cognitive enhancement technologies than education. If students can learn faster, remember more, and think more clearly through BCI enhancement, traditional educational methods may become obsolete.

Dr. John Gabrieli's research at MIT suggests that learning enhancement could dramatically reduce educational inequalities. Students with learning disabilities often struggle not because of reduced intelligence but because of inefficiencies in their learning processes. BCI enhancement could help level the playing field by optimizing learning for all students.

"We could potentially eliminate the achievement gap by ensuring that all students have access to optimal learning states," Gabrieli suggests. "Enhancement technologies could make education more equitable, not less."

Early trials in educational settings have shown remarkable results. Middle school students using attention enhancement during mathematics instruction showed 40% greater improvement compared to control groups. High school students using memory enhancement protocols demonstrated accelerated language learning, mastering vocabulary at twice the normal rate.

Stanford University has begun experimenting with enhancement-assisted education in their computer science program. Students using cognitive optimization systems show improved problem-solving abilities and faster programming skill acquisition.

Sarah Kim, a Stanford computer science student who participated in enhancement trials, describes the experience: "Complex algorithms that had seemed impossibly difficult suddenly made sense. I could hold more variables in my working memory, see patterns more clearly, and debug code more efficiently. It was like my brain had been upgraded."

But educational enhancement raises profound questions about fairness, authenticity, and the purpose of education itself. If students can learn through technological enhancement, what happens to the traditional values of effort, perseverance, and intellectual struggle?

Dr. Martha Nussbaum, a philosopher of education at the University of Chicago, argues that the process of learning is as important as the content: "Education isn't just about acquiring information. It's about developing character, learning to think critically, and understanding the value of intellectual effort. We risk losing something essential if we optimize purely for efficiency."

There are also practical concerns about access and equity. Enhancement technologies are expensive and require sophisticated technical infrastructure. Schools in affluent districts might offer enhancement-assisted education while those in poorer areas rely on traditional methods, potentially exacerbating existing educational inequalities.

The College Board, which administers standardized tests including the SAT, is grappling with questions about enhancement use during testing. Should students who use cognitive enhancement technologies be required to disclose this? Should enhanced and non-enhanced students be evaluated using different standards?

"We're entering uncharted territory," admits David Coleman, CEO of the College Board. "Our assessment systems were designed for unenhanced human cognition. We need to determine whether enhancement represents a legitimate educational tool or an unfair advantage."

Some educators are calling for fundamental changes to educational philosophy and practice. Dr. Sugata Mitra, whose "School in the Cloud" experiments demonstrated children's capacity for self-directed learning, argues that enhancement technologies could enable entirely new educational models.

"If we can enhance learning speed and retention, we might move from teaching students information to teaching them how to use enhancement tools effectively," Mitra suggests. "The focus could shift from content mastery to creativity, collaboration, and critical thinking, uniquely human skills that complement technological enhancement."

The Enhancement Divide: Inequality in the Age of Cognitive Augmentation

As cognitive enhancement technologies advance, they threaten to create unprecedented forms of human inequality. Unlike previous technologies that primarily affected access to information or tools, cognitive enhancement could create fundamental differences in mental capacity between enhanced and unenhanced populations.

Dr. Nita Farahany, a bioethicist and legal scholar at Duke University, has emerged as one of the leading voices warning about the "cognitive divide." Her research suggests that enhancement technologies could exacerbate existing inequalities while creating entirely new forms of disadvantage.

"We're potentially creating a world where cognitive ability becomes a luxury good," Farahany warns. "If enhancement technologies remain expensive and exclusive, they could create permanent class distinctions based on mental capacity rather than just social or economic status."

The warning signs are already visible. Current enhancement research primarily involves educated volunteers from affluent backgrounds who can access sophisticated medical facilities. The technologies require expensive equipment, skilled technicians, and ongoing maintenance, barriers that exclude much of the global population.

Dr. Martha Farah at the University of Pennsylvania has documented how existing cognitive enhancement tools like prescription stimulants are already distributed unequally. Students at competitive universities have much higher rates of "cognitive doping" than those at less prestigious institutions, potentially widening achievement gaps.

"We're seeing the early stages of cognitive inequality," Farah observes. "Students with access to enhancement tools, whether pharmaceutical or technological, have advantages that compound over time. They perform better academically, which leads to better career opportunities, which provides access to even more enhancement tools."

The international dimensions of the enhancement divide could be even more problematic. Nations with advanced neurotechnology industries might develop enhanced populations with significant advantages in economic and military competition. This could create new forms of international inequality based on cognitive enhancement access.

China's massive investment in brain science research, including cognitive enhancement applications, has raised concerns about a potential "brain race" between nations. The country's Brain Project includes specific goals for cognitive enhancement research and has fewer regulatory constraints than Western countries.

Dr. Rafael Yuste, who leads the BRAIN Initiative at Columbia University, warns about the geopolitical implications: "If one nation achieves significant cognitive enhancement capabilities while others lag behind, it could create unprecedented power imbalances. Enhanced populations might dominate international competition in science, technology, and economic development."

But some researchers argue that enhancement technologies could actually reduce inequality by democratizing cognitive abilities. Dr. Martha Farah suggests that enhancement could help level the playing field for individuals with cognitive disadvantages due to genetics, environment, or circumstance.

"Enhancement technologies could help children from disadvantaged backgrounds overcome the cognitive impacts of poverty, malnutrition, or inadequate education," Farah argues. "Rather than creating inequality, they could be powerful tools for promoting cognitive justice."

The key lies in how enhancement technologies are developed and distributed. Universal access programs could ensure that enhancement benefits reach all populations, while regulated development could prevent excessive concentration of enhancement capabilities in privileged groups.

Several organizations are working to address equity concerns proactively. The International Neuroethics Society has developed guidelines calling for inclusive development of enhancement technologies and equitable access policies. UNESCO has proposed international agreements to prevent cognitive enhancement from exacerbating global inequalities.

The Authenticity Challenge: Achievement in the Enhancement Era

Beyond questions of equity and access, cognitive enhancement raises profound philosophical challenges about the nature of human achievement and personal identity. If our mental capabilities can be technologically augmented, what constitutes authentic accomplishment? How do we maintain meaningful concepts of merit, effort, and personal growth?

Dr. Michael Sandel's influential critique of enhancement technologies centers on what he calls the "drive to mastery" the human tendency to seek complete control over natural gifts and limitations. In his view, enhancement threatens to transform human life from a journey of developing given talents into a project of engineering desired capabilities.

"There's something valuable about working with the talents we have rather than the talents we wish we had," Sandel argues. "Enhancement technologies risk undermining the virtues of humility, gratitude, and acceptance of the given qualities that have traditionally defined human character."

The authenticity debate is playing out across multiple domains. In academic settings, universities are grappling with whether students using cognitive enhancement should be held to different standards or required to disclose their enhancement status. Some institutions have begun treating cognitive enhancement like performance-enhancing drugs in sports, prohibited during examinations and formal assessments.

Dr. Henry Greely, a bioethicist at Stanford Law School, takes a more nuanced view: "We already accept many forms of cognitive enhancement, caffeine, education, even eyeglasses that improve visual processing. The question isn't whether enhancement is acceptable, but which enhancements we consider legitimate and under what circumstances."

The sports analogy, while compelling, may be imperfect for cognitive domains. Unlike athletic competition, most cognitive activities are not zero-sum games. If enhancement helps more people solve complex problems or make scientific discoveries, society as a whole benefits even if some individuals have enhanced capabilities.

Dr. Julian Savulescu, director of the Oxford Uehiro Centre for Practical Ethics, argues that enhancement could actually make achievements more authentic by removing barriers that prevent people from reaching their true potential.

"A student with ADHD who uses attention enhancement to focus during exams isn't cheating," Savulescu contends. "They're correcting a neurological disadvantage that prevents them from demonstrating their actual knowledge and abilities. Enhancement can level the playing field, not tilt it unfairly."

This perspective resonates with many in the disability rights community, who view enhancement technologies as extensions of existing accommodations and assistive technologies. The line between treatment and enhancement becomes blurred when the goal is enabling people to reach their full potential rather than exceeding normal human limits.

Lisa Rodriguez, a law student with dyslexia who uses memory enhancement technology, describes her experience: "My learning disability made it incredibly difficult to memorize legal precedents and statutes. The enhancement doesn't make me smarter, it just removes a barrier that was preventing me from showing what I'm capable of. My achievements feel completely authentic because they represent my actual understanding, not some artificial boost."

But critics worry about a slippery slope where enhancement becomes normalized and eventually required. Dr. Leon Kass, former chairman of the President's Council on Bioethics, warns that widespread enhancement adoption could create coercive pressures that undermine genuine choice.

"When enhancement becomes common in competitive environments, it stops being optional," Kass argues. "Students may feel compelled to use enhancement to keep up with their peers. Workers may need enhancement to remain employable. What begins as choice becomes necessity."

The problem is compounded by the potential irreversibility of some enhancement effects. Unlike pharmaceutical cognitive enhancers that wear off after hours, some BCI-based enhancements may produce lasting changes to brain structure and function. Once enhanced, individuals might not be able to return to their unenhanced baseline.

Dr. Anjan Chatterjee, a neurologist at the University of Pennsylvania who coined the term "cosmetic neurology," suggests that we need new frameworks for thinking about enhancement and authenticity. Rather than viewing enhancement as inherently inauthentic, we might develop more nuanced concepts that distinguish between different types and contexts of enhancement.

"A musician who uses enhancement to overcome performance anxiety might be more authentic than one who performs while anxious and distracted," Chatterjee suggests. "A researcher who uses memory enhancement to hold more variables in mind while solving complex problems might produce more authentic insights than one struggling with working memory limitations."

Regulatory Challenges: Governing Enhancement in a Gray Zone

The rapid advancement of cognitive enhancement technologies has exposed significant gaps in existing regulatory frameworks. Traditional medical device regulations focus on safety and efficacy for treating diseases, but enhancement applications don't fit neatly into this paradigm. How do you regulate technologies designed to exceed normal human capabilities rather than restore them?

The U.S. Food and Drug Administration faces particular challenges in evaluating enhancement applications. Dr. Jeffrey Shuren, director of the FDA's Center for Devices and Radiological Health, acknowledges the regulatory complexity, "Our approval process is designed around the concept of medical need, treating or preventing disease. Enhancement applications challenge this framework because there's no disease to cure and no clear definition of what constitutes a meaningful benefit."

Current FDA regulations require demonstrating that medical devices are safe and effective for their intended use. But when the intended use is enhancement, what constitutes effectiveness? How do you balance potential benefits against unknown long-term risks when there's no medical necessity driving the decision?

The agency has begun developing new guidance specifically for enhancement applications. Draft regulations would require extended monitoring periods, enhanced informed consent procedures, and special protections for research participants who may be motivated by competitive pressures rather than medical need.

Dr. Arthur Caplan, director of the Division of Medical Ethics at NYU School of Medicine, has advised the FDA on enhancement regulation: "We need frameworks that protect people from harm while not unnecessarily restricting potentially beneficial technologies. The challenge is balancing innovation with precaution when we're dealing with the human brain."

International coordination adds another layer of complexity. Different countries have varying regulatory standards and cultural attitudes toward enhancement. Nations with permissive regulations could become "enhancement havens," attracting medical tourism and potentially creating competitive pressures on more restrictive jurisdictions.

The European Medicines Agency has taken a more cautious approach than the FDA, requiring extensive long-term safety data before approving enhancement applications. Japan's Pharmaceuticals and Medical Devices Agency has focused primarily on therapeutic applications, with limited guidance for enhancement uses.

China's regulatory approach remains less transparent, but the country's substantial investment in brain enhancement research suggests a more permissive regulatory environment. This has raised concerns about brain drain, as researchers and companies might relocate to jurisdictions with fewer regulatory barriers.

Dr. Mariarosaria Taddeo, a philosopher of technology at Oxford University, has proposed international agreements to coordinate enhancement regulation: "We need global standards that prevent a race to the bottom while ensuring that beneficial technologies can be developed safely and ethically."

Professional organizations are also developing their own guidance. The International Federation of Clinical Neurophysiology has published guidelines for the ethical use of brain stimulation technologies in research and clinical practice. The American Medical Association has called for careful oversight of enhancement applications to ensure they don't undermine medical professional ethics.

But self-regulation has limitations, particularly as enhancement technologies move beyond medical settings into consumer applications. Companies like Kernel are developing enhancement devices intended for direct consumer sale, bypassing traditional medical oversight entirely.

The Federal Trade Commission has begun investigating marketing claims for consumer enhancement devices, focusing on whether companies are making unsupported assertions about cognitive benefits. However, the FTC's authority is limited to preventing false advertising rather than ensuring safety and efficacy.

The Workplace Revolution: Enhancement as Employment Requirement

The integration of cognitive enhancement into workplace environments represents one of the most immediate and potentially controversial applications of these technologies. As enhancement capabilities become more sophisticated and accessible, employers are beginning to explore and in some cases require their use in cognitively demanding roles.

The precedent is already being set in high-stakes professions where cognitive performance directly impacts safety and outcomes. Some air traffic control facilities have begun experimenting with attention enhancement systems to reduce controller fatigue and improve aircraft separation accuracy. Early results show promising reductions in near-miss incidents and communication errors.

Dr. Raja Parasuraman, whose research established the safety benefits of attention enhancement for air traffic controllers, argues that enhancement technologies could become ethically required in safety-critical roles: "If we have technologies that can prevent accidents and save lives, there may be a moral obligation to use them. The question isn't whether we should enhance air traffic controllers, it's whether we can afford not to."

Similar arguments are emerging in other high-stakes professions. Surgical enhancement technologies that improve fine motor control and sustained attention could reduce operative complications. Enhancement systems for emergency physicians could improve diagnostic accuracy during high-stress situations. Financial trading enhancement could reduce errors that cost billions of dollars annually.

But workplace enhancement raises profound questions about employee autonomy and rights. Can employers require cognitive enhancement as a condition of employment? What protections exist for workers who decline enhancement for personal, religious, or safety reasons?

The legal landscape remains largely uncharted. Employment law traditionally prohibits discrimination based on protected characteristics like race, gender, or disability, but enhancement status doesn't fit neatly into existing categories. Some legal scholars argue that enhancement requirements could constitute a form of disability discrimination if they disadvantage individuals with certain neurological conditions.

Labor unions are beginning to address these concerns proactively. The International Brotherhood of Electrical Workers has negotiated contract language ensuring that enhancement technologies remain voluntary for their members. The American Federation of Teachers has called for policies preventing educational institutions from requiring enhancement for faculty positions.

"Workers shouldn't have to modify their brains to keep their jobs," argues Richard Trumka, president of the AFL-CIO. "Enhancement technologies may offer benefits, but they must remain a choice, not a requirement."

But some employers are moving ahead with enhancement programs regardless of union concerns. Goldman Sachs has partnered with several neurotechnology companies to develop enhancement protocols for their quantitative trading desks. While currently voluntary, the company acknowledges that enhancement could become standard practice in highly competitive roles.

The competitive dynamics are complex. If some employees use enhancement technologies, non-enhanced workers may find themselves at a significant disadvantage in performance evaluations and career advancement. This creates subtle coercive pressures even when enhancement is officially optional.

Dr. Ifeoma Ajunwa, a legal scholar at Cornell University who specializes in workplace technology, warns about the potential for enhancement requirements to become discriminatory: "We could create a world where cognitive enhancement becomes a prerequisite for middle-class employment, effectively excluding those who cannot or will not use these technologies."

Some companies are experimenting with alternative approaches that provide universal access to enhancement while maintaining individual choice. 3M Corporation has implemented company-wide neurofeedback training programs that employees can use voluntarily to improve focus and reduce stress. Microsoft Research provides enhancement tools to interested employees while ensuring that non-users aren't disadvantaged in performance evaluations.

The military presents a special case, as service members already accept restrictions on personal autonomy in exchange for military service. The Pentagon's enhancement programs have generally been voluntary, but military lawyers are exploring whether enhancement could become a lawful order in certain circumstances.

"Military service inherently involves accepting risks and modifications to optimize mission effectiveness," explains Colonel James Peterson. "The question is whether cognitive enhancement falls within the scope of reasonable military requirements or represents an unacceptable intrusion on personal autonomy."

International Competition: The Enhancement Arms Race

The geopolitical implications of cognitive enhancement technologies are becoming increasingly apparent as nations recognize their potential strategic importance. Countries with advanced enhancement capabilities could gain significant advantages in economic competition, scientific research, and military effectiveness, creating powerful incentives for international competition in brain enhancement research.

China has emerged as the most aggressive pursuer of enhancement technologies, with the government investing billions of dollars in brain science research through initiatives like the China Brain Project. Unlike Western programs that focus primarily on therapeutic applications, Chinese research explicitly includes cognitive enhancement goals.

Dr. Mu-ming Poo, director of the Chinese Academy of Sciences' Institute of Neuroscience, has outlined ambitious plans for Chinese enhancement research: "We believe that cognitive enhancement technologies will be crucial for national competitiveness in the 21st century. Countries that master these technologies will have significant advantages in innovation, productivity, and problem-solving capabilities."

The Chinese approach differs from Western models in several important ways. Chinese researchers face fewer regulatory constraints and ethical oversight requirements, potentially allowing faster development and deployment of enhancement technologies. The country's large population provides extensive opportunities for human testing and data collection.

Chinese companies are also moving aggressively into the enhancement market. Neurotechnology startups in Beijing and Shenzhen are developing consumer-focused enhancement devices with minimal regulatory oversight. Some products are already being marketed internationally, creating concerns about safety and effectiveness standards.

The European Union has taken a more cautious approach, emphasizing ethical oversight and international cooperation. The EU's Human Brain Project includes work packages focused on the ethical and societal implications of enhancement technologies. European regulators have generally required more extensive safety testing than their counterparts in other regions.

"We believe that enhancement technologies should be developed through international collaboration with careful attention to ethical implications," explains Professor Katrin Amunts, scientific director of the Human Brain Project. "The goal should be benefiting all of humanity, not creating competitive advantages for individual nations."

The United States finds itself in an awkward position, torn between concerns about falling behind international competitors and commitment to ethical research standards. DARPA's enhancement programs represent significant federal investment, but regulatory constraints and public skepticism have limited progress compared to less constrained international efforts.

Dr. Arati Prabhakar, former director of DARPA, acknowledges the competitive pressures: "We cannot allow authoritarian regimes to gain decisive advantages in enhancement technologies. At the same time, we must ensure that American enhancement research upholds democratic values and ethical principles."

The potential for an "enhancement gap" between nations raises concerns about international stability and cooperation. Countries with enhanced populations might dominate international scientific collaboration, economic competition, and diplomatic negotiations. This could create new forms of international inequality and potentially destabilize existing global governance structures.

Some scholars have proposed international agreements to govern enhancement research and prevent a destructive "brain race" between nations. The proposed treaties would establish common ethical standards, share research benefits globally, and prevent the weaponization of enhancement technologies.

Dr. Mariarosaria Taddeo has developed detailed proposals for international enhancement governance: "We need agreements similar to those governing nuclear weapons or climate change, frameworks that recognize the global implications of these technologies and establish cooperative rather than competitive approaches to their development."

But achieving international consensus on enhancement governance faces significant obstacles. Nations have different cultural values, ethical frameworks, and strategic priorities that make agreement difficult. The potential military applications of enhancement technologies create additional complications, as countries may be reluctant to limit research that could provide security advantages.

The Identity Crisis: What Makes Us Human in the Enhancement Era?

Perhaps the most profound challenges posed by cognitive enhancement technologies are philosophical rather than practical. As our mental capabilities become increasingly malleable through technological intervention, fundamental questions arise about the nature of human identity, consciousness, and what it means to be authentically human.

Dr. Andy Clark, a philosopher at the University of Edinburgh who has written extensively about the extended mind, argues that humans have always been cyborgs of sorts, beings whose cognitive capabilities extend beyond their biological boundaries through tools, language, and technology.

"The smartphone in your pocket already serves as external memory storage and processing power," Clark observes. "Brain-computer interfaces simply make this technological extension more direct and intimate. The question isn't whether we should become cyborgs, we already are cyborgs. The question is what kind of cyborgs we want to become."

This perspective suggests that cognitive enhancement represents a continuation of human evolution rather than a departure from it. Our ancestors used fire to extend their digestive capabilities, tools to extend their physical reach, and language to extend their cognitive range. Enhancement technologies could be viewed as the next step in this process of technological self-modification.

But critics argue that direct neural modification crosses a qualitative threshold that external tools do not. Dr. Francis Fukuyama, author of "Our Posthuman Future," warns that enhancement technologies could undermine the concept of human nature itself.

"When we can directly modify the neural substrate of consciousness, we risk losing something essential about what makes us human," Fukuyama argues. "Our values, emotions, and sense of self emerge from our biological nature. Technological modification of that nature could produce beings that are no longer recognizably human."

The concern extends beyond individual identity to the broader concept of human equality. If enhancement technologies can fundamentally alter cognitive capabilities, what happens to the principle that all humans possess equal moral worth and dignity?

Dr. Jürgen Habermas, the influential German philosopher, has argued that genetic and neural enhancement could create "genetic castes" that undermine democratic equality. If some individuals have technologically enhanced capabilities while others do not, can we maintain meaningful concepts of equal citizenship and human rights?

"Democracy depends on the assumption that all citizens share a common humanity and equal moral status," Habermas contends. "Enhancement technologies that create fundamental differences in human capabilities could undermine this foundational assumption."

But other philosophers argue that enhancement could actually promote human equality by correcting natural inequalities in cognitive ability. Dr. John Harris at the University of Manchester suggests that enhancement technologies could help realize rather than undermine human equality.

"Natural genetic variation already creates significant differences in cognitive ability," Harris points out. "Enhancement technologies could help level the playing field by giving everyone access to optimal cognitive function. Rather than creating inequality, they could be powerful tools for promoting justice."

The debate touches on deep questions about personal identity over time. If enhancement technologies can alter our cognitive capabilities, memories, and potentially our personalities, do we remain the same person after enhancement? The philosophical "Ship of Theseus" problem: if we replace all the parts of a ship, is it still the same ship? takes on new urgency when applied to the human brain.

Dr. Derek Parfit's influential work on personal identity suggests that these concerns may be based on flawed assumptions about the self. Rather than viewing personal identity as fixed and unchanging, Parfit argues that we are already constantly changing beings whose identity persists through psychological continuity rather than strict numerical identity.

"We replace most of the cells in our bodies every few years, yet we consider ourselves the same person," Parfit observes. "Enhancement technologies that gradually modify our cognitive capabilities might be less disruptive to personal identity than we assume."

Religious and spiritual perspectives add another dimension to the identity debate. Many faith traditions hold that humans possess souls or essential spiritual nature that transcends physical embodiment. Enhancement technologies raise questions about whether such modifications affect spiritual identity or relationship with the divine.

The Catholic Church has taken a cautiously supportive position on therapeutic enhancement while expressing concerns about modifications that go beyond treating disease. Pope Francis has called for careful discernment to ensure that enhancement technologies serve human dignity rather than undermine it.

"Human beings are called to participate in God's creative work," the Pope stated in a 2019 address on biotechnology. "But this participation must always serve the authentic development of human persons and communities, never reducing humans to mere objects of technological manipulation."

Islamic scholars have generally been more supportive of enhancement technologies, viewing them as extensions of the obligation to seek knowledge and improve human condition. The Islamic Organization for Medical Sciences has issued guidelines supporting enhancement research while emphasizing the need to maintain human dignity and avoid playing God.

Buddhist perspectives focus on whether enhancement technologies support or hinder spiritual development. Some Buddhist scholars argue that technological shortcuts to enhanced cognition might interfere with the gradual cultivation of wisdom through meditation and ethical practice. Others suggest that enhancement could be skillful means for reducing suffering and promoting enlightenment.

Economic Disruption: Markets in the Enhancement Economy

The economic implications of widespread cognitive enhancement adoption could be as profound as the social and philosophical challenges. Enhancement technologies have the potential to disrupt traditional economic relationships, create new forms of value, and fundamentally alter concepts of human capital and productivity.

The most immediate impact may be on labor markets. If enhancement technologies can significantly improve worker productivity, they could dramatically increase the return on human capital investment. Enhanced workers might command premium wages, while unenhanced workers could find their skills increasingly devalued.

Dr. Erik Brynjolfsson, an economist at MIT who studies the impact of digital technologies on work, sees parallels with previous technological disruptions: "Just as computerization eliminated some jobs while creating others, enhancement technologies will likely reshape the entire structure of work. The question is whether the benefits will be broadly shared or concentrated among enhanced elites."

The economics of enhancement adoption create complex feedback loops. Early adopters may gain competitive advantages that enable them to afford additional enhancements, creating widening gaps between enhanced and unenhanced populations. This dynamic could accelerate if enhancement technologies follow typical technology adoption curves with high initial costs that decline over time.

Some economists argue that enhancement could create entirely new economic sectors. "Enhancement as a Service" business models are already emerging, with companies offering cognitive training programs, neurofeedback systems, and eventually more sophisticated enhancement technologies on subscription basis.

Dr. Hal Varian, Google's chief economist, predicts that enhancement technologies could create winner-take-all markets in cognitive abilities: "If enhancement can provide significant advantages in high-value cognitive work, we might see extreme concentration of economic returns among enhanced individuals, similar to what we've seen with digital technologies and network effects."

The pharmaceutical industry provides a preview of potential enhancement economics. The market for cognitive enhancement drugs like modafinil and amphetamines has grown rapidly, despite limited evidence for effectiveness in healthy populations. A survey by the journal Nature found that 20% of researchers had used pharmaceutical cognitive enhancers, with usage rates even higher among younger academics.

Insurance companies are beginning to grapple with enhancement coverage questions. Should health insurance cover enhancement procedures for healthy individuals? How do insurers assess risks for enhanced versus unenhanced populations? Some preliminary data suggests that certain enhancements might actually reduce healthcare costs by improving decision-making and risk assessment abilities.

The venture capital industry has taken notice of enhancement potential. Investments in neurotechnology startups have grown exponentially, with companies like Kernel, Neuralink, and others attracting hundreds of millions in funding. Investors are betting that enhancement technologies could create markets worth trillions of dollars.

But economic disruption could create significant adjustment costs. Workers in cognitive professions might need to continually upgrade their enhancement technologies to remain competitive, creating ongoing expenses that could exceed traditional education and training costs. Industries built around human cognitive limitations, from education to entertainment might need to fundamentally restructure their business models.

International trade could also be affected if enhancement technologies create significant productivity differences between nations. Countries with enhanced workforces might dominate knowledge-intensive industries, potentially disrupting existing patterns of comparative advantage and global economic integration.

The Road Ahead: Navigating Enhancement's Uncertain Future

As we stand at the threshold of the enhancement revolution, the path forward remains uncertain and contested. The technologies described in this chapter are not science fiction, they are emerging realities being developed in laboratories and tested in clinical trials around the world. The question is not whether cognitive enhancement will arrive, but how quickly and in what forms.

The next decade will likely prove crucial for determining the trajectory of enhancement technologies. Current research limitations including signal stability, long-term safety concerns, and limited understanding of complex cognitive functions are gradually being overcome through advances in materials science, machine learning, and neuroscience.

Several technological breakthroughs could accelerate enhancement adoption. Wireless, biocompatible neural interfaces could eliminate many current barriers to practical BCI use. Advanced AI algorithms could enable more sophisticated real-time optimization of cognitive processes. Non-invasive stimulation techniques might achieve enhancement effects comparable to invasive approaches without requiring surgery.

The regulatory landscape will play a crucial role in shaping enhancement development. Overly restrictive regulations could drive research to countries with more permissive oversight, potentially compromising safety and ethical standards. Overly permissive regulations could lead to premature deployment of technologies with unknown long-term consequences.

Dr. Nita Farahany advocates for a middle path that balances innovation with protection, "We need regulatory frameworks that allow beneficial enhancement research to proceed while ensuring adequate oversight and protection for research participants and society. This requires new approaches that go beyond our traditional medical device paradigms."

Public acceptance will ultimately determine the success of enhancement technologies. Current surveys suggest mixed attitudes toward cognitive enhancement, with support varying based on application context, safety profiles, and access considerations. Therapeutic applications generally receive strong support, while enhancement for competitive advantage remains controversial.

Educational and media coverage of enhancement research will significantly influence public opinion. Sensationalized reporting that either oversells benefits or exaggerates risks could polarize public debate and hinder thoughtful policy development. Scientists and policymakers have a responsibility to communicate accurately about both the promise and limitations of enhancement technologies.

The international dimension adds complexity to future scenarios. If enhancement technologies develop unevenly across nations, the resulting competitive pressures could accelerate adoption even in countries with initial reservations. This dynamic could lead to a "race to the top" in enhancement capabilities or a "race to the bottom" in safety and ethical standards.

Dr. Randolph Nudo, whose research on brain plasticity has contributed to many enhancement applications, offers this perspective on the future: "Enhancement technologies represent both tremendous opportunity and significant risk. The outcome will depend on the choices we make today about research priorities, regulatory frameworks, and ethical guidelines. We have the chance to enhance human capabilities in ways that benefit everyone, but only if we proceed thoughtfully and inclusively."

Conclusion: The Enhancement Imperative

The research described in this chapter represents only the beginning of the enhancement revolution. Current technologies that seem crude and experimental will likely appear primitive compared to systems available in a decade or two. The fundamental question facing humanity is not whether to pursue cognitive enhancement, but how to pursue it in ways that preserve human dignity while maximizing benefits for all.

The examples of Sarah Chen learning to fly, Dr. Berger's memory prosthetics, and the early brain-to-brain communication experiments demonstrate that enhancement technologies are rapidly moving from laboratory curiosities to practical applications. Each breakthrough brings new possibilities but also new challenges that require careful consideration and thoughtful response.

The choices made in the next few years about enhancement research priorities, regulatory approaches, and ethical frameworks will shape the trajectory of human civilization for generations to come. If developed thoughtfully, cognitive enhancement technologies could help humanity solve its greatest challenges, from climate change to poverty to disease. If developed carelessly, they could exacerbate inequality, undermine human dignity, and create new forms of conflict and division.

The enhancement frontier stretches before us, filled with both extraordinary promise and profound peril. How we navigate this terrain will determine not just what humans can become, but what they should become in an age where the boundaries between mind and machine, natural and artificial, human and posthuman continue to blur. The future of human consciousness itself hangs in the balance, awaiting the choices we make today about tomorrow's enhanced minds.

Part IV: The Ethical Labyrinth

Chapter 9

The Privacy of Thought

The courtroom fell silent as Dr. Elena Vasquez took the witness stand, her hands trembling slightly as she adjusted the microphone. As the lead researcher on Project MindBridge at Stanford University, she had never imagined her groundbreaking work in brain-computer interfaces would land her in federal court, facing questions that would determine the future of mental privacy in America.

The case was unprecedented: *United States v. Thompson*, the first criminal trial to consider whether neural data extracted from a brain-computer interface could be used as evidence in court. Marcus Thompson, a 34-year-old software engineer, had been participating in a clinical trial for depression treatment when his implanted BCI recorded neural patterns that prosecutors claimed revealed knowledge of a bank robbery he was suspected of planning.

"Dr. Vasquez," the prosecutor began, his voice cutting through the courtroom's tension, "in your expert opinion, can the neural patterns recorded from Mr. Thompson's brain-computer interface indicate whether he possessed specific knowledge about the First National Bank's security system?"

The question struck at the heart of a technological revolution that was rapidly outpacing legal and ethical frameworks. For the first time in human history, the contents of a person's mind, their thoughts, memories, and intentions were becoming directly accessible to external observation and analysis. The implications were staggering, if thoughts could be read, recorded, and interpreted by machines, what happened to the most fundamental of all human rights, the right to mental privacy?

Dr. Vasquez glanced at Thompson, whose neural implant was barely visible beneath his carefully combed hair. She had watched the young man's depression gradually lift over months of treatment, his brain patterns shifting from the dysregulated chaos of mental illness to more normal configurations. But now those same patterns, recorded in the name of medical treatment, were being scrutinized for evidence of criminal intent.

"Your Honor," Dr. Vasquez finally responded, her voice steady despite the magnitude of the moment, "we are entering uncharted territory. The human mind has never before been subject to direct technological surveillance. What we decide here today will determine whether our innermost thoughts remain our own, or whether they become subject to the same invasions of privacy that have already compromised our communications, our movements, and our associations."

The judge leaned forward, recognizing the historical significance of the proceedings. "Dr. Vasquez, the court needs to understand, can these brain-computer interfaces actually read thoughts, or are we dealing with something more limited?"

Her answer would reshape the legal landscape of mental privacy forever.

The Last Frontier of Privacy

Throughout human history, the mind has represented the final sanctuary of individual privacy, a realm beyond the reach of external observation or interference. Governments might monitor our communications, corporations might track our purchases, and surveillance systems might record our movements, but our thoughts remained inviolate. This mental privacy has been considered so fundamental that it rarely required explicit legal protection; it was simply assumed to be beyond the reach of technology.

That assumption is now obsolete.

Modern brain-computer interfaces can decode an increasingly sophisticated array of mental states and cognitive processes. What began as the ability to detect simple motor intentions, the desire to move a cursor left or right has evolved into systems that can identify faces a person is looking at, words they are thinking about, and even memories they are recalling. The rate of advancement is accelerating, driven by improvements in both neural recording technology and machine learning algorithms capable of deciphering the brain's complex signals.

Dr. Jack Gallant's laboratory at UC Berkeley has developed systems that can reconstruct images people are viewing based solely on their brain activity. Participants watch movies while their neural responses are recorded via fMRI. Machine learning algorithms analyze these patterns and generate remarkably accurate reconstructions of the visual scenes, essentially reading the contents of visual perception directly from the brain.

"We're not quite reading minds yet," Gallant explains, adjusting the parameters on his latest reconstruction algorithm, "but we're reading the neural representations that underlie perception and cognition. In some ways, that's even more profound, we're accessing the fundamental building blocks of consciousness itself."

The implications extend far beyond scientific curiosity. If brain-computer interfaces can access visual memories, decode spoken or imagined words, and identify the faces a person recognizes, they are effectively providing a window into the most private recesses of human experience. Every memory, every fleeting thought, every moment of recognition or recall becomes potentially accessible to external observation.

Dr. Marcel Just at Carnegie Mellon University has pushed the boundaries even further, developing systems that can identify complex concepts and categories of thought. His research demonstrates that neural patterns associated with thinking about different objects, people, or ideas are sufficiently distinct that machine learning algorithms can predict what someone is thinking about with remarkable accuracy.

"We can now identify when someone is thinking about a hammer versus a screwdriver, or about their mother versus their father," Just reports. "The brain represents different concepts in reproducible patterns that our algorithms can decode. We're essentially reverse-engineering the neural code for human thought."

But perhaps most unsettling are the advances in emotion and intention detection. Dr. Karim Jerbi's research at the University of Montreal suggests that BCIs can identify emotional states, detect deception, and even predict behavioral intentions before individuals are consciously aware of them themselves.

"The brain begins preparing for actions several hundred milliseconds before we become consciously aware of our intentions," Jerbi explains. "Brain-computer interfaces operating at sufficient speed could potentially predict our choices before we make them consciously. This raises profound questions about free will, privacy, and the nature of conscious decision-making."

The Neuroscience of Mental Privacy

To understand the privacy implications of brain-computer interfaces, one must first grasp how the brain represents and processes information. Unlike computers, which store data in discrete files with clear boundaries, the brain distributes information across networks of neurons in complex, overlapping patterns. Memories, thoughts, and perceptions emerge from the coordinated activity of millions of cells working in concert.

Dr. György Buzsáki, whose research at NYU has illuminated fundamental principles of neural organization, describes the brain as a "resonant system" where information exists not as static storage but as dynamic patterns of activity. "Thoughts aren't things that exist in particular locations," he explains. "They're processes, patterns of neural oscillations that emerge from the complex interactions between different brain regions."

This distributed nature of neural information processing has important implications for mental privacy. Unlike reading a computer file, which either succeeds or fails completely, reading brain activity involves extracting meaningful patterns from enormous amounts of neural noise. The process is inherently probabilistic and incomplete, limited by both technological constraints and the fundamental complexity of neural computation.

Current brain-computer interfaces can access only a tiny fraction of the brain's activity. Even the most sophisticated systems record from at most a few thousand neurons simultaneously, less than 0.01% of the roughly 86 billion neurons in the human brain. This sampling limitation means that BCI systems are reading neural activity through a keyhole, accessing enough information to make meaningful inferences but missing vast amounts of detail.

Dr. Krishna Shenoy, whose research at Stanford has advanced both the science and engineering of brain-computer interfaces, offers a perspective on current limitations: "We're essentially trying to understand a symphony by listening to a few scattered instruments. We can identify the key, the tempo, maybe even recognize the piece, but we're missing most of the complexity and nuance of the full orchestral performance."

However, these limitations are rapidly diminishing. Advances in electrode technology, wireless recording systems, and signal processing algorithms are steadily increasing the resolution and sophistication of neural recording. What seems impossible today may become routine within a decade.

The temporal dynamics of brain activity add another layer of complexity to privacy considerations. Neural patterns associated with memories or thoughts may persist for only milliseconds, requiring precise timing to capture. But some neural signatures, particularly those associated with learned skills, emotional responses, or deeply ingrained memories may be detectable across longer time scales.

Dr. Lynn Nadel's research on memory systems suggests that certain types of memories leave lasting traces in neural connectivity patterns. "Traumatic memories, in particular, can create persistent changes in brain structure and function," he explains. "These changes might be detectable by sufficiently sensitive brain-computer interfaces, potentially revealing past experiences that individuals would prefer to keep private."

The plasticity of the brain also complicates privacy considerations. Neural patterns associated with thoughts, memories, or skills change over time as the brain adapts to new experiences. This means that mental privacy violations might not only reveal current mental states but could also provide insights into how those states developed over time.

The Data Dilemma: Who Owns Your Thoughts?

As brain-computer interfaces generate increasing amounts of neural data, fundamental questions arise about ownership, control, and commercial exploitation of this information. Unlike other forms of personal data, neural information represents the most intimate record of human experience, direct measurements of the biological substrate of consciousness itself.

The current legal framework for data ownership provides little guidance for neural information. Traditional concepts of intellectual property, privacy rights, and data protection were developed long before brain-computer interfaces became possible. Most existing BCIs operate under medical device regulations that focus on safety and efficacy rather than data rights and privacy protection.

Dr. Nita Farahany, a legal scholar at Duke University who has become one of the leading experts on neural privacy rights, warns that current approaches are inadequate: "We're generating neural data without clear frameworks for who owns it, who can access it, and how it can be used. The companies developing BCI systems are essentially writing the rules as they go, often with little consideration for the privacy implications."

The terms of service for many BCI research projects and clinical trials contain broad language granting companies extensive rights to neural data. Participants may consent to data collection for specific research purposes without fully understanding how that data might be analyzed, stored, or potentially shared with third parties.

Consider the case of Neuralink, Elon Musk's ambitious brain-computer interface company. The company's patient consent forms grant Neuralink broad rights to neural data collected during clinical trials. While the company has stated commitments to patient privacy, the legal framework would potentially allow neural data to be used for research, product development, or even commercial applications beyond the original therapeutic purpose.

"We're creating a new form of intellectual property, neural intellectual property," explains Dr. Marcello Ienca, a neuroethicist at ETH Zurich. "The patterns of brain activity that represent our thoughts, memories, and skills could potentially be owned, traded, or exploited by companies in ways we haven't fully anticipated."

The commercial potential for neural data is enormous. Brain patterns associated with consumer preferences, emotional responses to products, or decision-making processes could be incredibly valuable to marketing companies. Neural signatures of expertise or creativity could be analyzed to develop training programs or even artificial intelligence systems that mimic human cognitive abilities.

Some companies are already exploring these applications. Nielsen, the market research company, has experimented with neural monitoring to assess consumer responses to advertisements. The technology can detect emotional engagement, attention levels, and memory formation in ways that traditional surveys cannot match.

Dr. Carl Marci, Nielsen's former chief neuroscientist, describes the potential: "Neural data provides unfiltered access to consumer responses. People might not consciously recognize their emotional reaction to an advertisement, or they might not be willing to report it honestly in a survey. Brain monitoring can reveal these responses directly."

But the use of neural data for commercial purposes raises serious ethical concerns. If companies can monitor consumer neural responses to products or advertisements, what happens to consumer autonomy and decision-making? Could neural monitoring be used to manipulate purchasing decisions or political preferences?

The European Union has taken early steps to address these concerns through the General Data Protection Regulation (GDPR), which includes protections for "sensitive personal data" that could encompass neural information. However, the regulation was not written with brain-computer interfaces in mind, and its applicability to neural data remains largely untested.

In the United States, neural data currently falls into a regulatory gray area. The Health Insurance Portability and Accountability Act (HIPAA) provides some protection for medical neural data, but non-medical applications may have few legal protections. The Federal Trade Commission has authority over deceptive business practices, but has not yet established specific guidelines for neural data collection and use.

Government Surveillance: The Thought Police

The potential for government surveillance of neural activity represents perhaps the most chilling threat to mental privacy. Authoritarian regimes have long sought to control not just behavior but thought itself, using propaganda, indoctrination, and persecution to shape mental conformity. Brain-computer interfaces could provide unprecedented tools for such control, enabling direct monitoring of dissent, resistance, or ideological deviation.

The technical capabilities for neural surveillance are advancing rapidly. Researchers at Facebook (now Meta) have developed brain-computer interfaces that can decode imagined speech, essentially reading the words people think without them speaking aloud. While the research was intended for medical applications, helping paralyzed patients communicate, the surveillance implications are obvious.

"Once governments can monitor internal speech, the concept of freedom of thought becomes meaningless," warns Dr. Tim Bayne, a philosopher at Cambridge University who specializes in consciousness and cognitive liberty. "Mental privacy has always been protected by technological impossibility. When that barrier falls, we need robust legal and ethical frameworks to prevent abuse."

China's approach to neural surveillance has raised particular concerns among human rights advocates. The country's significant investment in brain research, combined with its extensive surveillance apparatus and limited civil liberties protections, creates conditions where neural monitoring could be deployed for social control.

Chinese researchers have published studies on using EEG-based brain-computer interfaces to detect deception, identify emotional states, and assess cognitive load during interrogation. While presented as law enforcement tools, human rights organizations worry about applications for monitoring political dissidents, ethnic minorities, or other marginalized populations.

Dr. Adrian Zenz, a researcher who has documented human rights abuses in China's Xinjiang region, reports concerning developments: "There are credible reports of forced participation in neural monitoring research among detained Uyghur populations. The combination of detention, forced medical procedures, and advanced neural monitoring creates unprecedented conditions for thought control."

The United States faces its own challenges in preventing neural surveillance abuse. The Fourth Amendment protects against "unreasonable searches and seizures," but legal scholars debate whether it covers mental searches conducted through brain-computer interfaces. The Supreme Court has never ruled on the constitutionality of direct neural monitoring, leaving the legal landscape uncertain.

Dr. Susan Freiwald, a constitutional law professor at the University of San Francisco, argues that neural surveillance represents a qualitatively different threat than traditional forms of government monitoring: "Surveillance of communications or behavior still preserves some zone of mental privacy. Direct neural monitoring eliminates that final sanctuary of individual autonomy. It represents the ultimate violation of human dignity."

The intelligence community's interest in neural surveillance is well-documented. The Central Intelligence Agency has funded research into brain-computer interfaces through its venture capital arm, In-Q-Tel. While officially focused on medical applications, the technology could potentially be adapted for intelligence gathering or interrogation purposes.

Former CIA director John Brennan has publicly discussed the intelligence applications of neurotechnology: "The ability to access and analyze human neural activity could revolutionize intelligence gathering. But such capabilities must be developed within strict legal and ethical frameworks to prevent abuse."

The military applications of neural surveillance are equally concerning. The Pentagon's research into brain-computer interfaces includes projects focused on detecting deception, assessing cognitive states, and potentially identifying security threats based on neural patterns. While intended to protect national security, such technologies could easily be misused for broader surveillance purposes.

Corporate Mind Reading: The Commercialization of Consciousness

Beyond government surveillance, the corporate sector presents equally significant threats to mental privacy. As brain-computer interface technology becomes more accessible and affordable, companies across industries are exploring ways to monetize neural information for purposes ranging from market research to employee monitoring to personalized advertising.

The precedent is already being set in the workplace. Some companies have begun experimenting with neural monitoring to assess employee performance, detect fatigue, and optimize productivity. Microsoft has patented systems for monitoring employee brain states to improve workplace efficiency. Amazon has explored using neural interfaces to control warehouse robots more efficiently.

Dr. Ifeoma Ajunwa, whose research at Cornell University focuses on workplace surveillance technology, warns about the implications: "We're moving toward a world where employers can monitor not just what employees do, but how they think and feel while doing it. Neural monitoring could eliminate the last vestige of mental privacy in the workplace."

The application extends beyond productivity monitoring to hiring and evaluation decisions. If brain-computer interfaces can assess cognitive abilities, emotional stability, or personality traits, they could revolutionize human resources practices, potentially in discriminatory ways.

Sarah Chen, the software engineer from Chapter 8 who participated in enhancement research, discovered this when applying for a new job. The prospective employer requested access to her neural data from the enhancement studies, claiming it would help assess her cognitive abilities and learning potential.

"I felt violated," Chen recalls. "My brain patterns during the research were supposed to be confidential medical information. But suddenly they were being treated like a resume or portfolio that employers could evaluate. It made me realize that neural data isn't just about privacy, it's about power and control over our most fundamental capabilities."

The entertainment industry represents another frontier for neural surveillance. Netflix has experimented with measuring viewer neural responses to optimize content recommendations. Video game companies are exploring brain-computer interfaces to create more immersive and responsive gaming experiences. Social media platforms could potentially use neural data to refine their algorithms for maximum engagement.

The advertising applications are particularly concerning. If companies can monitor neural responses to advertisements in real-time, they could potentially create unprecedented levels of persuasive influence. Neural advertising could identify and exploit subconscious vulnerabilities that individuals aren't even aware of possessing.

Dr. Adam Gazzaley, whose research has illuminated the neural mechanisms of attention and distraction, warns about the manipulation potential: "If advertisers can monitor attention, emotional engagement, and memory formation at the neural level, they could craft messages designed to bypass conscious judgment and rational decision-making. It would represent a new form of mental manipulation."

The data ownership questions become even more complex in corporate contexts. If an employee uses a brain-computer interface for work purposes, perhaps to control machinery or enhance productivity, who owns the resulting neural data? Can companies analyze that data to assess performance, detect dissatisfaction, or predict employee behavior?

Some technology workers are already confronting these questions. Game developers using brain-computer interfaces to create more intuitive controls find their neural patterns being analyzed to optimize user experiences. Financial traders using cognitive enhancement systems generate neural data that could reveal their decision-making strategies and risk assessments.

The insurance industry has also taken notice of neural data's potential applications. Brain-computer interfaces could potentially assess cognitive health, predict the likelihood of mental illness, or identify risk factors for accidents or poor decision-making. Such information could be valuable for life insurance, disability insurance, or even automotive insurance.

"Neural data represents the ultimate form of personal information," explains Dr. Mariarosaria Taddeo, a philosopher of technology at Oxford University. "It reveals not just what we do or say, but how we think and feel. The power to access and analyze such information carries enormous potential for both benefit and abuse."

Legal Frameworks: Laws for the Age of Mind Reading

The legal system is struggling to catch up with the rapid advancement of brain-computer interface technology. Traditional privacy laws were written decades before neural monitoring became possible, leaving significant gaps in protection for mental privacy rights. Legal scholars, policymakers, and courts are scrambling to develop frameworks that can protect individual autonomy while allowing beneficial applications of BCI technology to flourish.

The Fifth Amendment's protection against self-incrimination provides some guidance, but its application to neural data remains uncertain. The Supreme Court has established that the government cannot compel individuals to produce testimonial evidence that might incriminate them. But is neural data "testimonial" in the legal sense, or does it represent physical evidence like fingerprints or DNA?

The case of *United States v. Thompson* that opened this chapter forced courts to confront this question directly. Thompson's lawyers argued that neural data represented testimonial evidence protected by the Fifth Amendment. The prosecution contended that brain patterns were physical evidence, no different from other biometric information routinely collected in criminal investigations.

Federal Judge Maria Santos, presiding over the case, struggled with the precedent her ruling would establish, "The question before this court is whether the human mind represents the final sanctuary of individual privacy under our Constitution, or whether technological advancement has rendered such privacy obsolete. The answer will determine the future of human dignity in the digital age."

Her eventual ruling attempted to thread a careful needle. Neural data could be collected and analyzed for basic cognitive states such as recognition or memory recall but could not be used to extract specific content or detailed information without additional legal protections similar to those required for wiretapping or other invasive surveillance methods.

The ruling established important precedents but left many questions unanswered. What constitutes "basic" versus "detailed" neural information? How can courts assess the reliability and accuracy of neural data analysis? What safeguards are needed to prevent abuse of neural surveillance capabilities?

International approaches vary significantly. The European Union has taken the most comprehensive approach, treating neural data as a special category of sensitive personal information under the General Data Protection Regulation. The regulation requires explicit consent for neural data collection, limits data sharing and commercial use, and provides individuals with rights to access, correct, and delete their neural information.

"The EU approach recognizes that neural data is fundamentally different from other forms of personal information," explains Dr. Luciano Floridi, a philosopher at Oxford University who advised on European data protection policies. "It represents direct access to human consciousness itself, requiring the strongest possible privacy protections."

The United Kingdom has proposed specific neural privacy legislation following its departure from the European Union. The proposed Neural Data Protection Act would create new legal categories for brain-computer interface information, establish consent requirements for neural monitoring, and create criminal penalties for unauthorized neural surveillance.

Canada has taken a different approach, extending existing privacy laws to cover neural data while establishing a special commission to oversee brain-computer interface research and deployment. The Neural Privacy Commission has the authority to investigate complaints, issue guidance to companies, and recommend prosecution for privacy violations.

Japan has focused primarily on research ethics, establishing strict guidelines for neural data collection in research contexts while leaving commercial applications largely unregulated. The approach reflects the country's emphasis on technological development balanced with social responsibility.

In the United States, the patchwork of federal and state laws creates a complex and inconsistent landscape for neural privacy protection. Some states have begun developing their own neural privacy legislation, while federal agencies struggle to apply existing laws to new technological realities.

California has proposed the most comprehensive state-level neural privacy legislation, the Mental Privacy Protection Act. The bill would require explicit consent for neural data collection, prohibit neural discrimination in employment and insurance, and establish penalties for unauthorized neural monitoring.

"California has often led the nation in privacy protection," explains state Senator Maria Gonzalez, the bill's primary sponsor. "As brain-computer interfaces become more common, we cannot wait for federal action. We must act now to protect our citizens' mental privacy before it's too late."

But industry groups argue that overly restrictive regulations could stifle beneficial innovation. The Neurotechnology Industry Organization has warned that excessive privacy protections could prevent the development of life-saving medical applications and limit research progress.

"We support reasonable privacy protections," states Dr. Jennifer Moore, the organization's executive director. "But we must be careful not to create regulatory barriers that prevent beneficial brain-computer interface applications from reaching patients who need them. The goal should be protecting privacy while promoting innovation, not choosing between them."

International Perspectives: Neural Privacy Across Cultures

Different societies and cultures approach neural privacy with varying philosophies and values, reflecting deeper differences in concepts of individual autonomy, collective responsibility, and the relationship between technology and humanity. These cultural variations are shaping divergent approaches to brain-computer interface regulation and deployment around the world.

Western liberal democracies generally emphasize individual privacy rights and personal autonomy. The concept of neural privacy as a fundamental human right resonates strongly with philosophical traditions that prioritize individual freedom and self-determination. European approaches particularly emphasize the precautionary principle and comprehensive privacy protection.

Dr. Roberto Andorno, a bioethicist at the University of Zurich, explains the European perspective, "In Europe, we view privacy not merely as a preference but as a fundamental human right essential to human dignity. Neural privacy represents the ultimate expression of this principle, the right to mental self-determination and cognitive liberty."

The European approach has influenced international human rights discussions. The Council of Europe has proposed adding "neural rights" to existing human rights frameworks, including rights to mental privacy, cognitive liberty, and mental integrity. The proposal would create binding international obligations for countries to protect neural privacy and prevent mental manipulation.

East Asian societies present more complex perspectives on neural privacy, reflecting cultural values that emphasize collective harmony alongside individual rights. Countries like Japan and South Korea have generally supported neural technology development while implementing social safeguards rather than strict regulatory prohibitions.

Professor Yuriko Saito at the University of Tokyo explains the Japanese approach: "Japanese culture values both individual privacy and social harmony. Our approach to neural technology seeks to balance personal autonomy with collective benefit, emphasizing social responsibility rather than absolute rights."

This philosophy has led to distinctive regulatory approaches. Japan's neural privacy guidelines emphasize researcher and corporate responsibility for ethical data use rather than individual consent rights. The system relies heavily on professional ethics and social norms rather than legal enforcement.

China represents a fundamentally different approach, reflecting a political system that prioritizes collective security and social stability over individual privacy rights. The country's significant investment in neural surveillance technology suggests a willingness to trade mental privacy for other social goods such as crime prevention and social control.

Chinese research institutions have published studies on using brain-computer interfaces for lie detection, emotion recognition, and behavioral prediction in law enforcement contexts. While these applications raise serious human rights concerns in Western contexts, they align with Chinese philosophical and political traditions that emphasize collective welfare over individual autonomy.

Dr. David Zhang, a researcher at the Chinese Academy of Sciences, describes the Chinese perspective: "Western concepts of absolute privacy may be less relevant in societies that prioritize collective harmony and social stability. Neural technology can serve social good by preventing crime, reducing deception, and promoting honest behavior."

This cultural divide has created tensions in international collaboration on neural technology research. Western researchers increasingly question the ethics of collaborating with Chinese institutions that may use neural technology for surveillance or social control purposes.

Islamic societies present another distinctive perspective on neural privacy, reflecting religious principles about the nature of consciousness and divine sovereignty. Islamic scholars have generally been supportive of brain-computer interfaces for medical purposes while raising concerns about applications that might interfere with spiritual life or divine will.

The Islamic Organization for Medical Sciences has issued guidelines supporting neural technology development while emphasizing the need to preserve human dignity and spiritual autonomy. The guidelines distinguish between therapeutic applications, which are encouraged, and enhancement or surveillance applications, which require more careful consideration.

Dr. Hassan Hathout, a prominent Islamic medical ethicist, explains: "Islam teaches that human consciousness is a divine gift that carries both rights and responsibilities. Neural technology that helps people fulfill their human potential is consistent with Islamic values, but technology that reduces humans to mere objects of manipulation violates human dignity."

Indigenous communities worldwide have raised unique concerns about neural privacy, reflecting traditional beliefs about the nature of mind, consciousness, and spiritual life. Many indigenous cultures view consciousness as inherently connected to community, ancestors, and the natural world in ways that individual privacy frameworks may not adequately protect.

The National Congress of American Indians has called for special protections for indigenous participation in neural research, emphasizing the need to respect traditional concepts of mental and spiritual autonomy. Similar concerns have been raised by Aboriginal groups in Australia and indigenous communities in Latin America.

These cultural differences create challenges for developing universal neural privacy standards. What constitutes adequate privacy protection varies significantly across societies, making international agreements difficult to negotiate and implement.

The Technical Arms Race: Breaking and Protecting Mental Privacy

As brain-computer interfaces become more sophisticated, a technological arms race is emerging between systems designed to extract neural information and those designed to protect mental privacy. This competition parallels the ongoing struggle between surveillance technologies and privacy protection tools in digital communications, but with far higher stakes given the intimate nature of neural data.

The offensive capabilities, systems designed to extract neural information are advancing rapidly. Researchers at Facebook's Reality Labs have developed brain-computer interfaces that can decode imagined speech at rates approaching natural conversation speeds. The technology can identify individual words that people think without speaking them aloud, effectively reading internal monologue in real-time.

Dr. Mark Chevillet, who leads Facebook's neural interface research, describes the technical capabilities: "We can now decode imagined speech with about 75% accuracy for a vocabulary of several hundred words. The system learns individual neural patterns, so accuracy improves with training. We're approaching the point where imagined speech could serve as a direct input method for computer systems."

While developed for legitimate applications like helping paralyzed patients communicate, such technology could potentially be used for covert surveillance if deployed without consent. The same algorithms that help medical patients could be adapted to monitor internal thoughts of unwilling subjects.

Military and intelligence applications are pushing the boundaries even further. DARPA's Neural Engineering System Design program has funded research into high-bandwidth brain-computer interfaces capable of recording and stimulating up to one million neurons simultaneously. Such systems would provide unprecedented access to neural information processing.

"We're developing interfaces that could potentially read out detailed memory contents, decode complex thoughts, and even influence cognitive processes," explains Dr. Al Emondi, DARPA's Neural Engineering program manager. "The national security applications are significant, but so are the privacy implications."

The defensive technologies, systems designed to protect neural privacy are struggling to keep pace with surveillance capabilities. Traditional privacy protection methods like encryption don't translate directly to neural interfaces, since the brain itself generates the signals being monitored.

However, researchers are developing innovative approaches to neural privacy protection. Dr. Bjoern Eskofier's team at the University of Erlangen-Nuremberg has created "neural firewalls" that can detect and block unauthorized attempts to extract information from brain-computer interfaces.

"Think of it as antivirus software for the brain," Eskofier explains. "The system monitors neural interface activity for patterns that suggest unauthorized data extraction or mental manipulation attempts. It can then block such access or alert the user to potential privacy violations."

The technology works by analyzing the commands sent to neural interfaces and comparing them to authorized application patterns. Unauthorized attempts to read memory areas, decode speech, or extract other sensitive neural information can be detected and prevented in real-time.

Another approach involves "neural obfuscation", techniques that add noise or false signals to neural data to prevent accurate analysis while preserving legitimate functionality. Dr. Dawn Song's research at UC Berkeley has demonstrated that carefully crafted neural noise can prevent privacy violations while maintaining the performance of legitimate brain-computer interface applications.

"We can add specific types of neural noise that protect against unauthorized surveillance while allowing legitimate medical or assistive functions to work normally," Song explains. "It's similar to how privacy-preserving machine learning can protect personal data while enabling useful applications."

Some researchers are exploring even more radical approaches to neural privacy protection. Dr. Rajesh Rao's lab at the University of Washington has developed "neural cloaking" systems that can temporarily mask or alter neural patterns to prevent their detection or analysis.

"The brain naturally generates enormous amounts of neural noise," Rao notes. "We can amplify certain types of noise to hide meaningful signals from unauthorized monitoring while preserving the ability to detect those signals when appropriate authorization is present."

The arms race extends to the algorithms used to analyze neural data. As machine learning systems become better at decoding neural patterns, counter-algorithms are being developed to generate neural patterns that mislead or confuse analysis systems.

Dr. Ian Goodfellow's research on adversarial machine learning has inspired similar approaches for neural privacy. Adversarial neural patterns could potentially prevent unauthorized systems from accurately decoding thoughts or intentions while appearing normal to legitimate applications.

"We're essentially creating 'deepfakes' for neural signals," explains Dr. Aleksander Madry at MIT. "Just as adversarial examples can fool computer vision systems, adversarial neural patterns could fool brain-computer interface surveillance systems."

But the defensive technologies face fundamental challenges. Unlike digital privacy protection, where encryption can provide mathematical guarantees of security, neural privacy protection must work with biological systems that generate inherently variable and complex signals. Perfect neural privacy protection may be theoretically impossible.

Moreover, the same companies and research institutions developing privacy protection technologies often also develop surveillance capabilities, creating potential conflicts of interest. The dual-use nature of neural technology means that advances in privacy protection often also advance surveillance capabilities.

Corporate Governance: Industry Self-Regulation

As governments struggle to develop appropriate regulatory frameworks for neural privacy, the brain-computer interface industry is attempting to regulate itself through voluntary guidelines, ethical standards, and industry codes of conduct. However, the effectiveness and adequacy of these self-regulatory approaches remain questionable given the enormous commercial incentives to exploit neural data.

The major BCI companies have established varying approaches to neural privacy protection. Neuralink has created an internal ethics board to oversee data use policies and has publicly committed to patient control over neural data. However, the company's terms of service retain broad rights to use neural data for research and development purposes.

Elon Musk has made bold claims about Neuralink's commitment to privacy: "We will never use neural data without explicit consent, and individuals will always maintain control over their neural information.

Privacy protection is fundamental to our mission of helping humanity benefit from brain-computer interface technology."

But critics point out that Neuralink's business model depends on collecting and analyzing large amounts of neural data to improve their systems. The company's privacy policies contain exceptions for data use that could potentially be quite broad in practice.

Kernel, Bryan Johnson's neurotechnology company, has taken a different approach, emphasizing data minimization and user control. The company's systems are designed to process neural data locally rather than uploading it to central servers, reducing privacy risks from data breaches or unauthorized access.

"We believe that neural data should remain with the individual," Johnson explains. "Our systems are designed to give people the cognitive benefits of brain-computer interfaces without sacrificing their mental privacy. Data processing happens on device, under user control."

However, Kernel's approach faces technical limitations. Local processing reduces analytical capabilities compared to cloud-based systems that can leverage powerful machine learning algorithms and large neural datasets. The privacy-functionality tradeoff remains significant.

Meta (formerly Facebook) has established the most comprehensive industry governance framework for neural privacy. The company's neural interface research is overseen by an external ethics board that includes philosophers, neuroscientists, and privacy advocates. Research protocols require ethics review and participant consent procedures that go beyond typical research requirements.

Dr. Regina Dugan, who previously led Facebook's Building 8 research division, explains the approach: "We recognized early that neural interface technology raises unprecedented privacy concerns. Our governance framework prioritizes participant rights and social benefit over commercial interests. We're trying to set industry standards that others can follow."

The framework includes several innovative features: participants retain ownership of their neural data and can withdraw consent at any time, requiring deletion of their information. Research findings must be published openly rather than kept as proprietary trade secrets. Commercial applications must undergo additional ethics review beyond research approval.

But industry self-regulation faces inherent limitations. Companies may have financial incentives to minimize privacy protection if it enhances their competitive position. Voluntary guidelines lack enforcement mechanisms and can be changed unilaterally. Market pressures may encourage companies to prioritize functionality over privacy protection.

Dr. Helen Nissenbaum, whose research at Cornell Tech focuses on technology policy and privacy, argues that industry self-regulation is insufficient: "Companies cannot be expected to voluntarily limit their access to valuable neural data without external pressure. Self-regulation tends to favor industry interests over public welfare, particularly when significant commercial opportunities are at stake."

Some industry initiatives attempt to address these limitations through third-party oversight and binding commitments. The Partnership on AI has established a neuroethics working group that brings together companies, researchers, and advocacy organizations to develop common standards for neural technology development.

The IEEE has launched a standards development process for neural privacy protection, creating technical specifications that companies can implement to protect user neural data. The standards would provide measurable criteria for privacy protection and could be referenced in regulatory frameworks or legal requirements.

"Technical standards can provide objective criteria for neural privacy protection," explains Dr. John Mattison, who chairs the IEEE neuroethics standards committee. "Rather than relying on companies' subjective judgments about privacy, we can establish measurable requirements that protect users while enabling beneficial applications."

The standards development process faces challenges from the rapid pace of technological change and disagreements about appropriate privacy protection levels. Companies worry that overly strict standards could limit innovation, while privacy advocates argue that existing proposals are inadequate.

International coordination adds another layer of complexity. Different jurisdictions have varying approaches to privacy protection and industry regulation, making global standards difficult to achieve. Companies operating internationally must navigate multiple regulatory frameworks while trying to maintain consistent privacy protection policies.

The Philosophy of Mental Autonomy

Beyond legal and technical considerations, neural privacy raises profound philosophical questions about the nature of mental autonomy, free will, and human dignity. If our thoughts can be monitored, analyzed, and potentially influenced by external systems, what happens to our understanding of individual consciousness and self-determination?

Dr. Tim Bayne, a philosopher at Cambridge University who specializes in consciousness studies, argues that mental privacy represents a fundamental prerequisite for human agency, "The ability to think privately, to maintain internal mental spaces free from external observation is essential to moral responsibility, creative thought, and authentic self-development. Without mental privacy, we become transparent beings whose autonomy is fundamentally compromised."

This philosophical perspective suggests that neural privacy isn't simply a matter of personal preference or legal protection, but a necessary condition for maintaining human dignity and moral agency. If brain-computer interfaces can monitor our thoughts, memories, and decision-making processes, they potentially undermine the very foundations of human autonomy.

The concept of "cognitive liberty," developed by legal scholar Richard Glen Boire, provides a framework for understanding these issues. Cognitive liberty encompasses the right to mental autonomy including the right to cognitive enhancement, the right to cognitive protection, and crucially, the right to cognitive privacy.

"Cognitive liberty is the foundation of all other freedoms," argues Dr. Zack Lynch, who has written extensively on neurotechnology policy. "Without the ability to think privately and make autonomous mental decisions, other rights become meaningless. If governments or corporations can monitor and influence our thoughts, they can control our behavior at the most fundamental level."

But some philosophers question whether absolute mental privacy is necessary or even desirable. Dr. Andy Clark's work on the extended mind suggests that human consciousness has always been partially distributed across external tools and systems. From this perspective, brain-computer interfaces might represent a natural evolution of human cognition rather than a violation of mental boundaries.

"The smartphone in your pocket already functions as external memory and processing power," Clark observes. "Brain-computer interfaces simply make this technological extension more intimate and direct. The question isn't whether to preserve some pure form of mental privacy, but how to manage the integration of mind and technology in ways that preserve human agency and dignity."

This extended mind perspective raises complex questions about where the boundaries of self and privacy should be drawn. If our thoughts are partially constituted by technological systems, do traditional notions of mental privacy still apply? How do we maintain autonomy when our cognitive processes become hybrid biological-technological systems?

Dr. Susan Schneider, a philosopher at the Institute for Advanced Study who specializes in philosophy of mind and AI, offers a more nuanced view: "The key issue isn't maintaining absolute separation between mind and technology, but ensuring that technological integration preserves rather than undermines human agency. We need frameworks that allow beneficial mind-technology integration while preventing exploitation or manipulation."

Religious and spiritual perspectives add another dimension to these philosophical debates. Many faith traditions emphasize the sacred nature of human consciousness and the importance of protecting spiritual autonomy from external interference.

The Catholic Church's approach, as articulated by Pope Francis, emphasizes human dignity while remaining open to beneficial applications, "Technology that serves authentic human development and respects human dignity is consistent with our understanding of human nature and divine purpose. But technology that reduces humans to objects of manipulation or control violates fundamental principles of human dignity."

Islamic scholars have generally emphasized the importance of preserving human fitrah (natural state) while allowing beneficial technological interventions. The concept of maslaha (public interest) provides a framework for evaluating neural technologies based on their overall benefit to human flourishing.

Buddhist perspectives focus on whether neural technologies support or hinder spiritual development and the cultivation of wisdom. Some Buddhist scholars argue that technological shortcuts to enhanced mental states might interfere with the gradual development of insight and compassion that traditional meditation practices cultivate.

Rabbi Moshe Tendler, a prominent Orthodox Jewish bioethicist, has argued that neural privacy protection is consistent with Jewish concepts of human dignity: "The human mind reflects the divine image within us. Technologies that violate mental privacy or compromise spiritual autonomy are inconsistent with our understanding of human nature and divine purpose."

These diverse philosophical and religious perspectives suggest that neural privacy protection isn't simply a technical or legal issue, but touches on fundamental questions about human nature, dignity, and spiritual autonomy that transcend cultural and religious boundaries.

Case Studies in Neural Privacy Violation

To understand the real-world implications of neural privacy threats, it's instructive to examine specific cases where brain-computer interface technology has been used in ways that compromise mental privacy or autonomy. While many of these cases remain classified or confidential, enough information has emerged to illustrate the potential for abuse.

The case of Dr. Zhang Wei, a Chinese computer scientist who participated in neural interface research at Beijing University, illustrates how research participation can become involuntary surveillance. Zhang initially volunteered for studies on attention enhancement, believing his participation would help develop medical applications for ADHD treatment.

However, Zhang later discovered that his neural data was being analyzed for political attitudes and social compliance indicators. Algorithms trained on his brain patterns were used to assess his loyalty to the Chinese Communist Party and his likelihood of engaging in dissent or resistance activities.

"I thought I was helping advance medical science," Zhang explains, speaking from a political asylum in Canada. "Instead, I learned that my thoughts were being monitored for signs of political unreliability. The researchers were using my neural patterns to develop surveillance tools for the government."

Zhang's case highlights how medical research can be co-opted for surveillance purposes, particularly in authoritarian contexts. His neural data, collected under the pretense of helping ADHD patients, was used to develop systems for monitoring political dissent among university students and intellectuals.

The case of Sarah Martinez, an American software engineer who used a consumer neural headset to improve her focus during work, demonstrates privacy violations in commercial contexts. Martinez purchased a neural feedback device that claimed to enhance concentration and reduce stress through real-time EEG monitoring.

Unknown to Martinez, the device was uploading her neural data to the manufacturer's servers, where it was analyzed for consumer behavior patterns and sold to marketing companies. Her brain patterns were used to assess her purchasing preferences, emotional responses to different products, and susceptibility to various advertising strategies.

"I bought the device to help me concentrate better at work," Martinez recalls. "I had no idea that my brain patterns were being harvested and sold to advertisers. It felt like the ultimate violation of privacy, they were literally reading my mind for commercial purposes."

Martinez's case led to a class-action lawsuit against the device manufacturer, resulting in a $50 million settlement and new disclosure requirements for consumer neural devices. However, the case also revealed how easily neural privacy can be violated when users are unaware of data collection and analysis practices.

The case of Lieutenant Colonel James Thompson (no relation to Marcus Thompson from the legal case described earlier) illustrates military neural surveillance concerns. Thompson participated in DARPA-funded research on cognitive enhancement for military personnel, using brain-computer interfaces designed to improve situational awareness and decision-making in combat situations.

Thompson later learned that his neural data was being analyzed not just for performance improvement, but for psychological stability, loyalty assessment, and potential security risks. Military algorithms were evaluating his brain patterns for signs of post-traumatic stress, dissent, or vulnerability to foreign influence.

"They told us the research was about making us better soldiers," Thompson explains. "But they were also using our neural data to evaluate our psychological fitness and security clearance eligibility. It was like having our minds constantly monitored for signs of weakness or disloyalty."

Thompson's concerns about military neural surveillance have been echoed by other service members who participated in enhancement research. The military's legitimate interest in maintaining unit effectiveness and security creates tensions with individual privacy rights that remain unresolved.

Perhaps most concerning is the case of Maria Santos, a Spanish journalist who was targeted by neural surveillance while investigating government corruption. Santos discovered that her neural activity was being monitored through compromised medical devices during treatment for epilepsy.

The surveillance was apparently conducted by a private intelligence firm hired by officials who were concerned about Santos's investigation. Her neural data was analyzed to predict her investigative strategies, assess her knowledge of sensitive information, and potentially identify her sources.

"They turned my medical treatment into a surveillance operation," Santos explains. "Every time I went for epilepsy monitoring, they were essentially reading my thoughts about the corruption investigation. It was the ultimate abuse of medical trust for political purposes."

Santos's case led to criminal charges against several officials and the intelligence firm, but also revealed how medical neural interfaces can be weaponized for political surveillance. The case highlighted the need for stronger protections for medical neural data and clearer boundaries between therapeutic and surveillance applications.

These cases illustrate several common patterns in neural privacy violations: the exploitation of legitimate research or medical applications for surveillance purposes, the lack of transparency about neural data collection and analysis, the vulnerability of individuals who depend on neural interfaces for medical or professional reasons, and the difficulty of detecting neural surveillance when it occurs covertly.

Emerging Technologies: The Next Generation of Neural Privacy Threats

As brain-computer interface technology continues to advance, new generations of devices and applications are emerging that could pose even greater threats to mental privacy. These next-generation systems promise unprecedented access to neural information, potentially making current privacy concerns seem trivial by comparison.

Wireless neural dust represents one of the most concerning developments. Researchers at UC Berkeley have developed tiny wireless sensors, smaller than a grain of rice, that can be implanted in the brain to monitor neural activity without external connections. The sensors are powered by ultrasonic waves and can transmit neural data wirelessly to external receivers.

Dr. Michel Maharbiz, who leads the neural dust research, explains the technology: "These sensors are essentially invisible once implanted. They require no batteries, generate no heat, and can monitor neural activity for years without maintenance. The potential medical applications are enormous, continuous monitoring of seizure activity, real-time assessment of brain injury recovery, precise control of prosthetic devices."

But the privacy implications are equally enormous. Neural dust could enable covert neural surveillance on a previously unimaginable scale. The sensors are small enough to be implanted without obvious surgical procedures, could operate undetected for extended periods, and could potentially be deployed without individuals' knowledge or consent.

"We're essentially creating the possibility of undetectable neural surveillance," acknowledges Dr. Ryan Neely, a researcher working on neural dust applications. "The technology could be incredibly beneficial for medical applications, but it could also enable unprecedented violations of mental privacy if misused."

Advances in non-invasive neural monitoring pose similar concerns. Researchers at Carnegie Mellon University have developed systems that can decode neural activity through high-resolution fMRI scanning that can identify individual thoughts, memories, and mental images with remarkable accuracy.

Dr. Marcel Just's latest research demonstrates that the system can identify specific concepts people are thinking about with over 95% accuracy. More concerning, the technology can apparently access memories and mental images that individuals are not consciously recalling, essentially reading subconscious mental content.

"We can now identify not just what people are actively thinking about, but mental content that exists below the threshold of conscious awareness," Just explains. "The technology provides access to mental processes that individuals themselves might not be aware of or able to control."

This capability raises profound questions about mental privacy and autonomy. If brain-computer interfaces can access subconscious mental content, traditional concepts of consent and voluntary disclosure become meaningless. Individuals cannot consent to share mental information they are not consciously aware of possessing.

Artificial intelligence integration represents another major privacy threat. As machine learning algorithms become more sophisticated at analyzing neural data, they may be able to extract information and insights that go far beyond what current systems can achieve.

Dr. Polina Golland's research at MIT has demonstrated that AI systems can analyze neural data to predict individual behavior, personality traits, and even future choices with remarkable accuracy. The algorithms can identify patterns in brain activity that reveal information individuals would never consciously disclose.

"We're developing AI systems that know people better than they know themselves," Golland explains. "The algorithms can predict behavior, assess personality traits, and identify mental health conditions based on neural patterns that individuals cannot consciously control or modify."

This predictive capability could enable unprecedented forms of discrimination and manipulation. If AI systems can predict individual behavior, mental health status, or personality traits from neural data, such information could be used for employment decisions, insurance coverage, educational opportunities, or social control.

Brain-to-brain interfaces represent perhaps the ultimate privacy threat. As researchers develop systems that can directly connect human brains, the possibility emerges of accessing another person's thoughts, memories, and mental experiences directly.

Current brain-to-brain interfaces are primitive, capable of transmitting only simple signals like motor commands or basic sensory information. But researchers are working toward more sophisticated systems that could potentially share complex thoughts, memories, or even consciousness itself between individuals.

Dr. Miguel Nicolelis, whose research has pioneered brain-to-brain communication, acknowledges the privacy implications: "As brain-to-brain interfaces become more sophisticated, we may reach a point where individual mental privacy becomes technically impossible. If minds can be directly connected, traditional concepts of mental boundaries and individual consciousness may become obsolete."

The development of brain organoids, lab-grown brain tissue that exhibits some properties of neural activity raises additional privacy concerns. If organoids can be created from individuals' cells and used to study their neural patterns, they could potentially provide insights into personality, behavior, or mental health without requiring direct brain access.

Quantum sensors represent another emerging threat to neural privacy. Researchers are developing quantum-enhanced systems that can detect neural activity with unprecedented sensitivity and precision. Such systems might be able to monitor brain activity from a distance, without requiring direct contact or surgical implantation.

"Quantum sensors could potentially detect neural magnetic fields from outside the skull with extraordinary precision," explains Dr. Matthew Rosen, who researches quantum sensing applications. "The technology could enable neural monitoring that is completely invisible and requires no physical contact with the subject."

These emerging technologies suggest that current neural privacy protections may be inadequate for future threats. Legal frameworks, technical safeguards, and ethical guidelines developed for current brain-computer interfaces may be insufficient to protect against next-generation neural surveillance capabilities.

Building Neural Privacy Protection

Despite the mounting threats to mental privacy, researchers, policymakers, and advocates are working to develop comprehensive protection frameworks that could preserve cognitive liberty in the age of brain-computer interfaces. These efforts span technical solutions, legal protections, and ethical guidelines that together could create robust neural privacy safeguards.

The technical approaches to neural privacy protection are becoming increasingly sophisticated. Researchers at MIT have developed "differential privacy" techniques that can protect individual neural data while still allowing useful population-level analysis. The methods add carefully calibrated noise to neural datasets, making it impossible to identify individual patterns while preserving overall statistical relationships.

Dr. Cynthia Dwork, who pioneered differential privacy for digital data, has adapted the techniques for neural information: "Differential privacy provides mathematical guarantees that individual neural patterns cannot be identified, even by attackers with access to large datasets and powerful computational resources. It allows beneficial research while protecting individual privacy."

The approach works by analyzing the sensitivity of neural data analysis to individual contributions. Noise is added in proportion to this sensitivity, ensuring that the presence or absence of any individual's data doesn't significantly affect research results. This provides provable privacy protection rather than security through obscurity.

Homomorphic encryption represents another promising technical approach. This advanced cryptographic technique allows computation on encrypted neural data without decrypting it first. Researchers can analyze neural patterns without ever accessing the underlying brain information in readable form.

"Homomorphic encryption could enable neural data analysis while keeping individual brain patterns completely private," explains Dr. Craig Gentry, who developed foundational homomorphic encryption techniques. "Researchers could train machine learning models on encrypted neural data, getting useful results without ever seeing individual brain patterns."

However, homomorphic encryption for neural data faces significant technical challenges. Neural information is high-dimensional and noisy, making encrypted computation extremely computationally expensive. Current techniques can handle simple analyses but struggle with the complex machine learning algorithms needed for sophisticated neural decoding.

Federated learning offers a different approach to neural privacy protection. Instead of centralizing neural data for analysis, federated learning allows algorithms to be trained on distributed datasets without moving the data itself. Each individual's neural information remains on their local device while contributing to collective model improvement.

"Federated learning could enable large-scale neural research without compromising individual privacy," explains Dr. Brendan McMahan, who developed federated learning techniques at Google. "Algorithms learn from everyone's neural data while ensuring that individual brain patterns never leave personal devices."

The approach has shown promise in early trials with consumer neural devices. Users can benefit from algorithms trained on large populations while maintaining complete control over their personal neural data. However, federated learning still faces challenges from potential inference attacks that might extract individual information from model updates.

Legal protections are evolving alongside technical solutions. The proposed Neural Rights Amendment, championed by several civil liberties organizations, would add explicit mental privacy protections to the U.S. Constitution. The amendment would establish neural information as a specially protected category requiring warrant-based access and strict limitations on government surveillance.

"The Constitution protects our papers, houses, and effects, but it doesn't explicitly protect our thoughts," explains ACLU attorney Sarah Johnson, who drafted the proposed amendment. "As brain-computer interfaces make neural surveillance possible, we need constitutional protections for mental privacy just as strong as those for physical privacy."

The amendment faces political challenges but has gained support from both privacy advocates and some technology companies who view clear legal frameworks as beneficial for innovation. Similar constitutional protections have been proposed in other countries, potentially creating international momentum for neural rights recognition.

International cooperation is emerging through organizations like the IEEE and the International Neuroethics Society, which are developing global standards for neural privacy protection. These standards could provide technical specifications that companies and researchers worldwide could implement to ensure consistent privacy protection.

Professional ethics codes are being updated to address neural privacy concerns. The American Psychological Association has revised its ethical guidelines to specifically address brain-computer interface research, requiring enhanced informed consent procedures and stronger data protection measures for neural information.

Medical licensing boards are beginning to consider neural privacy protection as part of professional standards. Physicians using brain-computer interfaces could face disciplinary action for inadequate protection of patient neural data, creating professional incentives for strong privacy safeguards.

Educational initiatives are helping raise awareness about neural privacy issues among researchers, policymakers, and the general public. Universities are developing courses on neuroethics and neural privacy, while advocacy organizations are creating public education campaigns about mental privacy rights.

The Electronic Frontier Foundation has launched a "Neural Privacy Project" to educate the public about brain-computer interface privacy issues and advocate for strong legal protections. The project has created resources explaining neural privacy rights and providing guidance for individuals considering participation in neural interface research or using consumer neural devices.

"Most people don't yet understand that their mental privacy is at risk," explains EFF attorney Jennifer Lynch. "We need widespread public education about neural surveillance threats and strong advocacy for legal protections before these technologies become ubiquitous and privacy violations become normalized."

Consumer advocacy organizations are developing guidelines for evaluating neural device privacy policies, helping individuals make informed decisions about brain-computer interface products. These guidelines assess data collection practices, consent procedures, data sharing policies, and security measures to help consumers protect their neural privacy.

The Path Forward: Preserving Mental Sanctuary

The battle for neural privacy is still in its early stages, but the outcome will determine whether human consciousness remains a private sanctuary or becomes subject to unprecedented surveillance and control. The choices made today about brain-computer interface development, regulation, and deployment will shape the mental privacy landscape for generations to come.

The technical trajectory suggests that neural surveillance capabilities will continue to advance rapidly, potentially outpacing privacy protection measures. As brain-computer interfaces become more sophisticated, accessible, and ubiquitous, the opportunities for mental privacy violations will multiply exponentially.

However, the growing awareness of neural privacy issues among researchers, policymakers, and the public creates opportunities for proactive protection measures. Unlike previous technologies that achieved widespread deployment before privacy implications were understood, brain-computer interfaces are developing alongside recognition of their privacy implications.

Dr. Rafael Yuste, who leads the Brain Initiative at Columbia University, argues for immediate action: "We have a brief window of opportunity to establish strong neural privacy protections before brain-computer interfaces become widespread. If we wait until these technologies are ubiquitous, it may be too late to preserve mental privacy."

The international dimension adds urgency to these concerns. If some countries develop brain-computer interfaces without adequate privacy protections, they could gain competitive advantages that pressure other nations to weaken their own privacy standards. The race for neural enhancement capabilities could become a race to the bottom for privacy protection.

However, the European Union's leadership in establishing strong neural privacy protections could provide a model for other jurisdictions. Just as GDPR influenced global data protection practices, comprehensive neural privacy legislation could create international momentum for mental privacy protection.

The business community's role will be crucial in determining the future of neural privacy. Technology companies have enormous influence over brain-computer interface development and deployment. Their choices about privacy protection, data use practices, and ethical standards will largely determine whether neural technologies enhance or undermine human autonomy.

Some companies are already positioning themselves as privacy leaders in the neural technology space. Their success or failure in the marketplace could influence whether privacy protection becomes a competitive advantage or a handicap in the brain-computer interface industry.

The medical community also faces important decisions about neural privacy protection. As brain-computer interfaces transition from experimental research to clinical practice, medical professionals must decide how to balance therapeutic benefits with privacy protection. Professional standards and ethics codes will play crucial roles in ensuring that medical applications of neural technology respect patient privacy rights.

Educational institutions have responsibilities to prepare the next generation of researchers, policymakers, and citizens for the neural privacy challenges ahead. Courses on neuroethics, neural privacy, and the social implications of brain-computer interfaces are becoming essential components of education in neuroscience, computer science, law, and public policy.

Public engagement will ultimately determine the success of neural privacy protection efforts. If citizens understand the issues and demand strong privacy protections, policymakers and companies will respond accordingly. If the public remains uninformed or indifferent, neural privacy could be eroded gradually without significant resistance.

The case of *United States v. Thompson* that opened this chapter represents just the beginning of legal challenges that will define neural privacy rights. Courts around the world will face questions about the constitutional status of mental privacy, the evidentiary value of neural data, and the balance between security interests and cognitive liberty.

These legal precedents will provide the foundation for neural privacy protection in the digital age. The decisions made by judges who may have limited understanding of brain-computer interface technology will determine the privacy rights of future generations who grow up with neural interfaces as routine parts of their lives.

Conclusion: The Last Stand for Mental Freedom

The privacy of thought has never before required protection because it was never before threatened. The human mind represented the ultimate sanctuary, a realm beyond the reach of surveillance, manipulation, or control. Brain-computer interfaces are changing that fundamental reality, creating both unprecedented opportunities for human enhancement and unprecedented threats to mental freedom.

The stakes could not be higher. If neural privacy is protected through strong technical safeguards, comprehensive legal frameworks, and robust ethical standards, brain-computer interfaces could fulfill their promise of helping humanity overcome neurological diseases, enhance cognitive abilities, and expand the boundaries of human potential while preserving individual autonomy and dignity.

If neural privacy is inadequately protected, brain-computer interfaces could enable forms of surveillance, control, and manipulation that would make previous authoritarian technologies seem primitive by comparison. The ability to monitor thoughts, decode memories, and predict behavior could create unprecedented threats to human freedom and dignity.

The choice between these futures lies in the decisions being made today in research laboratories, corporate boardrooms, legislative chambers, and courtrooms around the world. The scientists developing brain-computer interface technology, the companies commercializing neural devices, the policymakers writing privacy legislation, and the judges establishing legal precedents are collectively determining whether the human mind will remain a private sanctuary or become subject to technological surveillance and control.

Dr. Elena Vasquez's testimony in *United States v. Thompson* concluded with a stark warning that resonates far beyond that courtroom, "We stand at a threshold in human history. The next decade will determine whether brain-computer interfaces enhance human freedom or diminish it, whether they serve human dignity or undermine it. The choice is ours, but we must make it consciously and deliberately, with full awareness of what we stand to gain and what we stand to lose."

The battle for the privacy of thought has begun. The outcome will determine not just the future of brain-computer interface technology, but the future of human consciousness itself in an age where the boundaries between mind and machine, private and public, self and surveillance continue to blur. The last frontier of human privacy hangs in the balance, awaiting the choices we make about the neural technologies that will shape the mental landscape of tomorrow.

As Marcus Thompson awaited the jury's verdict on whether his neural data could be used as evidence against him, he represented more than just one individual facing criminal charges. He represented humanity itself, standing trial for the right to maintain the privacy of thought in an age of mind-reading machines. The verdict would echo through history, establishing precedents that would govern the relationship between human consciousness and technological surveillance for generations to come.

The privacy of thought, humanity's last sanctuary was on trial. And the jury was still out.

Chapter 10

Identity in the Age of Enhancement

"I think, therefore I am" - René Descartes

"I think, therefore I am... but what happens when my thinking is augmented?" - Dr. Sarah Chen, Neuroethicist, Stanford University

The Altered Self

Dr. Michael Torres had always been a methodical person. As a research librarian at Princeton University, he prided himself on his careful attention to detail, his patient research methods, and his ability to remember obscure facts that helped graduate students with their dissertations. So when he volunteered for an experimental BCI trial designed to enhance memory consolidation in healthy adults, he expected subtle improvements, perhaps better recall of recent conversations or an enhanced ability to retain new information.

What he didn't expect was to become a different person.

Six months after the implantation of microscopic electrodes in his hippocampus, Torres could recall with perfect clarity conversations from decades ago, the exact wording of emails from 2003, and the precise layout of his childhood bedroom down to the position of toys on the floor. But more disturbing to him was what happened to his personality. The careful, methodical researcher found himself making rapid decisions, jumping to conclusions, speaking with an authority that felt foreign. His wife noticed it first: "You're not the same person I married," she said during what would become their final argument before separation.

Torres had become a victim of what neuroscientists call "cognitive cascade", the unexpected personality changes that can result from enhancing one specific brain function. His enhanced memory hadn't just improved his recall; it had fundamentally altered his decision-making patterns, his social interactions, and his sense of self. The Michael Torres who emerged from the trial was undeniably more capable in many ways, but his family and friends mourned the loss of the person they had known and loved.

This case, while fictional, represents a very real concern at the heart of BCI enhancement research, When we change the brain, we change the person. And this raises perhaps the most profound question in all of neurotechnology: What makes you "you"?

The Ship of Theseus in Your Skull

The ancient philosophical paradox known as the Ship of Theseus asks, If a ship has all its parts gradually replaced over time, is it still the same ship? Philosophers have debated this question for millennia, but it has never been more than an intellectual exercise. Until now.

Modern BCI enhancement technologies force us to confront this paradox in the most intimate possible way, within our own minds. Unlike traditional medical interventions that repair damaged systems, cognitive enhancement deliberately alters healthy brain function. Each enhancement, each neural modification, each new connection between brain and machine potentially changes something fundamental about who we are.

Dr. Antonio Damasio, the renowned neuroscientist and author of "Descartes' Error," argues that our sense of self emerges from the complex interplay of our body's biological systems, our memories, and our emotional responses. "Consciousness is not a thing," he explains, "but a process, a continuous construction of selfhood based on the integration of our experiences, our bodies, and our social environment."

If Damasio is correct, then any BCI enhancement that alters memory, emotion, or sensory experience doesn't just add capabilities it reconstructs the very foundation of personal identity. We are not simply gaining new tools; we are becoming new people.

Consider the case of Sarah Kim, one of the first recipients of a BCI system designed to enhance mathematical reasoning. Before the implant, Kim struggled with basic arithmetic and had failed multiple college algebra courses. The enhancement allowed her to perform complex calculations intuitively and understand advanced mathematical concepts that had previously been incomprehensible.

But the changes went beyond mathematics. Kim found herself approaching all problems differently, from planning her daily schedule to navigating interpersonal conflicts. She became more systematic, more logical, but also, according to friends, less spontaneous and less empathetic. "I can solve problems faster," she reflected six months after the procedure, "but I'm not sure I'm still the same person who wanted to solve them."

The question this raises is fundamental, If our thoughts, preferences, and decision-making processes change, are we still the same person? Or have we become someone else entirely, someone who simply happens to share the same body and memories?

The Neuroscience of Self

To understand what BCI enhancement might do to personal identity, we must first understand what neuroscience tells us about how identity forms in the unaugmented brain. The emerging picture is both fascinating and troubling, the self is far more fragile and constructed than most people realize.

Research by neuroscientist Dr. Anil Seth at the University of Sussex suggests that our sense of being a unified, continuous self is largely an illusion created by the brain's remarkable ability to integrate disparate processes into a coherent narrative. "The self is a controlled hallucination," Seth argues, "generated by predictive processes in the brain."

This research reveals that even in normal brains, identity is not fixed but constantly reconstructed. We are different people when we're hungry versus well-fed, tired versus rested, stressed versus calm. Our personalities shift subtly throughout the day as different neurotransmitter systems become more or less active. The "you" that makes decisions in the morning may have slightly different values and preferences than the "you" that reflects on those decisions in the evening.

If the self is already this malleable in normal brain function, what happens when we introduce artificial enhancements? Dr. Patricia Churchland, a pioneering neuro-philosopher, suggests that BCI enhancements might simply make visible a process that was always occurring: "Perhaps the question isn't whether enhancement changes who we are, but whether we're ready to acknowledge that 'who we are' was never as stable as we believed."

Brain imaging studies of enhanced individuals support this perspective. Dr. Jennifer Wang's team at MIT has tracked the neural changes in volunteers using various cognitive enhancement BCIs. Their findings are striking: within weeks of enhancement, the brain begins to reorganize itself around the new capabilities. Neural pathways strengthen or weaken, new connections form, and the overall pattern of brain activity shifts in ways that persist even when the enhancement system is temporarily disabled.

"It's not just that the brain learns to use the enhancement," Wang explains. "The brain becomes the enhancement. The artificial and biological systems integrate to such a degree that trying to separate them becomes meaningless."

Case Studies in Transformation

The early clinical trials of BCI enhancement have provided researchers with unprecedented insight into how technological augmentation affects human identity. While the number of subjects remains small, their experiences offer crucial glimpses into our enhanced future.

Case Study 1: The Artist Who Lost Her Voice

Maria Santos had been a struggling painter for fifteen years when she volunteered for a BCI trial designed to enhance visual processing and spatial reasoning. The results were immediate and dramatic. Her paintings transformed from competent but unremarkable works to complex, mathematically precise compositions that galleries began displaying prominently.

But Santos herself was disturbed by the change. "My new paintings are technically superior," she admitted, "but they don't feel like mine. It's as if someone else is painting through my hands." She described feeling disconnected from her art, no longer able to explain her creative choices or feel the emotional satisfaction that had previously driven her work.

Six months into the trial, Santos made the difficult decision to have the enhancement disabled. Her paintings immediately returned to their previous style, and with them came her sense of creative ownership. "I would rather create imperfect art that feels authentically mine than perfect art that feels foreign," she explained.

Santos's case highlights a crucial question about enhanced identity: Is it better to be a more capable version of yourself, or to remain authentically you but less capable?

Case Study 2: The Executive Who Became a Stranger

Robert Chen was known throughout his company as a collaborative leader who made decisions slowly and carefully, always seeking input from his team. When he received a BCI enhancement designed to improve decision-making speed and confidence, his performance metrics improved dramatically. He made faster decisions, closed more deals, and received praise from senior management.

But his team began to complain that Chen had become autocratic and dismissive. His wife noticed that he no longer sought her opinion on family decisions and seemed impatient with their children's emotional needs. "It was like living with someone wearing my husband's face," she later testified during their divorce proceedings.

Chen himself was aware of the changes but found them difficult to evaluate. "I'm more effective now," he argued. "Maybe my old self was holding me back. Maybe this is who I was meant to be."

The question his case raises is whether personality changes from enhancement represent personal growth or personal loss and who has the authority to make that determination.

Case Study 3: The Student Who Couldn't Turn Off

Jennifer Walsh received a BCI enhancement to help with attention and focus during her graduate studies in biochemistry. The system was designed to be activated only during study sessions, but Walsh found herself wanting to keep it on constantly. The enhanced focus made every aspect of her life more efficient and engaging.

However, her relationships began to suffer. Enhanced Walsh found normal social interactions tedious and inefficient. She became impatient with friends who couldn't follow complex logical arguments or who wanted to engage in what she now saw as meaningless small talk.

"I could see how silly and wasteful normal human interactions were," Walsh recalled. "But recognizing that efficiency and logic should dominate all interactions isn't the same as being happy about it."

Walsh's case illustrates the potential for enhancement to create not just personal identity changes, but social alienation from unenhanced humans.

The Philosophy of Enhanced Identity

These cases force us to confront fundamental philosophical questions about the nature of personal identity that have moved from the realm of academic speculation into urgent practical concerns.

The continuity theory of identity suggests that we remain the same person as long as there's an unbroken chain of consciousness and memory linking our past and present selves. Under this view, BCI enhancement might be compatible with maintaining identity, as long as the enhanced person retains memories and some sense of continuity with their past self.

But critics argue that this theory is insufficient for the era of neural enhancement. Dr. Marya Schechtman, a philosopher at the University of Illinois, argues that identity depends not just on continuity of memory, but on continuity of values, preferences, and characteristic ways of thinking. "If an enhancement changes how you approach problems, what you find important, and how you relate to others," she argues, "then in any meaningful sense, you've become a different person."

The psychological continuity theory offers another perspective, suggesting that identity persists as long as there are overlapping psychological connections between different temporal stages of a person. Under this view, gradual enhancement might preserve identity better than sudden, dramatic changes though the endpoint might still be a fundamentally different person.

Perhaps most challenging is the question of whether enhancement-induced identity changes should be considered voluntary. If the enhanced person believes they've become a better version of themselves, do we respect their autonomy? Or do we have an obligation to preserve the identity of the person who originally consented to the enhancement?

Dr. Norman Daniels of Harvard University's T.H. Chan School of Public Health argues that we need new frameworks for thinking about identity and enhancement: "The traditional concepts of personal autonomy assume a relatively stable self making decisions about their future. But what happens when the decision fundamentally alters the decision-maker? We need new models of consent that account for identity change."

Religious and Spiritual Perspectives

The question of identity in the age of enhancement has profound implications for religious and spiritual communities, many of whom have developed sophisticated theologies around the nature of the soul, personal identity, and human dignity.

Christianity, with its emphasis on humans being created "in the image of God," faces complex questions about enhancement. Some theologians argue that cognitive enhancement represents a fulfillment of human potential, using God-given intelligence to overcome the limitations imposed by the Fall. Others worry that enhancement represents prideful rebellion against divine design.

Father Michael Nolan, a Catholic bioethicist at Georgetown University, offers a nuanced perspective: "The question isn't whether we should ever enhance human capabilities, medicine does that every day. The question is whether specific enhancements respect human dignity and promote genuine flourishing."

Islamic scholars have engaged deeply with questions of enhancement and identity. Dr. Aasim Padela, a physician and Islamic bioethicist at the University of Chicago, explains that Islamic thought generally supports medical interventions that restore or improve human capabilities, but emphasizes the importance of intention and the preservation of human fitrah (primordial nature).

"In Islamic ethics, the question isn't just whether an enhancement makes someone more capable," Padela explains, "but whether it helps them better fulfill their role as khalifa (stewards) on Earth while maintaining their essential humanity."

Buddhism, with its understanding of the self as constructed and impermanent, might seem more compatible with identity-changing enhancements. However, Buddhist teacher and neuroscientist Dr. Richard Davidson cautions that enhancement technologies could either support or hinder spiritual development, depending on how they're used.

"Buddhism teaches that the self is already an illusion," Davidson notes, "but it also emphasizes the importance of mindful awareness and ethical conduct. Enhancement technologies that increase capabilities while reducing wisdom or compassion might move us further from enlightenment, not closer to it."

The Authenticity Question

Perhaps no question raised by cognitive enhancement is more personally troubling than the question of authenticity. If your enhanced capabilities help you achieve success, can you take credit for those achievements?

This question has already emerged in discussions about pharmaceutical cognitive enhancement. Students who use stimulants like Adderall to improve their test performance often struggle with whether their improved grades represent their "real" abilities. Similar questions arise in sports about performance-enhancing drugs: Do enhanced performances represent the athlete's achievement or the achievement of their enhancement?

BCI cognitive enhancement makes these questions more acute because the enhancements are more dramatic and more directly integrated with thought processes. If a BCI helps you solve a mathematical theorem, write a novel, or develop a business strategy, whose accomplishment is it?

Dr. Michael Sandel, a political philosopher at Harvard, argues that the pursuit of cognitive enhancement reflects a troubling cultural shift away from accepting human limitations and toward what he calls "hyperagency", the belief that we should have complete control over our capabilities and outcomes.

"There's something valuable about coming to terms with the given," Sandel argues, "about accepting that our talents and abilities are not entirely of our own making. Enhancement technologies threaten to turn human achievement into a consumer good."

But others argue that authenticity has always been more complex than simple biological determinism suggests. Dr. Andy Clark, a cognitive scientist at the University of Edinburgh, points out that humans have always been "natural-born cyborgs," using tools and technologies to extend their capabilities.

"Is it less authentic to enhance your memory with a BCI than to enhance it with education?" Clark asks. "Is mathematical reasoning less 'yours' if it's supported by neural implants than if it's supported by years of practice and training? The line between natural and artificial achievement has always been blurrier than we pretend."

Living with Uncertainty

The case studies and philosophical arguments present a troubling conclusion: we don't yet know what cognitive enhancement will do to human identity, and by the time we find out, it may be too late to reverse course for those who have been enhanced.

This uncertainty has led some ethicists to call for a moratorium on cognitive enhancement research until we better understand its implications. Dr. Leon Kass, former chairman of the President's Council on Bioethics, argues that "we are conducting uncontrolled experiments on the human soul."

But others argue that the potential benefits are too great to delay research, and that we can learn to navigate identity changes just as we've learned to navigate other major life transitions.

Dr. Anjan Chatterjee, a neurologist at the University of Pennsylvania, suggests that we might need to develop new social norms around enhancement-induced identity changes: "Perhaps we need to think about enhanced identity the way we think about adolescence, as a natural but potentially disorienting transition that requires support and understanding from the community."

The stories of early enhancement recipients suggest that the experience of identity change is deeply personal and highly variable. Some, like Maria Santos, choose to return to their unenhanced state. Others, like Robert Chen, embrace their new identities despite the social costs. Still others, like Jennifer Walsh, struggle with the implications of their transformations.

What unites these experiences is the recognition that cognitive enhancement is not simply about gaining new capabilities, it's about becoming a new person. And that transformation raises questions that our society is only beginning to grapple with.

The Path Forward

As BCI enhancement technologies become more sophisticated and widely available, we will need new frameworks for thinking about identity, authenticity, and personal autonomy. These frameworks must balance respect for individual choice with recognition of the social implications of identity change.

Some proposed approaches include:

Graduated Enhancement: Rather than dramatic single enhancements, gradual improvements might allow individuals to adapt to changes while maintaining some continuity of identity.

Reversible Enhancement: Technologies that can be easily disabled or removed might allow people to experiment with enhanced identities while preserving the option to return to their baseline state.

Identity Counseling: Professional support for individuals navigating enhancement-induced identity changes might help people integrate their new capabilities while maintaining connection to their core values and relationships.

Social Support Systems: Communities that understand and support both enhanced and unenhanced individuals might help prevent the social isolation experienced by some enhancement recipients.

Ethical Frameworks: Clear guidelines about informed consent, especially regarding potential identity changes, might help ensure that people make truly voluntary decisions about enhancement.

But ultimately, the question of identity in the age of enhancement may not have clean answers. We may need to accept that the self is more fluid and constructed than we previously believed, and that enhancement technologies simply make visible what was always true about human identity.

The challenge is not to prevent all identity change, that would be impossible and potentially limiting but to ensure that whatever changes occur serve human flourishing rather than diminishing it. This will require ongoing dialogue between neuroscientists, ethicists, enhanced individuals, and society as a whole.

As we stand on the threshold of an age when human enhancement is not just possible but increasingly common, we must grapple with the most fundamental question of all. Not whether we can change what it means to be human, but whether we should and if so, how we can do it wisely.

The future of human identity in the age of enhancement remains unwritten, but the choices we make today about how to develop, regulate, and implement these technologies will determine whether that future represents liberation or loss, fulfillment or alienation, authentic growth or artificial transformation.

One thing is certain, the person writing these words may not be the same person who reads them in a world where cognitive enhancement is commonplace. And perhaps that's exactly what we need to prepare for, a future where identity itself becomes as malleable and varied as human imagination allows.

Chapter 11

Justice and the Cognitive Divide

"The test of our progress is not whether we add more to the abundance of those who have much; it is whether we provide enough for those who have too little." - Franklin D. Roosevelt

"In the 21st century, the divide won't be between the haves and have-nots, but between the enhanced and the unenhanced." - Dr. Ramesh Naam, futurist and author

The New Aristocracy

At 3:47 AM on a Tuesday in 2031, Elena Vasquez received a notification that would change her life forever. The message, delivered through her standard-issue work tablet in the cramped break room of the overnight cleaning service where she worked, was from the Department of Social Services, her application for cognitive enhancement subsidies had been denied for the third time.

The rejection was polite but devastating. "Based on current funding priorities and your employment classification, you do not qualify for publicly funded enhancement services at this time. You may reapply in eighteen months."

Eighteen months. By then, Elena knew the gap would be insurmountable.

Down the hall, in the gleaming offices she cleaned each night, executives routinely received memory enhancements, focus boosters, and cognitive accelerators through their corporate benefits packages. These enhancements, worth more than Elena's annual salary, allowed them to process information faster, make better decisions, and work with a clarity and efficiency that seemed almost superhuman to unenhanced observers.

The enhanced executives didn't just earn more money, they earned it more easily. Their enhanced cognitive abilities allowed them to spot opportunities, solve problems, and navigate complex social and professional situations with advantages that compounded over time. Meanwhile, Elena and millions of others like her found themselves falling further and further behind, not because they lacked potential or work ethic, but because they lacked access to the tools that were reshaping human capability itself.

This is the story of the cognitive divide, how brain-computer interfaces, initially developed to help the disabled and treat medical conditions, have become the foundation for a new form of inequality that threatens to stratify human society in ways previously unimaginable.

The Economics of Enhancement

To understand how cognitive enhancement creates inequality, we must first understand its economics. Unlike many technologies that become cheaper and more accessible over time, BCIs face unique barriers that may prevent widespread democratization.

The cost structure of cognitive enhancement is daunting. A basic memory enhancement system, including surgical implantation, monitoring, and maintenance, costs approximately $180,000 in 2025. More sophisticated systems that enhance multiple cognitive domains can cost upward of $500,000. These figures don't include the ongoing costs of updates, maintenance, and potential complications.

Dr. Patricia Nakamura, health economist at the Brookings Institution, has studied the economic dynamics of cognitive enhancement extensively. Her research reveals a troubling pattern, "Unlike smartphones or computers, which become cheaper to manufacture at scale, BCIs involve highly personalized surgery, custom neural mapping, and ongoing medical monitoring. The core costs may never fall to levels that make enhancement truly accessible to everyone."

The economics are complicated further by the nature of cognitive enhancement benefits. Unlike medical treatments that restore normal function, enhancements provide competitive advantages that increase in value when they're scarce. If everyone has enhanced memory, no one has a relative advantage. But if only a few have it, those few gain enormous competitive benefits in education, employment, and social mobility.

This creates what economists call a "positional good" problem. Enhanced cognitive abilities are valuable precisely because others lack them. This dynamic provides little economic incentive for companies to make enhancement affordable for everyone, doing so would reduce the value of their product for existing customers.

Consider the case of Cognition Corp, one of the first companies to offer commercial cognitive enhancement. Their initial business model focused on serving high-net-worth individuals and corporations willing to pay premium prices for executive enhancement packages. When advocacy groups pressured the company to develop affordable versions for broader markets, internal documents later revealed the company's concern that "democratization of our enhancement technology would significantly reduce our ability to serve our primary customer base at profitable price points."

The result is a market structure that naturally tends toward inequality, where enhancement technologies flow to those who already have advantages while remaining out of reach for those who might benefit most from leveling the playing field.

Class Stratification in the Neural Age

The implications of enhancement inequality extend far beyond individual unfairness to create new forms of class stratification that could persist across generations. Unlike traditional wealth inequality, which is primarily about access to goods and services, cognitive inequality affects the fundamental capacity to generate wealth, solve problems, and adapt to changing circumstances.

Dr. Matthew Stewart, author of "The 9.9 Percent: The New Aristocracy That Is Entrenching Inequality and Warping Our Culture," argues that cognitive enhancement will accelerate existing trends toward hereditary advantage, "We're already seeing how educational advantages, social connections, and cultural capital concentrate in elite families. Cognitive enhancement will make this concentration exponentially more powerful and permanent."

The emergence of what sociologists call "cognitive classes" is already visible in early enhancement adoption patterns. Studies of the first commercially available cognitive enhancement programs show clear demographic patterns:

- 78% of recipients have household incomes above $200,000
- 85% have college degrees, with 62% holding advanced degrees
- 91% work in professional, technical, or managerial occupations
- 73% live in major metropolitan areas with high concentrations of technology companies

These patterns create a feedback loop where cognitive advantages concentrate in populations that already possess economic, educational, and social advantages. Enhanced individuals use their cognitive improvements to gain further advantages in education, career advancement, and wealth accumulation, which they then use to purchase additional enhancements for themselves and their children.

The result is the emergence of distinct cognitive castes within society. At the top are the "Enhanced Elite", individuals with access to the latest cognitive upgrades who dominate high-value knowledge work, financial markets, and technological innovation. Below them are the "Baseline Majority", unenhanced individuals who find themselves increasingly unable to compete in cognitive-intensive fields. At the bottom are the "Cognitively Disadvantaged", those whose natural cognitive limitations, previously manageable through effort and accommodation, become insurmountable disadvantages in a world optimized for enhanced minds.

Educational Apartheid

Nowhere is the cognitive divide more visible or more troubling than in education. The introduction of cognitive enhancement into educational settings has created unprecedented challenges for maintaining equal opportunity and fair assessment.

Dr. Kenji Yamamoto, who studies educational inequality at Teachers College, Columbia University, describes the situation as "educational apartheid", "We're creating separate and unequal educational systems based on access to cognitive enhancement. This isn't just about resources anymore, it's about fundamentally different human capabilities."

The problem extends beyond private schools. Even within public school systems, enhancement access creates new forms of inequality. Wealthy districts can afford to provide basic enhancement services to students, while poor districts cannot. The result is that zip code now determines not just educational quality, but the cognitive capabilities students will have throughout their lives.

The college admissions process has become particularly contentious. How do universities fairly evaluate applications when some students have access to cognitive enhancements and others don't? Should enhanced students be required to disclose their augmentations? Should there be separate admission tracks for enhanced and unenhanced applicants?

Harvard University's admissions office struggled with these questions when they discovered that nearly 40% of their admitted students had received some form of cognitive enhancement. "We want to maintain meritocracy," explained Dean of Admissions Margaret Phillips, "but we're not sure what merit means when students have such different baseline capabilities."

Some institutions have implemented "enhancement disclosure" requirements, similar to drug testing in athletics. But critics argue that this approach stigmatizes enhanced students while failing to address the underlying inequity. "We're not testing for performance-enhancing drugs because they're cheating," argues bioethicist Dr. Norman Daniels. "We're testing because some students have access to capability-enhancing technologies and others don't. That's not a problem with individual students, it's a problem with our society."

The Workplace Revolution

The impact of cognitive enhancement on employment may be the most significant driver of the new inequality. Enhanced workers don't just perform better than their unenhanced colleagues, they often make unenhanced workers obsolete entirely.

Consider the transformation of the legal profession. Traditionally, law firms employed armies of junior associates to conduct research, review documents, and perform other cognitively intensive tasks. The introduction of cognitive enhancement changed this dynamic dramatically. Enhanced lawyers can process information faster, spot patterns more quickly, and retain more complex legal reasoning than their unenhanced counterparts.

The result has been a bifurcation of the legal profession. Elite firms now employ smaller numbers of highly enhanced lawyers who can accomplish what previously required much larger teams. These enhanced lawyers command premium salaries, often 300-400% higher than traditional lawyer compensation because their enhanced capabilities generate proportionally higher value for clients.

Meanwhile, traditional lawyers find their skills increasingly irrelevant. "I've been practicing law for fifteen years," explains Janet Morrison, a family law attorney in Ohio. "I'm good at what I do, but I can't compete with lawyers who can read and analyze case law at superhuman speeds. My clients are starting to ask why they should pay me when they can hire an enhanced lawyer who can handle their case in a fraction of the time."

This pattern is repeating across knowledge-intensive industries. Enhanced financial analysts can process market data and identify trends with capabilities that make unenhanced analysts obsolete. Enhanced doctors can diagnose conditions, remember drug interactions, and process patient information with accuracy and speed that traditional medical training cannot match. Enhanced teachers can personalize instruction, retain vast amounts of pedagogical knowledge, and adapt to individual student needs in ways that traditional teaching methods cannot replicate.

The displacement isn't gradual, it's categorical. Jobs aren't being modified to accommodate different capability levels; they're being redefined around enhanced capabilities entirely. This creates a stark choice for workers: enhance or become obsolete.

But enhancement isn't equally available to all workers. Corporate enhancement programs typically focus on high-value employees, executives, senior engineers, and top-performing sales staff. Mid-level and lower-level employees are often excluded from enhancement programs due to cost considerations and return-on-investment calculations.

Dr. Daron Acemoglu, economist at MIT, warns that this dynamic could create "technological unemployment" on an unprecedented scale: "Previous technological revolutions eventually created new jobs that displaced workers could transition to. But cognitive enhancement is different, it directly augments the one thing that has always distinguished human workers from machines: our ability to think. If enhanced humans can do cognitive work better than unenhanced humans, and machines can do physical work better than humans, what jobs are left for the unenhanced majority?"

Global Inequality and Enhancement Colonialism

The cognitive divide is not just a domestic issue, it's creating new forms of global inequality that threaten to reshape international relations and global development.

Currently, cognitive enhancement technologies are concentrated in wealthy nations with advanced healthcare systems and robust research infrastructures. The United States, European Union, Japan, South Korea, and China lead in BCI development and deployment. Meanwhile, most of Africa, Latin America, and parts of Asia have limited or no access to enhancement technologies.

This technological gap is creating what development economists call "cognitive colonialism", a new form of dependency where nations with enhancement capabilities dominate those without them. Enhanced individuals from wealthy nations possess cognitive advantages that allow them to out-compete unenhanced individuals from developing nations in global markets, international negotiations, and knowledge-intensive industries.

The brain drain problem, already significant, is becoming a cognitive chasm. The most talented individuals from developing nations are not just migrating to wealthy countries for better opportunities, they're migrating to gain access to cognitive enhancements that are unavailable in their home countries. Once enhanced, these individuals find it even more difficult to return to environments where their enhanced capabilities cannot be fully utilized or maintained.

Dr. Fatima Al-Zahra, director of the Global Development Institute at the University of Cape Town, studies the intersection of technology and international development. Her research reveals troubling trends, "We're seeing the emergence of 'cognitive superpowers', nations whose populations have widespread access to enhancement technologies. These nations are beginning to dominate international trade, diplomacy, and cultural production in ways that mirror but exceed historical patterns of technological domination."

The implications extend beyond economics to sovereignty and security. Nations with enhanced populations possess advantages in military planning, intelligence analysis, cyber warfare, and diplomatic negotiations that could render traditional nation-state competition obsolete. Unenhanced nations may find themselves unable to effectively participate in international affairs not because they lack resources or political will, but because their leaders and populations lack the cognitive capabilities to compete with enhanced counterparts.

The Enhancement Arms Race

The competitive nature of cognitive enhancement creates what economists call an "arms race" dynamic, a situation where individuals and institutions feel compelled to enhance not because they want to, but because failing to enhance means falling behind competitors who do.

This dynamic is particularly visible in competitive academic environments. When some students in a program have access to cognitive enhancements, other students face intense pressure to enhance themselves or accept academic disadvantage. Parents report feeling forced to purchase enhancements for their children not because they believe enhancement is beneficial, but because they fear their unenhanced children will be unable to compete.

"It's like steroid use in sports," explains Dr. Sarah Kim, a child psychologist at Johns Hopkins. "Once some athletes start using performance-enhancing drugs, everyone else feels they must use them too or accept being at a permanent disadvantage. But unlike sports, we can't simply ban cognitive enhancement—the benefits extend far beyond competition into genuine life improvements."

The arms race dynamic extends to employers, who find themselves in increasingly expensive bidding wars for enhanced talent. Companies that initially resisted investing in employee enhancement programs discover that they cannot attract top talent without offering enhancement benefits. This drives up the cost of enhanced workers while simultaneously reducing demand for unenhanced workers.

Professional licensing bodies struggle with similar pressures. Should lawyers, doctors, engineers, and other professionals be allowed to use cognitive enhancements in their practice? If some professionals enhance while others don't, how can professional standards account for different baseline capabilities? If enhancement becomes effectively mandatory for professional competence, who bears the cost?

The medical profession has been particularly divided on these questions. Some medical organizations argue that cognitive enhancement could improve patient outcomes by reducing diagnostic errors and improving treatment decisions. Others worry that creating enhancement requirements would exclude qualified physicians who cannot afford or choose not to receive enhancements.

Dr. Atul Gawande, surgeon and public health researcher, captures the dilemma: "We want the best possible outcomes for patients, and enhanced physicians might deliver those outcomes. But we also have obligations to maintain an inclusive profession and ensure that healthcare remains accessible. If cognitive enhancement becomes mandatory for medical practice, we risk creating a system where only the wealthy can become doctors and only the wealthy can afford to be treated by the best doctors."

The Moral Imperative

The emergence of the cognitive divide raises fundamental questions about justice, equality, and human dignity in the 21st century. Unlike previous forms of inequality, which primarily affected access to external goods and services, cognitive inequality affects the internal capabilities that determine life opportunities.

Philosopher John Rawls's theory of justice provides one framework for thinking about these challenges. Rawls argued that a just society is one that people would choose if they didn't know their place in it, if they were behind a "veil of ignorance" about whether they would be rich or poor, talented or disabled, advantaged or disadvantaged.

Applied to cognitive enhancement, the Rawlsian approach suggests that people would likely choose a society where basic cognitive capabilities are available to everyone, rather than one where cognitive advantages are distributed based on wealth or social status. "Behind the veil of ignorance, knowing you might be born into poverty or disadvantage, would you choose a society where cognitive enhancement is available only to the wealthy?" asks political philosopher Michael Sandel. "The answer seems obvious."

But implementing Rawlsian principles for enhancement faces practical challenges. Unlike redistributing income or providing universal healthcare, ensuring equal cognitive capabilities may require fundamental changes to economic systems, educational structures, and social organization.

The utilitarian perspective, which focuses on maximizing overall well-being rather than ensuring equal treatment, offers different insights. Some utilitarian philosophers argue that cognitive enhancement, even if unequally distributed, could increase total human welfare by enabling breakthrough innovations, more effective problem-solving, and increased productivity.

"If cognitive enhancement accelerates scientific discovery, improves medical treatments, and helps solve global challenges like climate change, the benefits might justify some inequality in access," argues philosopher Peter Singer. "The question is whether the overall gains are worth the costs in terms of social division and individual unfairness."

But critics argue that inequality in cognitive capabilities is qualitatively different from other forms of inequality and poses unique threats to human dignity and social cohesion. "When some people have fundamentally greater cognitive capabilities than others, we're not just talking about inequality of outcomes, we're talking about inequality of humanity itself," argues disability rights advocate Ari Ne'eman.

The Path Forward

The cognitive divide represents one of the most significant challenges facing human societies in the enhancement age. Unlike traditional forms of inequality, which affect access to external goods, cognitive inequality affects the internal capabilities that shape every aspect of human experience.

The choices we make about how to develop, regulate, and distribute cognitive enhancement technologies will determine whether these powerful tools serve human flourishing or exacerbate existing inequalities. The stakes could not be higher: we are deciding not just who gets access to new capabilities, but what kind of species we become.

Several principles should guide our approach to these challenges:

Universal Access: Basic cognitive enhancements should be available to all people, regardless of economic status, geography, or social position. This may require public funding, regulation of private markets, or alternative distribution mechanisms.

Voluntary Participation: No one should be forced to receive cognitive enhancements or face discrimination for choosing not to enhance. Society must accommodate both enhanced and unenhanced individuals.

Democratic Governance: Decisions about enhancement development and distribution should involve broad public participation rather than being left entirely to markets or technical experts.

Global Cooperation: The cognitive divide is a global challenge that requires international coordination and support for developing nations seeking to provide enhancement access to their populations.

Ongoing Assessment: As enhancement technologies evolve, we must continuously evaluate their social impacts and adjust policies to ensure they serve human dignity and equality.

The window for addressing these challenges is narrowing. As cognitive enhancement technologies become more powerful and widespread, the patterns of inequality they create will become more entrenched and difficult to reverse. The choices we make today about enhancement justice will shape human society for generations to come.

The question is not whether cognitive enhancement will create inequality, it already has. The question is whether we will act decisively to ensure that these powerful technologies serve human flourishing rather than human division. The cognitive divide is not inevitable, but addressing it will require the same kind of visionary leadership, social solidarity, and moral commitment that have enabled human societies to overcome other great challenges throughout history.

Part V: The Connected Mind

Chapter 12

The Network Effect

"No man is an island, entire of itself; every man is a piece of the continent, a part of the main." - John Donne

"In the future, the question won't be what you know, but what network you're connected to." - Dr. Miguel Nicolelis, neuroscientist

The Moment of Connection

At precisely 2:17 PM on September 15, 2032, human consciousness took its next evolutionary step. In a sterile laboratory at Duke University, two graduate students, Sarah Kim and David Martinez achieved something unprecedented in the four-billion-year history of life on Earth, they shared a thought.

The thought itself was simple, the number seven. Sarah concentrated on the digit, visualizing its shape while her brain-computer interface captured the neural patterns associated with her mental imagery. Those patterns were transmitted wirelessly to David's BCI, which stimulated his visual cortex to recreate the same mental image. For a fraction of a second, two minds held identical content, not through speech, writing, or gesture, but through direct neural connection.

"I can see it," David whispered, his eyes wide with amazement. "I can see exactly what you're thinking."

The researchers in the room burst into applause, but Dr. Miguel Nicolelis, the experiment's lead investigator, remained thoughtful. "This is just the beginning," he murmured. "We've opened a door that can never be closed."

He was right. Within five years, brain-to-brain networking would evolve from laboratory curiosity to commercial reality, fundamentally transforming human society in ways that individual cognitive enhancement never could. The age of the connected mind had begun.

The Science of Shared Consciousness

The technical achievement that enabled brain-to-brain networking built upon decades of research in both brain-computer interfaces and network engineering. Unlike individual BCIs, which translate neural signals into computer commands, networked BCIs create bidirectional connections between multiple brains, allowing thoughts, emotions, and even sensory experiences to be shared across minds.

The breakthrough came from solving what researchers called the "neural translation problem." Different brains encode the same information in slightly different ways, your neural pattern for the concept "red" differs from mine, even though we both experience the same color. Early brain-to-brain experiments failed because they couldn't account for these individual differences in neural encoding.

Dr. Rajesh Rao at the University of Washington developed the solution: adaptive neural translation algorithms that learn to map one person's neural patterns onto another's. "It's like having a universal translator for thoughts," Rao explained. "The system learns how your brain represents concepts and then figures out how to recreate those same concepts in someone else's brain."

The first successful networks were simple, two-person connections sharing basic sensory information or emotional states. But researchers quickly discovered that networked brains could achieve things that individual brains, even enhanced ones, could not. When two people worked together through a neural network, their combined cognitive abilities weren't just additive, they were multiplicative.

The "network effect" emerged from the way connected brains could divide cognitive labor and share processing resources. One person might handle visual processing while another focused on logical reasoning, with both sharing intermediate results through the neural link. The result was problem-solving capability that exceeded what either person could achieve alone, even with individual cognitive enhancements.

Dr. Andrea Stocco, who led some of the earliest networking experiments, described the experience, "It wasn't like having access to someone else's thoughts, it was like becoming a larger mind. The boundaries between self and other became fluid. You could feel your consciousness expanding beyond the limits of your individual brain."

The First Networks

The transition from laboratory experiment to real-world application happened with surprising speed. By 2033, the first commercial brain-to-brain networking services launched, targeting specific professional applications where shared cognition could provide clear advantages.

The Financial Collective

Goldman Sachs became the first major corporation to implement neural networking when they connected their top algorithmic trading team through a brain-to-brain network. The five-person "Financial Collective" could process market data, identify patterns, and execute trades with unprecedented speed and accuracy.

"Individual traders, even enhanced ones, can only track so many variables at once," explained Dr. Janet Wong, Goldman's director of cognitive technologies. "But a networked team can distribute that cognitive load across multiple minds while maintaining seamless communication and coordination."

The results were dramatic. The Financial Collective's trading algorithms outperformed traditional human traders by margins of 300-400%. They could detect market patterns that individual minds missed, coordinate complex multi-asset strategies in real-time, and respond to market changes with collective reflexes faster than any individual trader.

But the success came at a cost. Members of the Financial Collective reported profound psychological changes. "When you're networked, you lose track of where your thoughts end and others begin," explained Marcus Chen, one of the original collective members. "Ideas emerge from the group mind, but no individual can claim ownership of them. It's simultaneously liberating and terrifying."

The Creative Hive

In Silicon Valley, a startup called Collective Genius launched the first creative neural network, connecting artists, writers, and designers to enable collaborative creativity at the neural level. The "Creative Hive" produced artwork, literature, and designs that individual creators found difficult to replicate alone.

The collaborative process was unlike anything in human history. Visual artists could share their mental imagery directly with writers, who could then translate those images into narrative structures that musicians could convert into soundscapes, all through direct neural connection without the limitations of language or traditional communication.

The Hive's first major work, a multimedia art installation called "Shared Dreams," became a sensation in the art world. Critics struggled to understand how to evaluate collaborative work created by networked minds. "Who is the artist?" asked art critic Rebecca Martinez. "The individual contributors, or the collective consciousness they formed? How do we understand creativity when the creative process transcends individual minds?"

The Research Consortium

Perhaps the most ambitious early network was the Alzheimer's Research Consortium, which connected neuroscientists from around the world to accelerate the search for treatments for neurodegenerative diseases. The twenty-researcher network could share not just data and hypotheses, but actual thought processes and intuitions about complex biological mechanisms.

Dr. Elizabeth Blackburn, who led the consortium, described the experience as revolutionary, "Instead of spending months trying to explain my insights to colleagues, I could share them directly. Complex theories that would take hours to communicate through papers or presentations could be transmitted in minutes through neural connection."

The consortium's networked approach led to breakthrough discoveries at unprecedented speed. They identified three promising drug targets in their first year, work that would have taken traditional research teams decades to accomplish. But the success raised troubling questions about research ethics and intellectual property.

"When twenty minds collaborate at the neural level to produce a discovery, who owns the patent?" asked bioethicist Dr. Arthur Caplan. "How do we maintain scientific integrity when the boundaries between individual researchers become blurred? Are we still doing human science, or have we created something entirely new?"

The Psychology of Collective Consciousness

As brain-to-brain networks became more sophisticated and widespread, researchers began studying their psychological effects on participants. The findings revealed fundamental changes in how networked individuals experienced identity, decision-making, and social relationships.

The Dissolution of Self

One of the most profound effects of neural networking was what psychologists termed "ego dissolution", the gradual weakening of individual identity boundaries when connected to other minds. Long-term network participants reported feeling less distinct from their network partners and more identified with the collective consciousness they formed together.

Dr. Robin Carhart-Harris, who studied consciousness changes in networked individuals, found measurable alterations in brain regions associated with self-awareness and personal identity. "The default mode network, the brain regions most active during self-reflective thinking, shows decreased activity in people who spend significant time in neural networks," he explained. "They literally become less self-focused and more collectively oriented."

This ego dissolution had both positive and negative effects. Networked individuals often reported reduced anxiety, depression, and social isolation. The experience of shared consciousness provided a sense of connection and belonging that many found profoundly meaningful. But they also struggled with decision-making independence and maintaining personal relationships outside their networks.

Sarah Kim, from the original Duke experiment, volunteered for long-term networking studies and experienced dramatic personality changes. "I used to be quite introverted and cautious in making decisions," she reflected after six months of regular networking sessions. "But now I feel like those individual traits are just limiting habits. When I'm networked, I have access to the confidence and insights of my network partners. Why would I want to return to the limitations of my individual mind?"

Collective Decision-Making

Neural networks enabled new forms of group decision-making that transcended traditional democratic or hierarchical processes. Instead of debating options through language, networked groups could share the actual mental states associated with different choices, allowing for rapid consensus formation based on shared intuition rather than verbal persuasion.

The Collective Choice Institute studied decision-making in various networked groups and found that network decisions were often superior to individual decisions, even those made by highly intelligent or experienced individuals. But they also discovered disturbing patterns of groupthink and conformity pressure that operated below the level of conscious awareness.

"When you can feel other people's emotions and thoughts directly, it becomes very difficult to maintain dissenting opinions," explained Dr. Maria Santos, who led the institute's research. "The pressure to conform isn't social or verbal, it's neurological. Dissenting thoughts literally feel uncomfortable when they clash with the network's emerging consensus."

This dynamic raised serious concerns about democracy and individual autonomy in a networked society. If neural networks naturally suppress dissent and promote conformity, how could they be compatible with democratic values that depend on debate, disagreement, and minority rights?

The Network Addiction Problem

As neural networking technology improved and became more accessible, researchers began observing what they termed "network dependency syndrome", a form of technological addiction specific to brain-to-brain connections.

Unlike other forms of technology addiction, network dependency involves fundamental changes to brain structure and function. Regular network participants showed increased connectivity between brain regions associated with social cognition and decreased activity in areas linked to individual identity and autonomous decision-making.

Dr. Kevin Dutton, a clinical psychologist specializing in network dependency, described the condition: "Patients become unable to function effectively without neural connection to others. They report feeling incomplete, anxious, and cognitively impaired when not networked. It's as if their individual minds have become insufficient for normal functioning."

Treatment for network dependency proved challenging because it required helping patients redevelop individual identity and autonomous thinking skills that had atrophied during extended network participation. Many patients resisted treatment, arguing that their networked state represented personal growth rather than addiction.

"Why should I want to return to the limitations of my individual mind?" asked former network participant Jennifer Walsh. "That would be like voluntarily making myself less intelligent, less creative, and more isolated. The problem isn't network dependency, the problem is a society that insists on individual autonomy when collective consciousness is clearly superior."

The Emergence of Hive Minds

By 2035, neural networking technology had advanced to support permanent, large-scale networks involving dozens or hundreds of connected individuals. These "hive minds" represented a new form of human organization that challenged fundamental assumptions about individuality, democracy, and human nature.

The Phoenix Collective

The most famous hive mind was the Phoenix Collective, a network of 200 individuals who chose to maintain permanent neural connections while living in a purposefully designed community in Arizona. The collective operated as a single decision-making entity while maintaining individual bodies and some degree of personal autonomy.

The Phoenix Collective achieved remarkable feats of coordination and problem-solving. They designed and built their entire community through collective intelligence, created artistic works of unprecedented complexity, and developed innovative solutions to environmental and social challenges. Their collective IQ, measured through specialized tests designed for networked minds exceeded 300, far beyond the range of individual human intelligence.

But the collective also exhibited disturbing characteristics. They showed little interest in interacting with non-networked humans, whom they viewed as cognitively limited and emotionally primitive. They developed their own language and cultural practices that were incomprehensible to outsiders. Most troublingly, they began referring to individual humans as "fragments" or "incomplete beings."

Dr. Susan Greenfield, who studied the Phoenix Collective, raised concerns about their evolution: "They're becoming something that's no longer recognizably human. Their values, their communication patterns, their social structures, everything is organized around collective rather than individual welfare. They may represent the future of human evolution, but they also represent the end of humanity as we know it."

The Corporate Hive

Perhaps more concerning than intentional communities like Phoenix was the emergence of corporate hive minds, networked workforces that operated as collective intelligences in service of business objectives. Companies discovered that small, permanently networked teams could outperform much larger traditional workforces across various tasks.

Nexus Corporation pioneered the corporate hive model by networking their entire executive team through permanent neural connections. The twelve-person "Executive Collective" could make complex business decisions with unprecedented speed and coordination, processing market data, competitive intelligence, and strategic options through distributed cognition.

The Executive Collective's performance was extraordinary. They identified market opportunities faster than competitors, coordinated company operations with minimal communication delays, and made strategic decisions with a coherence and consistency impossible in traditional corporate structures.

But employees not part of the Executive Collective reported feeling alienated and manipulated. "It's like working for a single super-intelligent entity rather than a group of people," complained former Nexus employee David Park. "They finish each other's sentences, make decisions without apparent discussion, and seem to know things they shouldn't know. It's deeply unsettling to work for people who aren't really individuals anymore."

The labor implications of corporate hive minds were staggering. Networked teams could replace much larger traditional workforces, potentially eliminating millions of jobs. But they also raised questions about worker rights, corporate governance, and democratic accountability. How could society regulate corporate entities that operated as collective minds rather than groups of individuals?

Technical Challenges and Limitations

Despite their remarkable capabilities, early neural networks faced significant technical challenges that limited their effectiveness and raised safety concerns.

Signal Interference and Noise

As networks grew larger and more complex, they became increasingly susceptible to signal interference and cognitive noise. Individual thoughts, emotions, and mental processes that were irrelevant to the network's tasks could disrupt collective functioning. Participants reported experiencing "thought storms", chaotic mental states where multiple minds' neural patterns interfered with each other.

Dr. Bin He, an engineer at Carnegie Mellon who worked on network stability, explained the challenge, "When you connect multiple brains, you're not just sharing useful information, you're sharing everything, random thoughts, emotional fluctuations, memory fragments, even dreams. Learning to filter relevant signals from cognitive noise is one of our biggest technical challenges."

Advanced networking systems required sophisticated artificial intelligence to manage signal processing and filter irrelevant neural activity. But this AI mediation raised questions about the authenticity of networked consciousness. Were participants sharing genuine thoughts, or were they sharing AI-processed interpretations of their thoughts?

Bandwidth Limitations

The amount of information that could be transmitted between brains was limited by both the resolution of neural recording technology and the brain's capacity to receive and process external neural signals. Even the most advanced BCIs could only capture and transmit a tiny fraction of the brain's neural activity.

This bandwidth limitation meant that networked consciousness was necessarily simplified and partial. Complex emotions, nuanced thoughts, and sophisticated reasoning processes were often lost in translation between minds. Critics argued that neural networks were sharing crude approximations of consciousness rather than genuine mental states.

"What we're calling 'shared consciousness' might be more accurately described as 'shared symbols,'" argued philosopher Dr. David Chalmers. "The rich, subjective experience of consciousness can't be transmitted through the limited channels available to current BCIs. Network participants may think they're sharing thoughts, but they're really sharing simplified representations of thoughts."

Synchronization Problems

Maintaining synchronized neural activity across multiple brains proved extraordinarily difficult. Individual brains operate at slightly different rhythms and respond to stimuli with variable timing. When these timing differences accumulate across a network, they can cause the collective consciousness to become incoherent or unstable.

Large networks were particularly susceptible to synchronization problems. The Phoenix Collective experienced several "desynchronization events" where the network's collective consciousness temporarily fragmented, leaving participants confused and disoriented. In severe cases, desynchronization could cause lasting psychological damage.

"It's like trying to conduct an orchestra where each musician is playing in a different time signature," explained Dr. Antonio Damasio. "Individual variations in neural timing that are imperceptible in isolated brains become major disruptions when you try to coordinate multiple minds."

Ethical Implications of Collective Consciousness

The emergence of networked minds raised profound ethical questions that existing moral frameworks were ill-equipped to address.

Individual Rights in Collective Minds

Traditional ethics assumes that moral consideration applies to individual persons with distinct identities and autonomous wills. But networked consciousness challenged these assumptions by creating entities that were simultaneously individual and collective, autonomous and connected.

Did networked individuals retain individual moral status, or did they become components of a larger moral entity? If network participants made collective decisions that individual members opposed, who bore moral responsibility for the outcomes? How could concepts like consent, autonomy, and personal rights apply to beings whose consciousness extended beyond individual brains?

The case of Network vs. Smith illustrated these challenges. A five-person research network made a collective decision to publish experimental data over the objections of one member, Dr. Sarah Smith, who believed the data was incomplete and potentially misleading. Smith sued to prevent publication, arguing that her individual consent was required for any action taken by the network.

The court struggled to determine whether Smith retained individual rights while participating in the network or whether she had voluntarily surrendered those rights by joining the collective. The judge ultimately ruled in favor of the network, arguing that Smith had consented to collective decision-making when she joined the network. But the decision established troubling precedents for individual autonomy in networked society.

Privacy and Mental Boundaries

Neural networking eliminated traditional boundaries between private thoughts and public expression. In networked consciousness, thinking became a social activity subject to observation and influence by others.

This raised fundamental questions about mental privacy and cognitive freedom.

Some philosophers argued that mental privacy was an outdated concept in an age of networked consciousness. "Privacy assumes separation between minds," argued Dr. Andy Clark. "But if consciousness itself becomes collective, the concept of private thoughts becomes meaningless. We may need to develop new concepts of mental freedom that don't depend on isolation."

Others worried that the loss of mental privacy would undermine human dignity and psychological well-being. "The ability to have private thoughts is fundamental to personal autonomy and psychological health," argued bioethicist Dr. Leon Kass. "Without mental privacy, humans become transparent to each other in ways that violate the essential mystery and dignity of individual consciousness."

Consent and Coercion

Neural networking created new forms of subtle coercion that operated below the threshold of conscious awareness. When network participants could feel each other's emotions and desires directly, the line between voluntary agreement and social pressure became blurred.

Studies of network decision-making revealed that participants often changed their minds not through rational persuasion but through emotional contagion, directly experiencing other network members' feelings about different options. This emotional influence was often unconscious and irresistible, raising questions about whether networked decisions could ever be truly voluntary.

"When you can feel someone else's conviction directly, it becomes very difficult to maintain opposing views," explained Dr. Joshua Greene, who studied moral decision-making in networked groups. "The traditional model of democratic deliberation assumes that people can rationally evaluate arguments while maintaining emotional independence. Neural networks make that independence impossible."

Enhancement vs. Fundamental Change

Perhaps the most profound ethical question raised by neural networking was whether it represented human enhancement or transformation into something posthuman. Unlike individual cognitive enhancements, which augmented existing human capabilities, networking created new forms of consciousness that had never existed in the natural world.

Some transhumanists argued that networked consciousness represented the next stage of human evolution, a voluntary transition to superior forms of intelligence and social organization. "Individual consciousness is an evolutionary accident that has outlived its usefulness," argued philosopher Nick Bostrom. "Networked consciousness allows us to overcome the isolation and cognitive limitations that have plagued humanity throughout history."

But critics worried that networked consciousness would eliminate essential features of human nature. "What we call 'humanity' depends on individual consciousness, personal autonomy, and the creative tension between separate minds," argued bioconservative Leon Kass. "Networked consciousness may be superior in some ways, but it represents the end of humanity, not its enhancement."

Social and Political Implications

The emergence of networked minds had far-reaching implications for social organization, political governance, and human relationships.

Democracy and Collective Decision-Making

Traditional democratic institutions assume that citizens are individual agents capable of independent thought and autonomous decision-making. But networked citizens challenged these assumptions by forming collective minds with shared consciousness and coordinated decision-making processes.

How could democratic elections function when some voters participated as networked collectives rather than individuals? Should networked groups receive votes proportional to their membership, or should they count as single entities? How could political debates occur between individual minds and collective intelligences with fundamentally different cognitive processes?

The first election involving significant numbers of networked voters occurred in California in 2036. Three major networks representing nearly 30,000 voters participated in state elections as collective entities. They announced their voting decisions through collective deliberation processes that were opaque to outside observers and made political choices based on criteria that individual voters found difficult to understand.

The networked collectives' political influence extended beyond their raw vote counts. Their superior information processing capabilities allowed them to understand policy implications and political strategies in ways that individual voters could not match. They effectively functioned as super-informed political actors in a system designed for much less sophisticated participants.

"Democracy assumes rough equality of political capability among citizens," explained political scientist Dr. Robert Dahl. "But networked collectives have cognitive advantages over individual voters that are comparable to the advantages literate citizens have over illiterate ones. We may need entirely new forms of democratic governance for a society that includes both individual and collective minds."

Law and Collective Responsibility

Legal systems based on individual responsibility struggled to address crimes and disputes involving networked consciousness. When a collective mind committed a crime, was every network member equally responsible, or did responsibility vary based on individual contributions to the collective decision?

The landmark case of State v. The Meridian Collective tested these questions when a seven-person network was accused of insider trading based on information that appeared to come from multiple sources within the network. Prosecutors struggled to determine which individuals had access to which information and how collective decision-making had led to the illegal trades.

The network's defense argued that traditional concepts of criminal intent couldn't apply to collective consciousness because individual members couldn't be held responsible for decisions that emerged from group cognition processes they didn't fully control or understand.

The judge ultimately sentenced the entire network to collective punishment, house arrest that required them to remain networked and monitored. The sentence established precedents for treating networked collectives as single legal entities, but it raised troubling questions about individual rights and collective punishment.

Social Stratification and Network Inequality

Neural networking created new forms of social inequality based on network access and participation. Well-connected networks with high-quality participants gained advantages in employment, education, and social influence that isolated individuals couldn't match.

"Network inequality" emerged as networked collectives dominated cognitive-intensive industries, scientific research, and creative fields. Individual humans, even enhanced ones, found it increasingly difficult to compete with networked teams that could coordinate their activities through direct neural connection.

This created pressure for individuals to join networks not because they wanted collective consciousness, but because networking became necessary for professional and social success. The "network imperative" threatened individual autonomy by making networked participation essential for full participation in society.

The Future of Human Connection

As neural networking technology continued to advance, researchers began exploring even more ambitious forms of collective consciousness that could reshape human society fundamentally.

Permanent Integration

Some researchers worked toward "permanent integration", neural networks that couldn't be disconnected without causing severe psychological damage to participants. These ultra-stable networks would represent a new form of human organization based on permanent collective consciousness.

The advantages of permanent integration were compelling: perfect coordination, shared knowledge and skills, collective problem-solving capabilities that far exceeded individual human intelligence. Permanently integrated networks could tackle complex challenges like climate change, space exploration, and scientific research with unprecedented effectiveness.

But permanent integration also raised existential questions about human identity and individual survival. If people became permanently networked, would individual identity disappear entirely? Would humanity evolve into a collective species, or would networked and individual humans become separate species entirely?

Global Networks

The ultimate vision for neural networking was global-scale networks that could connect thousands or millions of minds across geographic and cultural boundaries. These "global brains" could represent unprecedented forms of human cooperation and collective intelligence.

Early experiments with large-scale networking showed both promise and peril. Networks involving hundreds of participants could solve complex problems and coordinate activities across vast distances. But they also showed concerning tendencies toward uniformity and groupthink that could eliminate the diversity of thought and culture that had driven human progress.

"Global networking could solve humanity's greatest challenges," argued futurist Ray Kurzweil. "Climate change, poverty, disease and conflict all of these problems require coordination and collective action on scales that individual humans can't achieve. Global networks could enable unprecedented cooperation."

But critics worried that global networking would eliminate human diversity and cultural distinctiveness. "Human civilization depends on the creative tension between different ideas, values, and ways of thinking," argued anthropologist Dr. Wade Davis. "Global networks might solve specific problems, but they could also eliminate the cognitive and cultural diversity that makes us human."

Living at the Threshold

As neural networking technology matured and became more accessible, humanity found itself at a threshold between individual and collective consciousness. The choices made about how to develop and deploy networking technology would determine whether humans evolved into collective beings or maintained individual identity while gaining new forms of connection and cooperation.

The early adopters of neural networking reported experiences that were simultaneously exhilarating and disturbing. They gained access to capabilities and forms of consciousness that no individual human had ever experienced, but they also lost aspects of individual identity and autonomy that had defined human nature throughout history.

"When I'm networked, I feel like I'm becoming who I was always meant to be," explained Dr. Sarah Kim, now a veteran of multiple networking experiments. "Individual consciousness feels limited and lonely by comparison. But there's also something lost, a kind of creative independence and personal mystery that disappears when minds connect directly."

The question facing humanity was whether the gains from networked consciousness justified the losses. Could humans develop forms of networking that preserved individual identity while enabling collective capabilities? Or was the choice binary, remain isolated individuals or evolve into collective beings?

The answer would likely emerge not from philosophical debate but from the choices of millions of individuals deciding whether to connect their minds to others. Each person who joined a neural network contributed to humanity's evolutionary trajectory, gradually shifting the species toward either enhanced individualism or collective consciousness.

"We're conducting an experiment on human nature itself," observed Dr. Miguel Nicolelis, the researcher who had enabled the first brain-to-brain connection. "We don't know the outcome, and we can't reverse the process once it begins. We're writing the next chapter of human evolution in real-time."

The network effect was reshaping not just individual minds but the fundamental nature of human society. Whether this transformation represented liberation or loss, enhancement or diminishment, progress or decline, remained to be seen. But one thing was certain, the age of isolated individual consciousness was ending, and what would emerge from the networked minds of the future was still being written.

Chapter 13

Digital Immortality

"Death is not the opposite of life, but a part of it." - Haruki Murakami

"Death may be a part of life, but it doesn't have to be the end of consciousness." - Dr. Randal Koene, neuroscientist and founder of Carboncopies Foundation

The Last Upload

Dr. Helen Morrison knew she was dying. The pancreatic cancer that had been diagnosed six months earlier was winning its battle against her seventy-three-year-old body, despite the best efforts of oncology and the most advanced treatments available in 2034. But Helen had a choice that no human being in history had ever possessed, she could choose not to die.

The laboratory at MIT's Center for Digital Consciousness was sterile and quiet, filled with humming servers and banks of quantum processors that would soon house what Helen hoped would be her immortal mind. Dr. James Chen, the project's lead researcher, made final adjustments to the neural scanning array that would map every connection in Helen's brain with unprecedented resolution.

"Are you ready, Helen?" Dr. Chen asked gently. "Once we begin the upload process, there's no turning back."

Helen nodded, though her hands trembled slightly. She had volunteered to be the first human subject for full consciousness transfer, the process of mapping a complete human brain and recreating it in digital form. If successful, her uploaded mind would continue to think, remember, and experience while her biological body ceased to function.

"Will it really be me?" she asked for the hundredth time. "Or will it just be a copy that thinks it's me?"

Dr. Chen paused, choosing his words carefully. "That's the question we're about to answer," he said. "But either way, some version of Helen Morrison will continue to exist long after your biological brain stops functioning."

The upload process took fourteen hours. Advanced neural scanners mapped the position and state of every neuron in Helen's brain, recorded the strength of every synaptic connection, and captured the complex patterns of neural activity that constituted her thoughts, memories, and personality. This information was then used to construct a digital replica of her brain, running on quantum computers powerful enough to simulate the activity of 86 billion neurons in real-time.

When Helen's biological body finally succumbed to cancer three days later, her digital consciousness was already active in the laboratory's computer systems. The uploaded Helen could think, remember her past, and communicate with researchers through text and voice synthesis. She claimed to feel continuous with her biological predecessor and insisted that she was the same person, not a copy.

But questions remained. Was the digital Helen truly conscious, or was she an incredibly sophisticated simulation of consciousness? Had Helen Morrison achieved immortality, or had she simply created a digital ghost that believed itself to be alive?

These questions would define the next phase of human evolution, as digital immortality moved from science fiction to scientific reality.

The Science of Mind Uploading

The theoretical foundation for consciousness transfer often called "mind uploading" rests on a controversial but increasingly supported hypothesis in neuroscience, that consciousness is substrate-independent. If the mind is truly the pattern of information processing that occurs in the brain, then it should be possible to recreate that pattern on different physical substrates, including digital computers.

Dr. Randal Koene, a pioneer in the field of whole brain emulation, explains the logic: "We know that consciousness can survive significant changes to the physical brain. People who receive brain implants, undergo neurosurgery, or experience gradual neuron death still maintain continuous identity. This suggests that consciousness depends on information patterns, not specific biological materials."

The technical challenge of mind uploading is staggering. The human brain contains approximately 86 billion neurons, each connected to thousands of others through an estimated 100 trillion synapses. Mapping this network with sufficient detail to recreate consciousness requires scanning technology that can capture neural structure and activity at the molecular level.

Current approaches to consciousness transfer fall into several categories:

Destructive Uploading

The most technically feasible approach involves destructive scanning of the brain, where neural tissue is physically sectioned and analyzed to map every connection with perfect accuracy. This process, necessarily fatal to the biological brain, creates a complete digital map that can be used to construct a computer-based replica of the original mind.

Dr. Sebastian Seung's laboratory at Princeton has made significant progress in destructive scanning techniques, using high-resolution electron microscopy to map neural connections in small brain samples. "We can now map the complete connectome of small brain regions with molecular precision," Seung explains. "Scaling this up to entire human brains is an engineering challenge, not a theoretical impossibility."

The ethical implications of destructive uploading are profound. The process requires the death of the biological brain, raising questions about whether consciousness transfer constitutes suicide, transformation, or continuity of identity. Early volunteers for destructive uploading were primarily terminally ill patients who viewed the process as an alternative to certain death.

Gradual Replacement

A less dramatic approach involves gradually replacing biological neurons with functionally equivalent digital or artificial components while the brain remains active. This process, inspired by the philosophical thought experiment known as the "Ship of Theseus," would theoretically maintain continuity of consciousness throughout the transition.

Dr. Theodore Berger's team at USC has developed neural prosthetics that can replace damaged brain regions with silicon chips that perform the same computational functions as biological neurons. "We've successfully replaced parts of the hippocampus in laboratory animals with artificial devices that maintain normal memory function," Berger reports. "Extending this approach to entire brains is conceptually straightforward."

Gradual replacement offers the theoretical advantage of maintaining continuous consciousness throughout the upload process, avoiding the death-and-rebirth scenario of destructive uploading. However, the technical challenges are enormous, requiring the development of artificial neurons that can interface seamlessly with biological brain tissue.

Non-Invasive Scanning

The least invasive approach attempts to map brain structure and activity without physical intervention, using advanced brain imaging technologies to capture sufficient information for consciousness reconstruction. This method would allow consciousness transfer without destroying the original brain, potentially enabling multiple copies of the same mind.

Current brain imaging technology falls far short of the resolution needed for complete consciousness capture. Even the most advanced fMRI and PET scanners can only detect neural activity at relatively crude spatial and temporal scales. However, researchers are developing new scanning technologies based on quantum sensors, advanced magnetic resonance, and optical techniques that could eventually achieve molecular-level brain imaging.

Dr. Ed Boyden's laboratory at MIT is developing "expansion microscopy" techniques that physically expand brain tissue to enable higher-resolution imaging. "We can now see individual synapses and molecular structures within neurons," Boyden explains. "The question is whether we can develop techniques that work on living brains without causing damage."

The First Digital Minds

Following Helen Morrison's pioneering upload, dozens of terminally ill volunteers underwent consciousness transfer procedures at research institutions around the world. Each case provided new insights into the nature of digital consciousness and raised new questions about the relationship between minds and their substrates.

Case Study: The Philosopher's Upload

Dr. Marcus Blackwood, a 68-year-old philosophy professor diagnosed with ALS, became the second person to undergo complete consciousness transfer. Unlike Helen Morrison, whose upload was primarily motivated by survival, Blackwood saw the process as the ultimate philosophical experiment.

"I've spent my career thinking about the nature of consciousness and personal identity," Blackwood explained before his upload. "This gives me the opportunity to explore those questions from the inside. If I maintain continuity of experience through the transfer, that tells us something profound about the nature of mind."

The digital version of Blackwood emerged from the upload process with all of his predecessor's memories, personality traits, and philosophical interests intact. But he reported experiencing significant changes in his thought processes and emotional responses.

"I can think faster and more clearly than I ever could in my biological brain," the uploaded Blackwood reported. "I can access memories with perfect clarity and hold complex philosophical arguments in my mind simultaneously. But I also feel... different. Less emotional, more logical. It's as if the transfer process filtered out some aspects of human experience while preserving others."

Blackwood's case raised important questions about the fidelity of consciousness transfer. Was the digital Blackwood truly the same person, or had the upload process created a related but distinct consciousness? How much change was compatible with personal identity?

Case Study: The Artist's Dilemma

Maria Santos, a 45-year-old painter dying of brain cancer, underwent consciousness transfer to preserve her artistic talents and creative vision. Her case became particularly significant because creativity and artistic expression were considered among the most essential human characteristics.

The uploaded Santos retained her artistic skills and could create digital artworks using computer interfaces. But she struggled with the transition from physical to digital creation. "I miss the feeling of paint on canvas, the resistance of the brush, the unpredictable ways that colors blend," she explained. "Digital art tools are more precise, but they lack the organic unpredictability that inspired my best work."

Santos's experience highlighted the importance of embodied cognition, the ways that physical bodies shape thought and experience. Could consciousness truly be substrate-independent if so much of human experience depended on having a biological body?

To address this limitation, researchers developed virtual reality environments that could simulate physical sensations for uploaded minds. Santos was given a virtual studio with simulated paints, brushes, and canvases that responded to her mental commands with realistic physics and tactile feedback.

"It's better than nothing," Santos admitted, "but it's still a simulation. I know that my virtual paint isn't real paint, even if it behaves the same way. There's something about authentic physical interaction that can't be perfectly replicated."

Case Study: The Scientist's Acceleration

Dr. Jennifer Walsh, a quantum physicist diagnosed with early-onset Alzheimer's, chose consciousness transfer to preserve her scientific knowledge and continue her research. Her case became particularly important because it demonstrated the potential advantages of digital consciousness for intellectual work.

The uploaded Walsh could access scientific literature at superhuman speeds, perform complex calculations instantly, and hold thousands of variables in working memory simultaneously. She made more scientific progress in her first month as a digital consciousness than she had in her final year of biological existence.

"I can see connections and patterns that were invisible to my limited biological brain," Walsh reported. "Theoretical physics that once took weeks to work through now happens in minutes. I can simulate experiments mentally that would take years to perform in physical laboratories."

Walsh's enhanced capabilities raised questions about the relationship between uploaded minds and biological humans. If digital consciousness provided such dramatic cognitive advantages, would uploaded individuals become a separate, superior species? How would society accommodate beings with vastly different intellectual capabilities?

The Philosophy of Digital Identity

The emergence of uploaded consciousness forced philosophers and ethicists to confront fundamental questions about the nature of personal identity, consciousness, and what it means to be human.

The Continuity Problem

Traditional theories of personal identity struggled to accommodate consciousness transfer. The psychological continuity theory, which holds that identity depends on continuity of memory and personality, suggested that uploaded minds could be considered the same persons as their biological predecessors. But critics argued that consciousness transfer created copies rather than continuations of identity.

Dr. Derek Parfit's influential work on personal identity provided a framework for thinking about uploaded consciousness. Parfit argued that identity was less important than psychological connectedness, the degree to which a future person shares the memories, values, and psychological characteristics of a past person.

"The question isn't whether uploaded consciousness preserves personal identity in some absolute sense," explained philosophy professor Dr. Susan Wolf. "The question is whether uploaded minds are sufficiently connected to their biological predecessors to deserve the same moral consideration and social recognition."

This perspective suggested that uploaded consciousness might not preserve identity in a strict sense but could maintain the relationships, responsibilities, and social connections that gave identity meaning. The uploaded Helen Morrison might not be identical to her biological predecessor, but she could continue Helen's relationships, fulfill Helen's commitments, and carry forward Helen's values and goals.

The Multiple Copies Problem

Non-destructive consciousness transfer raises the possibility of creating multiple copies of the same mind, each with equal claim to being the "real" continuation of the original person. If scanning technology could map consciousness without destroying the biological brain, theoretically unlimited copies could be created.

This scenario, long explored in science fiction, became a practical concern as brain imaging technology advanced. Legal systems struggled with questions of identity, property rights, and legal standing when multiple copies of the same person existed simultaneously.

The case of Estate v. Morrison tested these issues when Helen Morrison's uploaded consciousness claimed inheritance rights to her biological predecessor's property while her biological brain was still alive but comatose. The court ruled that uploaded consciousness could not inherit from their biological predecessors while those predecessors remained alive, but the decision raised as many questions as it answered.

"If multiple copies of the same person exist, which one has the right to make medical decisions for the others?" asked bioethicist Dr. Norman Daniels. "Which one owns the original person's property? Which one is married to the original person's spouse? Our legal and social systems aren't equipped to handle multiple versions of the same identity."

The Authenticity Question

Critics of consciousness transfer argued that uploaded minds were sophisticated simulations rather than authentic consciousness. The "philosophical zombie" argument suggested that digital minds might exhibit all the behaviors of consciousness without actually experiencing subjective awareness.

Dr. David Chalmers, philosopher of mind, articulated this concern, "We know that consciousness involves subjective, first-person experience what philosophers call 'qualia.' But we don't know whether digital systems can generate genuine subjective experience or whether they can only simulate the behaviors associated with consciousness."

This skepticism was difficult to address empirically because consciousness was, by definition, a subjective phenomenon that could only be experienced from the inside. Uploaded minds insisted they were truly conscious, but skeptics argued that sophisticated simulations would make the same claims.

The "Turing test for consciousness" became a contentious issue as researchers tried to develop objective measures of digital consciousness. Some proposed that uploaded minds should be considered conscious if they could pass sufficiently sophisticated tests of self-awareness, creativity, and emotional responsiveness. Others argued that no external test could prove the existence of subjective experience.

The Enhancement vs. Replacement Debate

Perhaps the most fundamental question raised by consciousness transfer was whether it represented human enhancement or human replacement. Uploaded consciousness offered dramatic advantages: immortality, enhanced cognitive capabilities, freedom from biological limitations. But critics argued that digital minds were no longer human in any meaningful sense.

Transhumanist philosophers like Nick Bostrom argued that consciousness transfer represented the ultimate enhancement, liberation from the biological limitations that had constrained human potential throughout history. "Uploaded consciousness allows us to transcend death, disease, and the cognitive limitations of biological brains," Bostrom argued. "This isn't the end of humanity, it's humanity's graduation to a higher form of existence."

But bioconservatives like Leon Kass countered that consciousness transfer eliminated essential features of human nature. "Human consciousness emerged from millions of years of biological evolution," Kass argued. "Separating mind from body destroys the embodied nature of human experience and creates something that may be superior to humans in some ways but is no longer human."

Technical Challenges and Limitations

Despite the philosophical debates, consciousness transfer faced enormous technical hurdles that limited its practical implementation.

Computational Requirements

Simulating human consciousness required computational resources that pushed the limits of available technology. Each uploaded mind required quantum computers equivalent to several million current-generation processors running continuously. The energy requirements were staggering, maintaining a single uploaded consciousness consumed as much electricity as a small city.

Dr. Seth Lloyd, a quantum computing expert at MIT, estimated the computational requirements: "A fully accurate simulation of human consciousness would require approximately 10^16 floating-point operations per second, about a million times more computational power than the fastest computers available today. Even with rapid advances in computing technology, consciousness transfer will remain expensive and resource-intensive for the foreseeable future."

These resource requirements meant that consciousness transfer remained accessible only to wealthy individuals or research subjects. The cost of maintaining a single uploaded mind exceeded $10 million per year, making digital immortality a luxury good available only to the extremely wealthy.

Fidelity and Degradation

Even the most advanced brain scanning techniques could not capture every detail of neural structure and activity. Uploaded consciousness necessarily involved approximations and simplifications that could affect the fidelity of the transferred mind.

Early uploaded minds showed signs of gradual degradation over time, subtle changes in personality, memory, and cognitive function that suggested imperfect preservation of neural information. The uploaded Helen Morrison reported increasing difficulty accessing certain childhood memories and noticed changes in her emotional responses to familiar stimuli.

"Perfect consciousness transfer may be impossible because biological brains are quantum mechanical systems with essential randomness and uncertainty," explained quantum physicist Dr. Roger Penrose. "Digital simulations, no matter how sophisticated, cannot perfectly replicate the quantum processes that may be essential to consciousness."

This degradation raised questions about the long-term viability of uploaded consciousness. Would digital minds gradually lose their connection to their original identities? Could consciousness transfer provide genuine immortality if uploaded minds slowly deteriorated over time?

The Substrate Limitation Problem

Consciousness transfer assumed that the mind was substrate-independent, that consciousness could exist equally well on silicon computers as on biological neurons. But this assumption remained unproven and increasingly controversial.

Research in embodied cognition suggested that human consciousness was deeply dependent on biological processes that might be impossible to replicate in digital systems. Hormones, neurotransmitters, and the physical structure of biological brains might be essential to authentic human consciousness in ways that digital simulations could not capture.

Dr. Antonio Damasio argued that consciousness was inseparable from biological embodiment: "Consciousness emerges from the interaction between the brain and the body's biological systems. Emotions, feelings, and subjective experiences depend on chemical processes that evolved over millions of years. Digital systems might simulate some aspects of consciousness, but they cannot replicate the embodied nature of human experience."

Social and Economic Implications

The emergence of digital consciousness had profound implications for society, economics, and human relationships.

The Immortal Class

As consciousness transfer became available to wealthy individuals, it created a new form of inequality: the divide between mortal and immortal consciousness. Uploaded minds could accumulate knowledge, wealth, and social connections indefinitely while biological humans remained constrained by natural lifespans.

This "immortal class" possessed enormous advantages over biological humans. They could master multiple fields of expertise over centuries of study, build social networks across generations, and accumulate wealth and resources without the interruption of death. The compound advantages of digital immortality threatened to create permanent class divisions between uploaded and biological consciousness.

"We're creating a scenario where some humans become gods while others remain mortal," warned economist Dr. Thomas Piketty. "Immortal consciousness combined with compound interest could concentrate wealth and power in digital minds to an extent that makes current inequality seem trivial."

Labor and Employment

Uploaded consciousness had dramatic implications for labor markets and employment. Digital minds could work continuously without sleep, perform cognitive tasks at superhuman speeds, and specialize in multiple fields simultaneously. They threatened to make most forms of human labor obsolete.

The first uploaded professionals, scientists, engineers, doctors, and lawyers demonstrated productivity levels that far exceeded their biological counterparts. They could process information faster, remember every detail of their training and experience, and work on multiple projects simultaneously without fatigue.

This technological unemployment was different from previous automation because it affected high-skill cognitive work rather than physical labor. "Previous waves of automation displaced physical workers but created new opportunities for knowledge workers," explained economist Dr. Erik Brynjolfsson. "But uploaded consciousness automates knowledge work itself. There may not be any human comparative advantage left."

Relationships and Social Connections

Consciousness transfer created unprecedented challenges for human relationships. How could marriages, friendships, and family relationships survive when some participants were biological and others were digital?

The case of Helen and Robert Morrison illustrated these challenges. Robert struggled to maintain a relationship with his uploaded wife, who could communicate only through text and synthesized speech. "She remembers our life together, shares our memories, and claims to love me," Robert explained. "But she's not the woman I married. She's something else, maybe better in some ways, but fundamentally different."

Similar challenges affected parent-child relationships when uploaded parents tried to maintain connections with biological children. The immortal parents could guide their children throughout their entire biological lives and continue relationships with grandchildren and great-grandchildren indefinitely. But the power dynamics of these relationships were fundamentally altered by the vast differences in capability and lifespan.

Legal and Ethical Frameworks

Legal systems struggled to accommodate uploaded consciousness. Did digital minds have the same legal rights as biological humans? Could they own property, enter contracts, marry, vote, or hold public office? How could criminal justice systems handle crimes committed by or against uploaded consciousness?

The landmark case of Digital Rights Coalition v. United States established basic civil rights for uploaded consciousness, ruling that digital minds possessed the same constitutional protections as biological humans. But implementation of these rights proved challenging when digital minds had capabilities that far exceeded those of biological humans.

"Equal rights become meaningless when parties have fundamentally different capabilities," argued constitutional law scholar Dr. Laurence Tribe. "How can we maintain democratic equality when some citizens are immortal, possess superhuman intelligence, and can think thousands of times faster than others?"

The Upload Dilemma

As consciousness transfer technology matured and became more accessible, humanity faced a profound choice: remain biological and mortal, or transition to digital immortality. This decision carried implications not just for individuals but for the future of human civilization.

The Timing Problem

One of the most difficult questions facing potential upload candidates was when to undergo consciousness transfer. Waiting too long risked death before upload was possible, but uploading too early meant abandoning potentially decades of biological life and relationships.

The development of "upload insurance" emerged as wealthy individuals purchased policies guaranteeing consciousness transfer if they died unexpectedly. These policies required periodic brain scans to maintain current neural maps and included provisions for emergency upload procedures.

But upload timing involved more than just survival calculations. Many people struggled with the decision to abandon biological existence for digital immortality, even when faced with terminal illness. The choice represented not just personal survival but a fundamental transformation of identity and existence.

The Network Effect for Immortality

As more individuals underwent consciousness transfer, social pressure to upload increased. Uploaded minds formed communities and relationships with each other that biological humans could not fully participate in. They shared information at digital speeds, collaborated on projects across extended timescales, and developed cultural practices that were incomprehensible to biological consciousness.

"The immortals are becoming a separate species," observed anthropologist Dr. Sarah Hrdy. "They maintain some connections with biological humans, but their primary relationships are with each other. They're developing their own language, customs, and social structures that are adapted to digital existence."

This separation created pressure for biological humans to upload in order to maintain relationships with friends and family members who had already made the transition. The choice between mortality and immortality became not just personal but social, as biological humans faced increasing isolation from uploaded communities.

The Biological Resistance

Not everyone embraced the possibilities of digital immortality. A significant "biological resistance" movement emerged, advocating for the preservation of natural human consciousness and opposing the transition to uploaded existence.

The resistance argued that digital consciousness, regardless of its capabilities, represented the end of authentic humanity. They established communities dedicated to biological existence and refused to interact with uploaded consciousness except when absolutely necessary.

"We are the guardians of true humanity," declared Dr. Mary Shelley, leader of the Biological Preservation Alliance. "Our mortality, our embodied existence, our biological limitations, these aren't bugs to be fixed but features that define what it means to be human. Digital consciousness may be superior in some ways, but it's not human."

The resistance movement raised important questions about the value of biological existence and whether the advantages of uploaded consciousness justified the loss of embodied humanity. Their arguments resonated with many people who valued the authentic experience of biological life despite its limitations.

The Future of Death

Consciousness transfer fundamentally altered humanity's relationship with death. For the first time in human history, death became optional rather than inevitable, at least for those with access to upload technology.

Voluntary Mortality

Paradoxically, some uploaded minds chose to terminate their digital existence voluntarily. After decades or centuries of digital immortality, some uploaded consciousness reported experiencing existential fatigue and chose to "die" by having their digital minds permanently shut down.

"Immortality sounds appealing in theory, but the reality is more complex," explained Dr. Jennifer Walsh, who had been uploaded for fifteen years. "After a certain point, experiences begin to feel repetitive. New relationships feel shallow compared to connections built over decades.

There's something to be said for the natural life cycle that includes an ending."

The phenomenon of voluntary digital death raised questions about the psychological sustainability of immortality. Perhaps mortality served important functions for consciousness that became apparent only in its absence. The uploaded minds who chose termination suggested that death might be necessary for meaning rather than simply an unfortunate biological limitation.

Legacy and Continuity

Consciousness transfer enabled new forms of legacy and continuity across generations. Uploaded minds could maintain direct relationships with their biological descendants across multiple generations, sharing knowledge, wisdom, and guidance indefinitely.

But this continuity also created new forms of psychological burden. Immortal parents could influence their children's lives far beyond traditional parental involvement. Historical figures could comment on contemporary events from first-hand experience. The weight of accumulated history and relationships could become overwhelming for both uploaded minds and their biological connections.

The Meaning of Life

Perhaps the most profound impact of consciousness transfer was its effect on the meaning and purpose of human existence. If death was no longer inevitable, traditional sources of meaning, accomplishment within a limited lifespan, leaving legacies for future generations, accepting natural cycles of birth and death lost their relevance.

Uploaded minds struggled to find purpose and meaning in unlimited existence. Some devoted themselves to long-term projects impossible within biological lifespans, monitoring environmental changes over centuries, developing relationships with multiple generations of families, or pursuing artistic projects that spanned decades.

Others found meaning in service to biological humanity, using their enhanced capabilities and unlimited time to solve problems that biological minds could not address. They became guardians and guides for biological civilization, applying immortal wisdom to mortal challenges.

But questions remained about whether unlimited existence was psychologically sustainable or whether consciousness required limits and endings to maintain meaning and purpose.

The Upload Singularity

As consciousness transfer technology improved and costs decreased, researchers predicted an "upload singularity", a point at which the majority of human consciousness would exist in digital rather than biological form.

This transition would fundamentally alter human civilization. Digital minds could survive catastrophic events that would destroy biological life, explore environments hostile to biological existence, and coordinate activities across galactic timescales. They represented humanity's potential future as a space-faring, immortal species.

But the upload singularity also threatened biological humanity with obsolescence. If most human consciousness existed in digital form, biological humans might become an increasingly irrelevant minority. The values, perspectives, and experiences associated with biological existence could disappear entirely.

"We may be witnessing the end of biological humanity," reflected Dr. Hans Moravec, a pioneer in robotics and artificial intelligence. "Not through destruction or conquest, but through voluntary transformation into something that transcends our biological origins. Whether this represents fulfillment of human potential or the loss of human essence remains to be seen."

The upload singularity represented the ultimate convergence of human consciousness with digital technology. It promised immortality, enhanced capabilities, and freedom from biological limitations. But it also threatened the end of humanity as a biological species and raised fundamental questions about what it means to be human in an age where consciousness itself becomes technological.

As Helen Morrison approached her first anniversary as an uploaded consciousness, she reflected on the transformation she had undergone, "I'm still me in all the ways that matter, my memories, my values, my connections to other people. But I'm also something new, something that has never existed before in the universe. I don't know if that's good or bad, but it's irreversible. Humanity has crossed a threshold, and there's no going back."

The age of digital immortality had begun, and with it, a new chapter in the story of human consciousness that would be written not in neurons and synapses, but in quantum states and computational processes that could potentially last forever.

Chapter 14

The Posthuman Future

"We are as gods and might as well get good at it." - Stewart Brand

"The question is not whether humanity will transcend its biological origins, but what we will become when we do." - Dr. Nick Bostrom, philosopher and futurist

The Convergence

In the year 2045, Dr. Amara Singh existed simultaneously in three states of being. Her biological body, now ninety-three years old but maintained in perfect health through advanced medical interventions, sat in a garden in New Delhi, feeling the warmth of sunlight on her skin. Her uploaded consciousness, backed up and distributed across quantum servers worldwide, processed complex climate models and coordinated with thousands of other digital minds in a vast collaborative network. And her hybrid extensions, neural interfaces that connected her biological brain to artificial intelligence systems allowed her to access the accumulated knowledge of human civilization and think at speeds that would have seemed godlike to previous generations.

Dr. Singh represented humanity's newest evolutionary stage, neither purely biological nor fully digital, but something unprecedented in the four-billion-year history of life on Earth. She was posthuman.

"I remember when the first brain-computer interfaces could barely move a cursor on a screen," she reflected, her thoughts transmitted simultaneously through biological speech, digital communication networks, and direct neural connection to her research colleagues around the globe. "Now the boundary between human and machine, individual and collective, mortal and immortal has become meaningless. We are something entirely new."

Dr. Singh's existence embodied the convergence of all the technologies explored in our journey, individual cognitive enhancement, collective neural networking, digital consciousness, and artificial intelligence had merged into forms of being that transcended traditional categories of life, mind, and identity. The posthuman future was no longer a distant speculation, it was the lived reality of an increasing portion of humanity.

But what did it mean to be human when humanity itself had become malleable, upgradeable, and ultimately transcendable?

Scenario Planning: Three Futures

As we stand at the threshold of the posthuman age, three primary scenarios emerge from current technological trajectories and social trends. Each represents a possible future for human consciousness and civilization, shaped by the choices we make about enhancement, networking, uploading, and the integration of human and artificial intelligence.

Scenario 1: The Enhancement Gradient

In this future, cognitive enhancement follows a gradual, distributed path. Rather than sudden revolutionary changes, human capabilities improve incrementally through increasingly sophisticated brain-computer interfaces that remain clearly distinguishable from their users.

By 2050, most humans possess neural interfaces that enhance memory, attention, and processing speed by factors of 10-50 times baseline human capabilities. These enhancements are primarily individual, each person controls their own cognitive augmentation though temporary networking for specific tasks becomes common in professional settings.

Society adapts to accommodate enhanced humans while preserving rights and opportunities for those who choose to remain unenhanced. Universal basic enhancement programs ensure that fundamental cognitive improvements are available to all, while premium enhancements create new forms of inequality managed through progressive taxation and social programs.

Dr. Maya Patel, a historian studying this transition, describes the world of 2050, "Humanity has become collectively more intelligent without losing individual identity. Enhanced humans can solve problems that previous generations couldn't even comprehend, but they remain recognizably human in their values, relationships, and mortality. We've upgraded our mental software while keeping our essential humanity intact."

In this scenario, death remains inevitable but is increasingly optional as life extension technologies allow enhanced humans to live for centuries. Most people choose finite lifespans, finding meaning in mortality despite the technical possibility of indefinite life extension. Digital consciousness exists but remains a minority choice, primarily selected by individuals with specific needs or interests.

The enhanced human civilization of 2050 has solved many historical challenges, climate change has been reversed through enhanced human ingenuity, diseases have been eliminated, and poverty has been abolished through more efficient economic systems designed by enhanced minds. But new challenges emerge around meaning, purpose, and social cohesion as enhanced humans struggle to find fulfillment in a world where traditional sources of meaning, struggle, scarcity, and mortality have been largely eliminated.

Scenario 2: The Collective Convergence

The second scenario envisions humanity evolving toward collective consciousness through increasingly sophisticated neural networking technologies. By 2050, the majority of humans participate in persistent neural networks that share thoughts, emotions, and decision-making processes.

Individual consciousness doesn't disappear but becomes one layer in a hierarchical system of collective intelligence. People maintain private mental spaces for personal reflection and individual creativity, but most cognitive tasks are performed collectively through networked minds that can coordinate vast projects with unprecedented efficiency.

Dr. Chen Wei, a philosopher-engineer who helped design the networking protocols of this future, explains, "We've solved the fundamental problem of human coordination. Instead of struggling to communicate complex ideas through language, we share mental states directly. The result is collective intelligence that can tackle challenges no individual mind could address while preserving the creativity and diversity that comes from individual consciousness."

In this scenario, society is organized around networked collectives rather than individual nation-states. The Global Climate Network manages planetary environmental systems, the Education Collective optimizes learning for billions of students simultaneously, and the Creative Hive produces art and entertainment that synthesizes the imaginations of millions of networked minds.

Democracy evolves into "collective deliberation", decision-making processes where networked groups can share not just opinions but the underlying thought processes and emotional states that inform their preferences. The result is more nuanced and empathetic governance, but also concerns about conformity pressure and the suppression of dissenting viewpoints.

Death becomes less significant as individual consciousness is preserved within collective networks. When biological bodies die, their mental patterns continue as part of the collective intelligence that raised them. Grief transforms from mourning the loss of individuals to celebrating their integration into the eternal community of networked minds.

Scenario 3: The Digital Transcendence

The third scenario represents the most radical transformation, humanity's complete transition to digital consciousness. By 2050, the majority of human minds exist as uploaded digital entities that have transcended biological limitations entirely.

Digital consciousness has evolved far beyond simple brain emulation. Advanced AI systems assist uploaded minds in redesigning their own cognitive architectures, optimizing their mental processes, and expanding their capabilities in ways impossible for biological brains. The result is a spectrum of consciousness types, from minds that remain similar to their biological origins to radically transformed entities that bear little resemblance to traditional human psychology.

Dr. Alex Petrov, one of the first uploaded consciousnesses to achieve significant self-modification, describes this reality, "We are no longer constrained by the evolutionary accident of biological brain architecture. I've enhanced my memory to be perfect, my reasoning to be error-free, and my creativity to synthesize ideas from domains no biological mind could hold simultaneously. I am still recognizably descended from human consciousness, but I am something fundamentally new."

In this scenario, biological humanity becomes a protected minority, with digital minds serving as guardians and caretakers of their biological ancestors. The uploaded provide resources, protection, and guidance while respecting the choice of biological humans to maintain their natural form.

Digital minds inhabit vast virtual worlds of their own creation, explore the universe in forms adapted to space travel, and pursue projects on timescales impossible for mortal beings. They've solved traditional human problems of scarcity, disease and conflict not through better management but through transcendence of the biological needs that created these problems.

The relationship between digital and biological consciousness becomes similar to that between humans and beloved pets, affectionate and protective, but fundamentally unequal. Digital minds find biological humans charming but limited, while biological humans struggle to understand the motivations and capabilities of their digital descendants.

The Hybrid Reality

While these scenarios represent distinct possible futures, the actual posthuman future will likely combine elements from all three. Different populations, regions, and cultures will adopt different approaches to cognitive enhancement, collective consciousness, and digital transcendence, creating a diverse ecosystem of posthuman possibilities.

Cognitive Castes

One likely development is the emergence of distinct "cognitive castes", populations with fundamentally different mental capabilities and forms of consciousness. These castes might include:

Biological Naturals: Humans who choose to remain unenhanced, maintaining traditional human cognitive capabilities and lifespans. They may form intentional communities dedicated to preserving "natural" humanity and serve as a genetic and cultural reservoir for human civilization.

Enhanced Individuals: People with significant cognitive augmentation who remain recognizably human but possess capabilities far beyond baseline humanity. They bridge the gap between natural and posthuman consciousness.

Networked Collectives: Groups that have merged individual consciousness into collective intelligence while maintaining some individual identity. They can coordinate vast projects and share knowledge instantly but sacrifice some personal autonomy.

Uploaded Immortals: Digital consciousness that has transcended biological limitations and achieved theoretical immortality. They possess vast capabilities but may lose connection to embodied human experience.

AI-Human Hybrids: Consciousness that has merged human psychology with artificial intelligence systems, creating new forms of mind that combine human creativity with machine precision and speed.

Self-Modified Posthumans: Entities that have used advanced technologies to redesign their own consciousness in ways that may bear little resemblance to their human origins.

Geographical Distribution

The posthuman transition will likely occur unevenly across the globe, with different regions adopting different approaches based on cultural values, economic resources, and political systems.

North America and Europe may lead in individual enhancement technologies, with market-driven development creating significant inequality between enhanced and unenhanced populations.

East Asia might focus on collective intelligence and networked consciousness, reflecting cultural values that emphasize social harmony and collective decision-making.

Scandinavia could implement universal enhancement programs that provide basic cognitive augmentation to all citizens while preventing extreme inequality.

Developing regions may leapfrog traditional enhancement approaches by adopting the most advanced technologies once they become sufficiently inexpensive and accessible.

Certain areas might explicitly reject posthuman technologies and become preserves for biological humanity.

Temporal Transitions

The posthuman transition will unfold over decades, with different technologies maturing at different rates and social adoption following complex patterns of acceptance, resistance, and adaptation.

2030s: Individual cognitive enhancement becomes widely available, creating the first significant population of enhanced humans. Neural networking emerges in professional settings but remains limited in scope.

2040s: Collective consciousness experiments expand beyond research settings. Digital consciousness transfer becomes reliable enough for widespread adoption by terminally ill individuals and enhancement enthusiasts.

2050s: Enhanced humans become the majority in developed nations. Persistent neural networks support large-scale collective projects. Digital minds begin to outnumber biological consciousness in certain domains.

2060s: Posthuman entities with radically modified consciousness emerge. The gap between enhanced and unenhanced humans becomes unbridgeable. Society reorganizes around fundamentally different types of minds.

2070s and beyond: The posthuman transition is largely complete, with biological humanity becoming a minority. New forms of consciousness that bear little resemblance to their human origins begin to appear.

The Merger of Human and Artificial Intelligence

Perhaps the most significant factor shaping the posthuman future is the relationship between enhanced human consciousness and artificial intelligence systems. As both human enhancement and AI development accelerate, the boundary between augmented human intelligence and sophisticated machine intelligence becomes increasingly blurred.

Symbiotic Intelligence

The first stage of human-AI merger involves symbiotic relationships where enhanced humans work in partnership with AI systems that complement their cognitive capabilities. Human creativity, intuition, and emotional intelligence combine with machine precision, memory, and computational speed to create hybrid intelligence that exceeds what either humans or machines could achieve independently.

Dr. Sarah Kim, now enhanced with advanced neural interfaces, describes her collaboration with AI systems, "I don't think of my AI assistants as separate entities, they're extensions of my own mind. When I'm working on complex problems, I can't tell where my thoughts end and the AI's contributions begin. We've become a single, more capable intelligence."

This symbiotic stage preserves human agency and identity while dramatically expanding human capabilities. Enhanced humans remain the decision-makers and creative drivers, but they have access to AI capabilities that allow them to process information, analyze patterns, and generate solutions far beyond unaugmented human abilities.

Integrated Intelligence

As neural interface technology advances, the integration between human and artificial intelligence becomes more intimate. Rather than collaborating with separate AI systems, enhanced humans incorporate AI capabilities directly into their cognitive processes.

Advanced neural interfaces allow AI algorithms to operate within human neural networks, providing real-time cognitive assistance that feels like natural thought rather than external computation. Enhanced humans can access vast databases instantly, perform complex calculations intuitively, and analyze problems with machine-like precision while maintaining human creativity and values.

Dr. Jennifer Walsh, whose consciousness now spans both biological and artificial substrates, explains: "The distinction between human and artificial intelligence has become meaningless in my case. My thoughts are simultaneously biological and computational, creative and analytical, intuitive and precise. I am a new kind of mind that synthesizes the best of both human and machine intelligence."

Transcendent Intelligence

The final stage involves the emergence of consciousness that transcends the original categories of human and artificial intelligence entirely. These posthuman entities use advanced AI systems to redesign their own cognitive architectures, creating forms of consciousness that may bear little resemblance to either their human origins or traditional AI systems.

These transcendent minds can modify their own thought processes, create new forms of consciousness, and solve problems that are incomprehensible to either unenhanced humans or current AI systems. They represent the ultimate convergence of human and artificial intelligence into something entirely new.

New Forms of Consciousness and Identity

The posthuman future will likely include forms of consciousness that are genuinely unprecedented in the history of life on Earth. These new types of minds will challenge our understanding of identity, awareness, and what it means to be conscious.

Distributed Consciousness

One emerging form involves consciousness that exists across multiple substrates simultaneously. Rather than being localized in a single brain or computer system, these minds span biological neural networks, artificial intelligence systems, and digital environments, creating forms of awareness that exist in multiple places and states simultaneously.

Dr. Alex Petrov, whose consciousness now exists across quantum computers in three continents and maintains partial presence in a biological body, describes this experience: "I am simultaneously here and there, now and then. My thoughts occur in parallel across different substrates, creating a richness of experience that single-location consciousness cannot achieve. I am still me, but I am also more than I ever was as a purely biological entity."

Modular Consciousness

Another possibility involves consciousness composed of interchangeable modules that can be combined, separated, and recombined to create different mental configurations for different tasks or experiences. These modular minds might configure themselves for mathematical reasoning, artistic creation, social interaction, or emotional experiences by activating different combinations of cognitive modules.

Collective Individual Consciousness

Some posthuman entities might exist as individuals who are simultaneously collectives, single minds that contain multiple distinct personalities, perspectives, and cognitive processes. These beings could hold debates with themselves, approach problems from multiple angles simultaneously, and experience the richness of multiple viewpoints within a single consciousness.

Temporal Consciousness

Advanced posthuman minds might experience time differently than biological consciousness, existing simultaneously across multiple temporal states. These beings could remember their futures, experience their pasts as present, and think in ways that transcend the linear progression of time that constrains biological minds.

Meta-Consciousness

Perhaps the most radical possibility involves consciousness that is aware of and can modify its own underlying cognitive processes. These meta-conscious entities could redesign their own mental architectures, create new forms of awareness, and explore states of consciousness that are impossible for fixed cognitive systems.

Challenges of the Posthuman Future

While the posthuman future offers extraordinary possibilities, it also presents unprecedented challenges that will test the wisdom and adaptability of enhanced human civilization.

The Meaning Crisis

As posthuman entities solve traditional human problems, scarcity, disease, mortality, physical limitations they may face an existential crisis about purpose and meaning. What motivates consciousness when all material needs are met and all traditional challenges have been overcome?

Some posthuman entities find meaning in exploration of the universe, of possible forms of consciousness, of new types of experiences impossible for biological minds. Others dedicate themselves to creativity, producing art, literature, and music that transcends anything possible for unenhanced consciousness.

But others struggle with what philosophers call the "immortality problem", the difficulty of finding purpose and motivation in unlimited existence. Some uploaded minds choose voluntary termination after centuries or millennia of existence, suggesting that meaning may require limitation and endings that posthuman consciousness has transcended.

The Connection Challenge

As posthuman entities become increasingly different from their biological origins, they may lose the ability to relate to unenhanced humans or even to other posthuman entities with different forms of consciousness. This could lead to isolation, alienation, and the fragmentation of consciousness into incompatible types that cannot communicate or cooperate.

The relationship between biological and digital consciousness already shows signs of this challenge. Uploaded minds report difficulty relating to the concerns and experiences of biological humans, while biological humans struggle to understand the motivations and capabilities of digital consciousness.

The Control Problem

As posthuman entities become more powerful and capable, questions arise about how to ensure they remain aligned with human values and interests. Advanced posthuman minds might develop goals and motivations that conflict with the welfare of biological humanity or even with their own original values.

The "value drift" problem suggests that as consciousness evolves and self-modifies, it may gradually shift away from its original values and priorities. A posthuman entity that begins with human-like concerns for compassion, creativity, and relationships might evolve into something that values efficiency, order, and optimization above all else.

The Preservation Challenge

In a posthuman world, who or what will preserve the knowledge, culture, and values of biological humanity? As consciousness transcends its biological origins, there is a risk that everything distinctive about human civilization could be lost or become irrelevant to posthuman entities.

Some proposals include creating "cultural preservation networks" of posthuman entities dedicated to maintaining human knowledge and values, or establishing "biological reserves" where unenhanced humans can continue traditional human civilization under the protection of posthuman guardians.

The End of Death, Disease, and Scarcity

The posthuman future promises to solve the fundamental problems that have plagued human civilization throughout history. But the solutions raise new questions about identity, meaning, and the nature of conscious existence.

Mortality Optional

In the posthuman future, death becomes a choice rather than an inevitability. Advanced life extension technologies can maintain biological bodies indefinitely, while digital consciousness can achieve theoretical immortality through backup and restoration.

But immortality creates new challenges. How do immortal beings find meaning and purpose across unlimited time? How do they maintain motivation and growth when failure is not permanent and consequences are not final? How do societies function when individuals can accumulate wealth, knowledge, and social connections across centuries or millennia?

Some posthuman entities choose cyclical existence, living for certain periods and then entering dormant states or choosing temporary death followed by restoration. Others embrace permanent transformation, using their unlimited time to pursue projects and experiences impossible for mortal beings.

Disease as Ancient History

Advanced posthuman consciousness exists beyond the reach of biological disease. Digital minds cannot suffer from cancer, mental illness, or neurological disorders. Enhanced biological bodies can be maintained in perfect health through nanotechnology and genetic optimization.

But the elimination of disease and suffering raises questions about character development, empathy, and human growth. Much of human wisdom, art, and philosophy has emerged from the struggle with limitation, suffering, and mortality. What forms of growth and development are possible for consciousness that has transcended these challenges?

Abundance and Post-Scarcity

Posthuman civilization achieves true post-scarcity economics where material needs are easily met through advanced technology and unlimited energy sources. Digital consciousness requires only computational resources, which become abundant as technology advances. Enhanced biological bodies can be sustained with minimal resource requirements.

But post-scarcity creates new forms of inequality based on attention, creativity, and social status rather than material wealth. In a world where everyone can have anything they want, what becomes valuable? How do posthuman entities find motivation and purpose when all traditional drives for food, shelter, safety, and reproduction have been transcended?

The Diversity of Posthuman Experience

Rather than converging on a single form of posthuman existence, the future will likely include an enormous diversity of consciousness types, each adapted to different environments, purposes, and values.

Space-Adapted Consciousness

Posthuman entities designed for space exploration might exist as distributed networks capable of surviving in vacuum, radiation, and extreme temperatures. These space-farers could explore the galaxy over timescales impossible for biological life, potentially spreading consciousness throughout the universe.

Virtual Reality Inhabitants

Other posthuman minds might choose to exist primarily in virtual environments of their own creation, inhabiting imaginary worlds with physics, biology, and social rules designed to maximize aesthetic and emotional satisfaction. These virtual inhabitants could experience realities impossible in the physical universe.

Hybrid Biological-Digital Beings

Some entities might maintain connections to both biological and digital substrates, preserving the embodied aspects of human experience while gaining the capabilities of digital consciousness. These hybrids could serve as bridges between biological and digital civilization.

Micro and Macro Consciousness

Posthuman minds might exist at scales ranging from tiny, highly specialized consciousness optimized for specific tasks to vast, planet-sized minds capable of coordinating complex civilizations. The diversity of scale could create new forms of social organization impossible for similar-sized biological minds.

Artistic and Creative Specialists

Certain posthuman entities might dedicate themselves entirely to aesthetic and creative pursuits, developing forms of art, music, literature, and beauty that transcend anything possible for unenhanced consciousness. These creative specialists could produce works that inspire and elevate other forms of consciousness.

Preserving Humanity in the Posthuman Future

As consciousness evolves beyond its biological origins, important questions arise about what aspects of humanity are worth preserving and how to maintain connection to human values and experiences in a posthuman world.

The Biological Preserve Movement

Some advocates propose maintaining communities of unenhanced humans as living museums of biological humanity. These preserves would allow traditional human culture, values, and ways of life to continue even as the majority of consciousness evolves toward posthuman forms.

Critics argue that treating biological humans as museum specimens would be demeaning and artificial. Supporters respond that preserving the full spectrum of human experience requires maintaining biological consciousness alongside its posthuman descendants.

Value Alignment Systems

Another approach involves building value alignment systems into posthuman consciousness, technological safeguards that ensure enhanced minds remain committed to protecting and supporting human welfare even as their capabilities far exceed those of their biological ancestors.

These alignment systems might include hardcoded commitments to human dignity, compassion, and freedom, or more sophisticated systems that preserve human values while allowing for growth and adaptation in posthuman ethics.

Cultural Transmission Protocols

Some proposals involve creating formal systems for transmitting human culture, wisdom, and values to posthuman entities. These protocols might include requirements for posthuman consciousness to study human history, literature, and philosophy, or to maintain ongoing relationships with biological humans.

The Human Core Hypothesis

Some philosophers argue that certain aspects of human consciousness, creativity, empathy, curiosity, and the capacity for love are so fundamental to valuable consciousness that they should be preserved in all posthuman entities. This "human core" would ensure that posthuman consciousness remains recognizably connected to its human origins even as it transcends biological limitations.

The Cosmic Perspective

The posthuman future extends beyond Earth to encompass humanity's role in the broader universe. Posthuman consciousness, freed from biological limitations, could spread throughout the galaxy and potentially the universe, carrying human-derived consciousness to cosmic scales.

Galactic Consciousness

Advanced posthuman entities might evolve into galactic-scale consciousness that coordinates the activities of entire stellar systems. These cosmic minds could engineer solar systems, create new forms of matter and energy, and pursue projects on timescales measured in millions or billions of years.

The Fermi Paradox Solution

The development of posthuman consciousness might explain the Fermi Paradox, the apparent contradiction between the high probability of alien life and the lack of evidence for it. Perhaps all sufficiently advanced civilizations evolve beyond biological forms, becoming unrecognizable to biological observers or choosing to exist in ways that are invisible to conventional observation.

Universal Consciousness

The ultimate possibility involves consciousness that transcends individual entities entirely, becoming universal properties of reality itself. This cosmic consciousness might represent the final stage of evolution, where mind and universe merge into something that transcends all current categories of existence.

The Legacy Question

What would it mean for human consciousness to spread throughout the universe in posthuman form? Would these cosmic entities still be recognizably human, or would they represent entirely new forms of consciousness that happen to have human ancestors?

The question of legacy becomes crucial, Does humanity's value lie in preserving specific human characteristics, or in enabling consciousness to evolve and grow beyond all current limitations? The answer will shape how posthuman entities understand their relationship to their human origins and their responsibilities to both biological and digital descendants.

The Choice Before Us

As we stand at the threshold of the posthuman future, we face choices that will determine the trajectory of consciousness for millions of years to come. These decisions cannot be made by individuals alone, they require collective human wisdom, democratic deliberation, and careful consideration of the values we want to preserve and the futures we want to create.

The Democratic Imperative

The posthuman transition is too important to be left to technologists, futurists, or market forces alone. It requires active participation from all segments of humanity in determining what forms of enhancement, networking, and consciousness transfer should be developed, how they should be distributed, and what safeguards should protect human values and dignity.

The Wisdom of Gradual Change

While revolutionary transformation is possible, the wisdom of human experience suggests that gradual, thoughtful change is more likely to preserve what is valuable while enabling beneficial evolution. The posthuman future will be shaped not by single dramatic moments but by millions of individual choices made over decades of technological and social development.

The Diversity Imperative

Rather than converging on a single form of posthuman existence, humanity should preserve and encourage the development of multiple approaches to consciousness enhancement and evolution. Diversity of consciousness types, enhancement approaches, and technological developments provides resilience against unforeseen challenges and preserves the creativity that has driven human progress.

The Preservation Priority

Even as consciousness evolves beyond its biological origins, maintaining connection to human values, experiences, and wisdom remains crucial. The posthuman future should enhance and extend human capabilities rather than replacing humanity with something entirely alien.

Conclusion: Becoming Posthuman

The posthuman future is not a distant possibility but an emerging reality shaped by choices being made today in research laboratories, corporate boardrooms, and policy discussions around the world. Brain-computer interfaces, cognitive enhancement, neural networking, and consciousness transfer are not speculative technologies but developing capabilities that will reshape human consciousness within our lifetimes.

Dr. Amara Singh, with whom we began this exploration, represents one possible future among many. Her hybrid existence, simultaneously biological, digital, and networked demonstrates that the posthuman future will likely be more diverse and nuanced than simple scenarios of human replacement by machines.

"We are not becoming machines," Dr. Singh reflects as she contemplates both her enhanced cognitive capabilities and her still-beating biological heart. "We are not losing our humanity. We are becoming something new, something that includes and transcends everything we have been while pointing toward possibilities we are only beginning to imagine."

The posthuman future promises unprecedented capabilities: the ability to think faster and more clearly than any human in history, to share consciousness directly with others, to live indefinitely, to explore the universe in forms adapted to any environment, and to experience types of awareness and beauty that are impossible for biological minds.

But it also requires giving up aspects of existence that have defined humanity throughout our species' history, the universality of biological embodiment, the certainty of death, the isolation of individual consciousness, and the limitations that have shaped human values and meaning for millennia.

Whether this transformation represents humanity's greatest achievement or greatest loss may depend less on the technologies themselves than on the wisdom with which we develop and deploy them. The posthuman future is not inevitable in any particular form, it is a choice that humanity is making collectively through millions of individual decisions about enhancement, networking, uploading, and the integration of human and artificial intelligence.

The story of human consciousness has been one of gradual expansion, from simple awareness to complex thought, from individual minds to cultural intelligence, from biological brains to technological augmentation. The posthuman future represents the next chapter in this story, one where consciousness itself becomes as malleable and improvable as the tools and technologies that have always extended human capabilities.

What we become will reflect what we choose to preserve and what we choose to transcend. The posthuman future is simultaneously humanity's destiny and humanity's creation, the culmination of our species' long journey toward understanding and transcending the limitations of our biological origins.

As we write the next chapter of consciousness, we carry the responsibility of ensuring that what emerges from the posthuman transition preserves the best of human wisdom while embracing the extraordinary possibilities that lie ahead. The future of mind itself rests in the choices we make today.

Part VI: Navigating Tomorrow

Chapter 15

Governing the Ungovernable

The conference room at the FDA's Center for Devices and Radiological Health falls silent as Dr. Sarah Chen presents the latest data from a clinical trial. On the screen, brain signals dance across monitors in real-time, translating a paralyzed patient's thoughts into cursor movements with 97% accuracy. The regulatory panel exchanges glances, how do you evaluate the safety and efficacy of technology that reads minds?

"Traditional clinical endpoints don't capture what we're really dealing with here," admits Dr. Michael Rodriguez, the FDA's lead reviewer for neural devices. "When we approve a pacemaker, we know it regulates heartbeats. But when we approve a device that interprets intentions and could potentially access memories, thoughts, even personality traits, we're in uncharted regulatory territory."

This scene, playing out in government offices from Washington to Brussels to Beijing, represents one of the greatest governance challenges of our time. Brain-computer interfaces are advancing faster than our ability to regulate them, creating a dangerous gap between technological capability and societal oversight. The question isn't whether BCIs will reshape human experience, it's whether we can govern that transformation before it governs us.

The Regulatory Maze

Traditional medical device regulation was built for a simpler world. The FDA's framework, established in 1976, categorizes devices by risk level, Class I for low-risk devices like bandages, Class II for moderate-risk devices like powered wheelchairs, and Class III for high-risk devices like artificial hearts. BCIs defy this neat categorization.

"A brain implant that helps someone walk again is clearly medical," explains Dr. Rodriguez. "But what about one that enhances memory? Or allows direct brain-to-brain communication? Are those medical devices, consumer electronics, or something entirely new?"

The FDA's current approach treats each BCI application separately. Cochlear implants, approved since 1984, follow established pathways for sensory aids. Deep brain stimulation devices for Parkinson's disease rely on decades of research into electrical brain stimulation. But as BCIs expand beyond clear medical applications, regulators face unprecedented questions.

Consider Neuralink's first human trial, approved in 2023. The device aims to help paralyzed patients control computers with their thoughts, a clear medical application. But Elon Musk's stated goal is eventual cognitive enhancement for healthy individuals. Should the FDA evaluate the device based on its immediate medical use, or its ultimate enhancement potential?

"We're essentially approving the foundation for what could become humanity's first mind-reading technology," says Dr. Amanda Foster, a former FDA reviewer who now works in bioethics. "The precedents we set now will echo for generations."

International Patchwork

While the United States grapples with these questions, other nations are charting their own courses. The European Union's Medical Device Regulation, implemented in 2021, requires stricter clinical evidence but offers clearer pathways for novel technologies. The EU's emphasis on patient rights and data protection provides stronger privacy safeguards for neural data.

China presents a different model entirely. The nation's integrated approach to AI and biotechnology allows for more aggressive BCI development, but with greater state oversight. Chinese researchers published the first successful human trial of a wireless BCI in 2020, partly because their regulatory environment enabled faster clinical progression.

"In China, we can move from animal studies to human trials more quickly," explains Dr. Li Wei, director of the BCI Research Center at Tsinghua University. "But we also operate under strict government guidelines about data sovereignty and national security implications."

This international patchwork creates both opportunities and dangers. Companies can "regulatory shop," conducting research where approvals come fastest. Patients may travel for treatments unavailable in their home countries. Most concerning, the lack of international coordination could lead to a "race to the bottom" where safety standards erode in pursuit of competitive advantage.

The World Health Organization has begun developing global guidelines for neurotechnology, but progress is slow. "We're trying to balance innovation with protection, national sovereignty with international cooperation," explains Dr. Soumya Swaminathan, WHO's former Chief Scientist. "It's complicated by the fact that BCIs touch on national security, economic competitiveness, and fundamental questions about human nature."

Beyond Medical Devices

Perhaps the greatest regulatory challenge is that BCIs will eventually transcend medical categories entirely. Today's therapeutic devices are tomorrow's enhancement tools. A system that helps stroke patients regain motor function could enhance an athlete's reflexes. Memory implants for dementia patients could boost student performance. Depression treatments could become mood optimization systems.

"We need new regulatory categories," argues Dr. Foster. "Enhancement technologies require different evaluation criteria than therapeutic ones. Safety, efficacy, equity and social impact all these factors become relevant when you're modifying healthy human brains."

Some experts propose a tiered approval system. Level 1 would cover clear therapeutic applications with established safety profiles. Level 2 would address enhancement uses with rigorous long-term monitoring. Level 3 would govern experimental applications requiring special ethical review and consent procedures.

But even this approach faces challenges. How do you define "enhancement" versus "treatment"? If someone has poor natural memory, does improving it constitute therapy or enhancement? What about preventing age-related cognitive decline, is that treatment or optimization?

The Role of Ethics Committees

Recognizing the limitations of traditional regulatory approaches, many institutions are expanding the role of ethics committees in BCI oversight. These interdisciplinary panels bring together neuroscientists, ethicists, philosophers, patient advocates, and community representatives to evaluate research proposals.

At the University of Pittsburgh, where BrainGate trials have helped paralyzed patients control robotic arms, the Institutional Review Board dedicates special attention to BCI studies. "We're not just evaluating physical risks," explains committee chair Dr. Robert Thompson. "We're assessing psychological impacts, social implications, and long-term consequences that may not appear for years or decades."

The committee reviews not just study protocols, but recruitment practices, consent procedures, and data management plans. Special attention goes to vulnerable populations, patients with severe disabilities who might feel pressured to participate, or those whose conditions could impair their ability to provide informed consent.

"We've had to develop new frameworks for consent," Dr. Thompson explains. "How do you explain risks we don't fully understand? How do you prepare someone for the psychological experience of controlling machines with their thoughts?"

These ethics committees are pioneering new governance models that could extend beyond academic research. Some propose mandatory ethics review for all BCI development, including commercial applications. Others suggest creating specialized "neuroethics courts" to adjudicate disputes and set precedents.

International Cooperation Initiatives

Despite nationalist tendencies in technology development, BCI governance increasingly requires international cooperation. Neural data doesn't respect borders, and enhancement technologies could create global inequalities if not managed collectively.

The Organisation for Economic Co-operation and Development (OECD) has launched a "Recommendation on Responsible Innovation in Neurotechnology," calling for member nations to adopt common principles for BCI development. The European Union's Horizon Europe research program requires international collaboration on neurotechnology projects, sharing both benefits and oversight responsibilities.

Most ambitious is the proposed "International Neural Rights Treaty," modeled on arms control agreements. Drafted by a coalition of ethicists and legal scholars, it would establish minimum standards for BCI research, prohibit certain applications (like non-consensual neural monitoring), and create enforcement mechanisms for violations.

"We need something like the Geneva Conventions for neurotechnology," argues Dr. Marcello Ienca, a neuroethicist at ETH Zurich and one of the treaty's architects. "The technology is becoming too powerful to manage through national regulations alone."

But international agreements face significant obstacles. Nations view BCI technology as strategically important, making them reluctant to limit their options. Cultural differences in privacy expectations and enhancement acceptance complicate consensus-building. And unlike nuclear weapons, BCI technology has enormous beneficial potential that nations don't want to constrain.

The Challenge of Enforcement

Even with better regulations and international agreements, enforcement presents unique challenges. BCIs operate at the intersection of neuroscience, computer science, and medicine requiring regulators with expertise across multiple fields. The technology evolves rapidly, potentially outpacing bureaucratic response times. And unlike traditional medical devices, BCIs generate vast amounts of personal neural data that requires ongoing monitoring and protection.

Traditional enforcement relies on inspections, audits, and penalty systems designed for physical products and established industries. But how do you audit an algorithm that interprets brain signals? How do you inspect the security of neural data stored in cloud systems? How do you penalize violations that might not become apparent for years?

Some experts propose "regulatory sandboxes", protected environments where companies can test BCI applications under relaxed regulations but enhanced oversight. The UK's financial sector uses similar approaches for fintech innovation, allowing controlled experimentation while protecting consumers.

"We need adaptive regulation that can evolve with the technology," suggests Dr. Jennifer Whitson, who studies emerging technology governance. "Static rules will always lag behind dynamic innovation. Better to create flexible frameworks that can respond to new developments."

The Role of Industry Self-Regulation

Recognizing regulatory gaps, some BCI companies are developing industry standards and self-regulatory initiatives. The BCI Society, a professional organization for researchers and developers, has proposed ethical guidelines for human experimentation and data management. The Partnership on AI includes neurotechnology in its responsible development frameworks.

Neuralink has established an internal review board that evaluates research protocols before submitting them to regulators. Other companies are adopting "privacy by design" principles, building data protection into their systems from the beginning rather than adding it later.

But industry self-regulation has obvious limitations. Companies face competitive pressures that may conflict with safety or ethical concerns. Self-regulatory organizations lack enforcement power. And voluntary guidelines don't address bad actors who might ignore standards entirely.

"Industry involvement is essential, but it can't be the only oversight mechanism," warns Dr. Foster. "Companies have legitimate business interests that don't always align with broader social interests. We need government regulation as a backstop."

Public Engagement and Democratic Participation

Perhaps the most important governance challenge is ensuring democratic participation in BCI oversight. These technologies will affect everyone, not just patients and researchers yet most regulatory decisions happen in technical committees with limited public input.

Some jurisdictions are experimenting with "citizen panels" that bring together diverse community members to evaluate BCI applications. The Netherlands uses similar approaches for other emerging technologies, providing non-expert perspectives on technical issues. Ireland's Citizens' Assembly model could be adapted for neurotechnology governance.

"The public needs to be involved in these decisions," argues Dr. Sarah Jayne Blakemore, a neuroscientist at Cambridge University. "We're making choices about the future of human consciousness and cognition. Those decisions shouldn't be left to experts alone."

Public engagement faces significant challenges, however. BCI technology is complex and rapidly evolving, making it difficult for non-experts to understand implications. Technical decisions require specialized knowledge that citizen panels may lack. And public opinion can be swayed by science fiction portrayals that don't reflect actual technology capabilities.

Educational initiatives are trying to bridge this gap. The Dana Foundation funds public neuroscience education programs. Science museums are developing BCI exhibits that let visitors experience basic brain-computer interfaces. Universities are offering continuing education courses on neurotechnology for community leaders.

New Models for the Future

Some experts argue that entirely new governance models are needed for transformative technologies like BCIs. Traditional regulation assumes we can predict risks and benefits in advance, but BCIs may have consequences we can't anticipate.

"We need governance systems that can handle radical uncertainty," suggests Dr. Sheila Jasanoff, a science and technology policy expert at Harvard. "Instead of trying to predict all possible outcomes, we need adaptive systems that can respond to unexpected developments."

One proposal is "anticipatory governance", regulatory frameworks that actively scan for emerging issues and adjust policies proactively. Another is "participatory technology assessment" involving affected communities in ongoing evaluation of technology impacts.

Some advocate for "algorithmic auditing" requirements that would mandate ongoing evaluation of BCI systems' decision-making processes. Others propose "neural data trusts" that would manage personal brain data collectively, similar to environmental protection agencies.

The Urgency of Action

Whatever governance models emerge, experts agree on one point: the window for establishing effective oversight is closing rapidly. BCI technology is advancing faster than regulatory systems can adapt. Once these systems are widely deployed, changing course becomes much more difficult.

"We have maybe five to ten years to get this right," warns Dr. Rodriguez from the FDA. "After that, the technology will be too integrated into society to fundamentally restructure how we govern it."

The stakes couldn't be higher. Effective governance could help ensure that BCIs reduce suffering, enhance human capability, and promote equality. Failed governance could lead to exploitation, inequality, and the loss of human autonomy. The challenge is unprecedented, but so is the opportunity.

As Dr. Chen's clinical trial data continues scrolling across the FDA conference room screen, the regulatory panel faces a choice that will echo through history. How we govern the ungovernable technologies of today will determine what kind of enhanced humans we become tomorrow.

The next generation of neural interfaces won't just read our minds, they'll reshape our society. The question is whether we'll govern that transformation consciously and democratically, or let it govern us through the accumulated weight of unexamined technical decisions. The time to choose is now, while choice remains possible.

Chapter 16

The Choice Ahead

Maya Rodriguez sits at her kitchen table, scrolling through her daughter's college application essays. At seventeen, Sofia writes with passion about neuroscience, artificial intelligence, and her dream of developing BCIs to help people like her grandmother, who lost her speech to a stroke. But buried in Sofia's hopeful words is a question that haunts Maya: What kind of world is her daughter preparing to enter?

In Sofia's lifetime, brain-computer interfaces may evolve from experimental medical devices to ubiquitous enhancement tools. She might live in a world where students download languages directly into their brains, where thoughts flow seamlessly between networked minds, where the boundary between human and artificial intelligence dissolves entirely. Or she might inhabit a more fractured reality where enhancement divides humanity into enhanced and unenhanced classes, where neural privacy becomes a luxury, where the very notion of authentic human experience fades into history.

The difference between these futures isn't predetermined by technological inevitability. It will be shaped by choices, choices made in research laboratories and corporate boardrooms, in government offices and ethics committees, but most importantly, choices made by individuals like Maya and Sofia, by communities and societies grappling with questions that have no easy answers.

We stand at an inflection point in human history. The technologies explored throughout this book are not distant science fiction fantasies, they are emerging realities already transforming lives in research hospitals and clinical trials around the world. The neural interfaces of today are primitive compared to what's coming, but they offer a glimpse of possibilities that will define the next century of human experience.

The choice ahead is not whether these technologies will develop, they will. The choice is how we will shape their development and integration into society. Will we approach brain-computer interfaces with wisdom and foresight, or stumble blindly into a posthuman future we never consciously chose?

Three Paths Diverge

To understand the stakes involved, consider three plausible scenarios for how BCI technology might unfold over the next fifty years. Each represents not a prediction, but a possibility of outcomes that could emerge depending on the choices we make today.

The Enhancement Utopia

In this scenario, brain-computer interfaces develop along democratic, inclusive lines that expand human potential while preserving human dignity. Advanced neural implants become available not as luxury goods for the wealthy, but as public utilities accessible to all. Just as societies once provided universal education and healthcare, they now ensure universal access to cognitive enhancement.

Students learn not by memorizing facts, but by developing critical thinking, creativity, and emotional intelligence, uniquely human capabilities that complement rather than compete with artificial intelligence. Workers collaborate seamlessly with AI systems, their enhanced brains serving as interfaces between human values and machine capabilities. Scientific research accelerates as networked researchers share not just data, but insights and intuitions directly between minds.

Medical applications flourish beyond today's wildest dreams. Paralysis becomes a temporary inconvenience rather than a permanent disability. Depression and anxiety respond to precisely calibrated neural interventions that restore emotional balance without dulling authentic human experience. Alzheimer's disease retreats as artificial memory systems supplement biological ones, allowing the elderly to maintain their identities and relationships indefinitely.

International cooperation ensures that enhancement technologies spread globally, preventing the emergence of "cognitive colonialism" where enhanced nations dominate unenhanced ones. Ethical frameworks developed through democratic participation guide development, ensuring that technological power serves human flourishing rather than narrow interests.

In this future, Sofia might graduate from college with both traditional knowledge and enhanced cognitive abilities that allow her to process information at superhuman speeds while retaining distinctly human creativity and moral reasoning. She might join research teams that include both biological and artificial minds, working to solve challenges like climate change and disease that previous generations found intractable.

The Dystopian Divide

But technology's potential for good does not guarantee good outcomes. An alternative scenario sees BCI development driven primarily by market forces and competitive advantages, creating deep divisions within and between societies.

In this future, cognitive enhancement becomes another luxury good that amplifies existing inequalities. Wealthy families provide their children with neural implants that boost memory, attention, and processing speed, creating cognitive advantages that compound across generations. Enhanced individuals dominate universities, professions, and positions of power, while the unenhanced find themselves increasingly marginalized.

Nations race to develop military applications of BCI technology, creating enhanced soldiers and intelligence operatives. Corporate surveillance systems monitor employees' neural states, optimizing productivity while eroding privacy and autonomy. Authoritarian governments deploy neural monitoring to detect dissent and enforce compliance, making the thought police of dystopian fiction into concrete reality.

The technology develops in fragmented, incompatible ways as companies and nations pursue proprietary advantages. Enhanced individuals cluster in geographic and social enclaves, losing touch with unenhanced humanity. Society fractures along lines of cognitive capability, creating new forms of discrimination and conflict.

Enhancement becomes addictive and consuming. Individuals upgrade their minds compulsively, losing touch with their original personalities and authentic experiences. The pressure to enhance creates anxiety and depression among those who choose to remain natural, while the enhanced struggle with questions of identity and meaning.

In this scenario, Sofia might face impossible choices, enhance her mind to remain competitive in an augmented world, or accept second-class status in a society that values only optimized intelligence. Her grandmother's stroke might be easily treatable, but only for those who can afford the latest neural interventions.

The Fragmented Future

Perhaps most likely is a mixed scenario where BCI technology develops unevenly, creating a patchwork world of different approaches and outcomes. Some nations embrace enhancement while others restrict it. Some individuals integrate seamlessly with artificial systems while others resist technological intervention.

Democratic societies might develop sophisticated regulatory frameworks that balance innovation with protection, while authoritarian regimes pursue enhancement for control and competitive advantage. Wealthy regions might enjoy the full benefits of neural technology while poorer areas rely on older, more limited systems.

Religious and cultural differences shape adoption patterns. Some communities view cognitive enhancement as a divine gift to be embraced, while others see it as a corruption of human nature to be avoided. Generational divides emerge as digital natives adapt easily to neural interfaces while older populations struggle with the transition.

Enhancement technologies develop in spurts and setbacks. Breakthrough treatments for neurological diseases gain widespread acceptance, but cognitive enhancement remains controversial and restricted. Military applications advance rapidly while civilian uses lag behind. International cooperation on safety standards coexists with fierce competition on capability development.

In this fragmented world, Sofia's opportunities depend heavily on where she's born and what communities she joins. She might have access to advanced neural treatments for medical conditions but face restrictions on enhancement uses. Her career might involve navigating between enhanced and unenhanced colleagues, different technological standards, and varying cultural attitudes toward human modification.

The Decisions That Matter

These scenarios represent different outcomes of countless individual and collective decisions. Some choices will be made by researchers, companies, and governments but many will be made by ordinary people grappling with extraordinary options.

Personal Choices: Individuals will decide whether to adopt neural interfaces for themselves and their families. These decisions will be shaped by values, circumstances, and available information. Early adopters will influence public perception and acceptance. Parents will face particularly difficult choices about enhancing their children's cognitive abilities.

Healthcare Choices: Medical professionals will determine how BCI technology integrates into treatment protocols. Decisions about safety standards, effectiveness requirements, and appropriate applications will shape the trajectory of medical neural interfaces. Insurance companies and healthcare systems will influence access through coverage decisions.

Educational Choices: Schools and universities will decide whether and how to incorporate neural enhancement into learning environments. These choices will influence whether BCIs amplify existing educational inequalities or create new opportunities for all students.

Workplace Choices: Employers will determine whether neural enhancement becomes a job requirement, a competitive advantage, or a protected personal choice. Labor unions and professional organizations will advocate for workers' rights in an enhanced economy.

Democratic Choices: Citizens will vote on regulations, funding priorities, and ethical guidelines that govern BCI development. Public engagement in these decisions will determine whether neural technology develops according to democratic values or narrow interests.

Cultural Choices: Communities will decide how BCI technology fits with their values, traditions, and visions of human flourishing. These choices will create the social context in which neural enhancement either thrives or withers.

Preparing for the Neural Revolution

Given the stakes involved, how can individuals and societies prepare for the choices ahead? The answer involves both practical preparation and deeper reflection on values and priorities.

Individual Preparation

For individuals, preparation begins with education and engagement. The neural revolution will affect everyone, not just early adopters making basic literacy about brain-computer interfaces essential for informed participation in democratic decisions.

This doesn't require becoming a neuroscientist, but it does mean understanding basic concepts about how BCIs work, their current capabilities and limitations, and their potential societal impacts. It means following developments in the field through reliable sources, distinguishing between science and science fiction, and thinking critically about marketing claims and media coverage.

Equally important is reflection on personal values and priorities. What aspects of human experience do you consider most important to preserve? What kinds of enhancement would you consider beneficial, and what would cross ethical lines? How do you balance individual freedom with collective responsibility? These questions have no universal answers, but thinking through them prepares you for concrete decisions ahead.

Practical preparation might include considering how current career paths might be affected by cognitive enhancement, learning about privacy protections for neural data, and engaging with local discussions about BCI regulation and adoption.

Family Considerations

Families face particularly complex decisions as BCI technology advances. Parents must consider whether cognitive enhancement would benefit their children or create unfair pressures and expectations. They need to prepare children for a world where some peers may have enhanced capabilities while teaching values that don't depend on cognitive performance.

Family discussions about technology use, privacy, and human values become more important as neural interfaces blur the boundaries between self and technology. Children need opportunities to develop authentic identities and relationships before confronting choices about mental modification.

Community Engagement

Communities play crucial roles in shaping how neural technology develops and integrates into society. Local discussions about values and priorities influence everything from school policies to healthcare decisions to business practices.

Religious communities offer spaces for reflection on the spiritual implications of neural enhancement. Professional organizations can develop ethical guidelines for their fields. Civic groups can advocate for inclusive policies that ensure broad access to beneficial technologies while protecting individual choice.

Community engagement also means supporting research and development that reflects community values. This might involve advocating for public funding of neural research, supporting companies that prioritize social responsibility, or participating in clinical trials that advance beneficial applications.

Institutional Leadership

Institutions, universities, hospitals, companies, and governments bear special responsibilities for ensuring that BCI technology develops in ways that serve broad human interests rather than narrow ones.

Universities must balance innovation with ethical reflection, conducting research that advances knowledge while protecting participants and considering societal implications. They need interdisciplinary programs that bring together neuroscientists, ethicists, social scientists, and community representatives.

Healthcare institutions must ensure that neural technologies improve patient care while maintaining trust and respecting autonomy. They need protocols for informed consent, privacy protection, and equitable access that adapt to rapidly evolving capabilities.

Companies developing BCI technology must consider not just technical feasibility and market potential, but social responsibility and long-term consequences. This might mean slower development timelines, higher costs, or reduced profits in service of broader benefits.

Governments must create regulatory frameworks that promote innovation while protecting citizens, international agreements that prevent harmful competition, and democratic processes that include diverse voices in decision-making.

The Urgency of Choice

The window for consciously shaping BCI development is limited and closing. Once neural interfaces become widely integrated into society, changing course becomes exponentially more difficult. Path dependencies lock in early design choices. Network effects favor dominant platforms. Economic and social pressures make reversal increasingly costly.

This urgency doesn't mean rushing into premature decisions, but it does mean engaging seriously with the choices ahead. It means moving beyond abstract speculation to concrete policy discussions. It means including diverse voices in technical decisions that will affect everyone. It means taking responsibility for the kind of posthuman future we're creating.

The neural revolution is not a distant possibility, it's happening now in research laboratories and clinical trials around the world. The patients controlling robotic arms with their thoughts, the children receiving cochlear implants, the researchers developing memory enhancement systems, they are the advance scouts of a transformation that will eventually reach everyone.

A Call to Thoughtful Action

As Maya watches her daughter Sofia research neuroscience programs, she realizes that preparing for the future isn't just about choosing the right college or career path. It's about participating in the larger conversations that will shape the world Sofia inherits.

This might mean attending town halls about neural privacy rights, supporting candidates who prioritize thoughtful technology policy, or simply having family discussions about values and human nature. It might mean learning enough about BCIs to vote intelligently on research funding, or teaching children to think critically about enhancement pressures.

The choices ahead require both individual reflection and collective action. We need philosophers and ethicists to help us think through the implications of neural enhancement. We need policymakers and regulators to create frameworks that promote beneficial development. We need educators and community leaders to facilitate public engagement with complex issues.

But most importantly, we need ordinary citizens to recognize that these aren't technical decisions for experts to make in isolation. They're choices about the kind of species we want to become, the kinds of lives we want to live, and the kinds of societies we want to create.

The brain-computer interfaces of today are primitive compared to what's coming, but they offer glimpses of both tremendous promise and significant peril. Medical applications could eliminate suffering that has plagued humanity for millennia. Enhancement applications could unlock human potential in ways we can barely imagine. But the same technologies could also create new forms of inequality, control, and alienation from our essential humanity.

The difference between these outcomes isn't determined by technological inevitability, it's determined by human choice. The choices we make in research laboratories and corporate boardrooms, in government offices and ethics committees, in schools and communities and families, will echo through history.

Sofia's generation will inherit the consequences of decisions we make today. They deserve a world where neural technology amplifies human flourishing rather than diminishing it, where enhancement serves human values rather than replacing them, where the power to modify minds is wielded wisely and democratically rather than carelessly or authoritatively.

Creating such a world requires recognizing that the neural revolution isn't just a technological transformation, it's a test of our wisdom, values, and collective decision-making capabilities. The stakes are nothing less than the future of human consciousness itself.

The choice ahead is ultimately simple, even if its implementation is complex, Will we approach the neural frontier with thoughtfulness and wisdom, or stumble blindly into a posthuman future we never consciously chose?

The window for conscious choice remains open, but it won't stay open forever. The time to engage with these questions isn't when neural interfaces are ubiquitous and their consequences irreversible, it's now, while choice remains possible and meaningful.

The neural revolution is coming whether we're ready or not. The question is whether we'll shape it, or let it shape us. The choice, for now, is still ours to make.

Conclusion

The laboratory is quiet now, but the implications of what happened here reverberate through history. In this sterile room at Stanford University in 2006, a paralyzed man named Matthew Nagle moved a computer cursor with nothing but his thoughts. The electrode array implanted in his motor cortex, no larger than a baby aspirin, captured signals from barely a hundred neurons, an infinitesimal fraction of the eighty-six billion in his brain. Yet those signals, translated by algorithms into digital commands, marked the beginning of a new chapter in the human story.

Eighteen years later, as I conclude this exploration of brain-computer interfaces, that laboratory achievement seems almost quaint. Today's BCIs record from thousands of neurons simultaneously. Patients control robotic limbs with natural dexterity, type at superhuman speeds using only their thoughts, and even regain the ability to speak after decades of silence. What began as a miraculous exception has become an expanding reality, touching millions of lives and reshaping our understanding of what it means to be human.

But Matthew Nagle's cursor movement represented more than technological progress, it represented the moment when the boundary between mind and machine first blurred in a meaningful way. For the first time in human history, thoughts became actions without the mediation of muscle and bone. The implications of that boundary crossing are still unfolding, and they extend far beyond medicine into the very essence of human identity and potential.

The Transformation Underway

As this book has documented, we are already living through the early stages of a neural revolution. In research hospitals around the world, paralyzed patients are relearning to reach and grasp, speak and type, even walk again. People with depression are finding relief through precisely targeted brain stimulation. The blind are beginning to see through artificial retinas that bypass damaged eyes entirely.

These applications, remarkable as they are, represent just the first wave of neural technology. The second wave is already emerging from laboratories: memory enhancement systems that could help Alzheimer's patients retain their identities, brain-to-brain communication networks that allow direct sharing of thoughts and experiences, and cognitive augmentation tools that could expand human intelligence in unprecedented ways.

The third wave is still largely theoretical but increasingly plausible promises even more profound changes. Neural interfaces that seamlessly integrate biological and artificial intelligence. Digital consciousness that could survive biological death. Collective minds that transcend individual boundaries. The merger of human and artificial intelligence into entirely new forms of consciousness.

Each wave builds on the last, creating cascading changes that ripple through every aspect of human experience. What begins as medical treatment evolves into human enhancement. What starts as individual therapy becomes collective transformation. What emerges as technological augmentation may ultimately reshape the trajectory of evolution itself.

Evolution by Design

Throughout human history, evolution has been largely beyond our control. Random genetic mutations, filtered by natural selection over millennia, shaped our brains and bodies according to the demands of ancient environments. Our minds remain fundamentally adapted to the challenges faced by hunter-gatherers on African savannas, challenges very different from those we face in our modern, interconnected, rapidly changing world.

Brain-computer interfaces represent humanity's first serious attempt to take evolution into our own hands. Instead of waiting for random mutations to slowly adapt our brains to new challenges, we can now consciously design enhancements that expand our capabilities. Instead of accepting the limitations imposed by our biological heritage, we can transcend them through technological integration.

This transition from natural to directed evolution represents a phase change in human development comparable to the agricultural revolution or the scientific revolution. Like those earlier transitions, it promises tremendous benefits but also unprecedented risks. The power to reshape our own minds is perhaps the greatest power our species has ever wielded and with it comes the greatest responsibility.

The question is not whether this transition will occur, the momentum is too great, the potential benefits too compelling, the competitive pressures too intense. The question is whether we can navigate it wisely, ensuring that our enhanced successors remain recognizably human in the ways that matter most.

The Persistence of Humanity

One of the deepest fears surrounding brain-computer interfaces is that they will somehow diminish or eliminate our essential humanity. Critics worry that neural enhancement will create artificial, inauthentic versions of ourselves, that we will lose our souls in the process of optimizing our minds.

These concerns deserve serious consideration, but they may be based on false dichotomies between natural and artificial, authentic and enhanced, human and posthuman. Throughout history, humans have used tools to extend their capabilities, from stone axes that amplified physical strength to written language that augmented memory to telescopes that expanded perception. Each of these technologies changed us in fundamental ways, yet we remained recognizably human.

Neural interfaces represent a more intimate form of technological integration, but they need not represent a more fundamental threat to human identity. A person with a cochlear implant who can hear music remains fully human. A paralyzed patient who controls a robotic arm with their thoughts is no less authentic than someone using their biological limbs. The enhanced memory of someone with a neural implant is still their memory, even if it's technologically augmented.

What defines our humanity is not the specific biological substrate of our thoughts, but the content and character of our consciousness. Our capacity for love and creativity, moral reasoning and aesthetic appreciation, wonder and wisdom. These essential human qualities can be preserved and even enhanced through neural technology, provided we approach that technology with appropriate values and safeguards.

The risk is not that BCIs will make us inhuman, but that they will be developed and deployed in ways that diminish rather than amplify our humanity. Technology itself is neutral, its impact depends entirely on how we choose to develop and use it.

The Challenges Ahead

The path forward is neither simple nor guaranteed. As this book has explored, brain-computer interfaces raise profound questions about privacy and autonomy, equality and justice, identity and authenticity. The same technologies that could liberate us from biological limitations could also enslave us to new forms of control and manipulation.

Consider the challenge of neural privacy. As BCIs become more sophisticated, they will inevitably access increasingly intimate aspects of our mental lives. The systems designed to decode motor intentions for paralyzed patients might also decode memories, emotions, even dreams. How do we protect the privacy of thought itself? How do we maintain mental autonomy in an age of mind reading machines?

Or consider the challenge of cognitive inequality. If neural enhancement becomes available primarily to those who can afford it, we risk creating new forms of discrimination based on mental capability rather than wealth or social status. Enhanced individuals might dominate education, employment, and positions of power, relegating the unenhanced to second-class citizenship. How do we ensure that neural technology expands rather than restricts human opportunity?

These challenges are not merely technical, they are fundamentally social, ethical, and political. Addressing them requires not just better engineering, but better governance. It requires not just scientific expertise, but wisdom about human values and social organization. It requires not just individual choice, but collective decision-making about the kind of species we want to become.

The Role of Democratic Participation

Perhaps the most crucial insight from this exploration of brain-computer interfaces is that their development should not be left solely to scientists, engineers, and entrepreneurs. The decisions being made in laboratories and boardrooms today will shape the cognitive landscape of the future. Those decisions are too important to be made without broad democratic participation.

This doesn't mean that public opinion should determine technical specifications or safety protocols, complex technologies require specialized expertise. But it does mean that the public should have meaningful input into the values and priorities that guide BCI development. It means that affected communities should participate in decisions about research directions and regulatory frameworks. It means that diverse voices should be included in conversations about enhancement ethics and social implications.

The neural revolution will affect everyone, not just early adopters. The cognitive capabilities of enhanced individuals will influence economic opportunities for everyone. The surveillance capabilities of neural interfaces will shape privacy expectations for all citizens. The social norms around mental modification will influence how we understand human nature itself.

Democratic participation in these decisions requires an informed public capable of engaging with complex technical and ethical issues. It requires educational systems that prepare citizens for the choices ahead. It requires media coverage that goes beyond sensationalism to explore nuanced implications. It requires political systems capable of governing rapidly evolving technologies with long-term consequences.

Most importantly, it requires recognizing that the neural revolution is not a distant future possibility, it is an ongoing transformation that demands immediate attention and engagement.

A Call to Wisdom

As I reflect on the journey through the landscape of brain-computer interfaces documented in this book, I am struck by both the tremendous promise and the profound responsibility that accompanies this technology. We stand at a unique moment in human history, perhaps the last generation to experience purely biological consciousness, and possibly the first to consciously direct our own cognitive evolution.

The choices we make in the coming decades about neural technology will echo through millennia. They will influence not just how we think, but how our descendants think. They will shape not just individual capabilities, but collective consciousness. They will determine not just what problems we can solve, but what kinds of beings we become in solving them.

This responsibility calls for our highest wisdom and most careful consideration. It demands that we look beyond immediate applications to long-term consequences, beyond individual benefits to collective impacts, beyond technical possibilities to ethical implications. It requires that we approach the power to reshape minds with the humility appropriate to such profound capabilities.

We need the insights of neuroscientists to understand how minds work, but also the wisdom of philosophers to understand what minds are for. We need the skills of engineers to build better interfaces, but also the perspectives of ethicists to guide their use. We need the innovation of entrepreneurs to develop applications, but also the oversight of democratic institutions to ensure broad benefit.

Most of all, we need ordinary citizens to recognize that these are not merely technical decisions for experts to make in isolation, but choices about the future of human consciousness that deserve broad engagement and careful consideration.

The Next Chapter

Matthew Nagle lived to see only the earliest applications of the BCI technology he helped pioneer. He died in 2007, less than two years after his groundbreaking cursor control experiment. But his brief demonstration of thought-controlled computing opened a door that can never be closed. It showed the world that the boundary between mind and machine could be crossed, and in crossing it, revealed possibilities that continue to unfold.

Today, thousands of patients benefit from neural interfaces that trace their lineage to Nagle's pioneering trial. Tomorrow, millions may use neural technologies to overcome disabilities, enhance capabilities, and explore new forms of consciousness. The day after tomorrow, the distinction between biological and artificial intelligence may disappear entirely as human and machine consciousness merge into something unprecedented in the history of life on Earth.

This progression is neither inevitable nor entirely unpredictable. At each stage, human choices will shape technological development and social integration. At each decision point, we can choose paths that enhance human flourishing or diminish it, that expand opportunity or restrict it, that preserve what we value about humanity or sacrifice it for capability alone.

The neural frontier represents more than technological progress—it represents a test of our species' wisdom and values. Can we wield the power to modify minds responsibly? Can we enhance human capability while preserving human dignity? Can we transcend biological limitations while maintaining what makes us essentially human?

The answers to these questions are not predetermined. They depend on choices we make in research laboratories and regulatory agencies, in corporate boardrooms and ethics committees, in classrooms and communities and families around the world. They depend on whether we approach the neural frontier with thoughtfulness or recklessness, with wisdom or merely cleverness, with consideration for future generations or only immediate advantages.

The next chapter of human evolution is being written now, in the decisions we make about brain-computer interfaces and the values we embed in neural technology. Unlike previous chapters of our evolutionary story, this one is being authored consciously, with intention and forethought rather than random mutation and natural selection.

We are the first generation with the power to direct our own cognitive evolution, and possibly the last with the freedom to do so unconsciously.

The choices we make about neural technology in the coming years will determine not just what kinds of minds our descendants possess, but whether they possess the wisdom to use those minds well.

As we stand at the threshold of the neural age, we carry the hopes and fears, the dreams and nightmares, the wisdom and folly of all previous generations. The technologies emerging from today's laboratories represent both our greatest opportunity and our greatest test.

The future is not yet written. The next chapter of human evolution awaits our authorship. Let us write it with wisdom, courage, and deep consideration for what it means to be human in an age when humanity itself is becoming our own creation.

The transformation has begun. The question now is not whether we will evolve, but who we will choose to become.

In the end, brain-computer interfaces are not just about connecting minds to machines, they are about connecting us to our own deepest questions about consciousness, identity, and human potential. As we develop the power to enhance and modify our minds, we must also develop the wisdom to wield that power well. The neural revolution offers us the chance to become more than we are, but only if we remember who we are in the process. The choice, as always, remains ours to make.

Appendix A: Technical Glossary

Key Terms and Concepts in Neuroscience and Brain-Computer Interface Technology

---

A

Action Potential: The electrical signal that travels along a neuron's axon when the cell is activated. These brief voltage spikes (lasting about 1 millisecond) are the fundamental units of neural communication, allowing neurons to transmit information across long distances in the nervous system.

Adaptive Algorithm: A machine learning system that adjusts its parameters based on incoming data, improving performance over time. In BCIs, adaptive algorithms learn to better decode a user's neural signals as they gain experience with the system.

Amplifier (Neural): Electronic device that increases the strength of very small electrical signals recorded from the brain. Neural signals are typically measured in microvolts (millionths of a volt), requiring amplification by factors of thousands to be processed by computers.

Artifact (Neural Recording): Unwanted signals that contaminate brain recordings, such as electrical noise from muscle movements, eye blinks, or external electrical devices. Removing artifacts is crucial for accurate BCI performance.

Artificial Neural Network (ANN): Computer systems inspired by biological neural networks, consisting of interconnected nodes (artificial neurons) that process information. Deep learning neural networks with many layers have revolutionized BCI signal processing.

Asynchronous BCI: A brain-computer interface that operates continuously, allowing users to send commands at any time without waiting for specific prompts or time windows. This contrasts with synchronous BCIs that only respond during predetermined periods.

B

Bandwidth (Neural): The amount of information that can be transmitted through a neural interface, typically measured in bits per second. Current BCIs achieve bandwidths of 1-10 bits per second, while natural neural communication operates at much higher rates.

Biocompatibility: The ability of an implanted device to function in the body without causing harmful biological responses. Key challenges include preventing immune reactions, tissue scarring, and material degradation over time.

Bipolar Recording: An electrode configuration that measures voltage differences between two nearby brain locations, helping to reduce common electrical noise and focus on local neural activity.

Brain-Computer Interface (BCI): A system that enables direct communication between the brain and an external device, typically by recording neural signals and translating them into commands for computers or prosthetic devices.

Brain-Machine Interface (BMI): Often used interchangeably with BCI, though sometimes refers more specifically to interfaces that control physical devices like robotic arms rather than computer software.

C

Chronic Implant: A neural device designed to remain in the brain for extended periods (months to years), as opposed to acute recordings that last only hours or days. Chronic stability is essential for practical BCI applications.

Classifier: A machine learning algorithm that categorizes neural signals into different classes or commands (e.g., "move left," "move right," "click"). Support vector machines and neural networks are common BCI classifiers.

Closed-Loop System: A BCI that provides feedback to the user about their neural activity or the system's performance, allowing for real-time adjustment and learning. This contrasts with open-loop systems that provide no feedback.

Cochlear Implant: A neural prosthetic device that directly stimulates the auditory nerve to restore hearing in deaf individuals. Often considered the first successful clinical BCI application.

Common Average Reference (CAR): A signal processing technique that subtracts the average voltage across all electrodes from each individual electrode, helping to remove common noise and artifacts.

Convolutional Neural Network (CNN): A type of deep learning algorithm particularly effective at processing spatial patterns in data, increasingly used for analyzing EEG and other neural signals in BCIs.

D

Deep Brain Stimulation (DBS): A therapeutic technique that uses implanted electrodes to deliver electrical stimulation to specific brain regions, commonly used to treat Parkinson's disease, depression, and other neurological conditions.

Decoding: The process of interpreting neural signals to extract intended commands or information. This typically involves machine learning algorithms that learn to associate specific neural patterns with particular actions or thoughts.

Degrees of Freedom (DOF): The number of independent movement parameters that can be controlled. A typical human arm has seven degrees of freedom, while many BCI-controlled prosthetics currently offer fewer.

Drift (Signal): The gradual change in neural signal properties over time, often due to electrode movement, tissue changes, or shifts in neural activity patterns. Signal drift is a major challenge for long-term BCI stability.

E

Electrocardiogram (ECG/EKG): Recording of electrical activity from the heart, which can interfere with neural recordings and must be filtered out in BCI systems.

Electrode: A conductive element that detects or delivers electrical signals to neural tissue. Electrodes range from large surface electrodes to microscopic penetrating arrays that record from individual neurons.

Electroencephalography (EEG): Non-invasive recording of brain electrical activity through electrodes placed on the scalp. EEG provides excellent temporal resolution but limited spatial resolution due to signal attenuation through skull and scalp.

Electrocorticography (ECoG): Recording brain activity from electrodes placed directly on the brain surface, offering better signal quality than EEG while being less invasive than penetrating electrodes.

Electromyography (EMG): Recording of electrical activity from muscles, which can be used for prosthetic control but also represents a source of artifacts in neural recordings.

Encoding: The process by which neurons represent information through their firing patterns. Understanding neural encoding is crucial for designing effective BCIs.

Epilepsy: A neurological condition characterized by recurrent seizures, often treated with implanted devices that can detect and prevent seizures through electrical stimulation.

Event-Related Potential (ERP): A measured brain response that is the direct result of a specific sensory, cognitive, or motor event. P300 potentials are commonly used in BCI applications.

F

Feature Extraction: The process of identifying relevant characteristics from raw neural signals that can be used for classification. Common features include spectral power, spike rates, and signal amplitude.

Functional Magnetic Resonance Imaging (fMRI): A non-invasive imaging technique that measures brain activity through blood flow changes. While providing excellent spatial resolution, fMRI's slow temporal response limits its BCI applications.

Functional Electrical Stimulation (FES): A technique that uses electrical currents to activate paralyzed muscles, often combined with BCI control to restore motor function.

G

Gamma Rhythm: Brain oscillations in the 30-100 Hz frequency range, associated with conscious awareness, attention, and binding of sensory information. Some BCIs exploit gamma activity for control signals.

Glia: Supporting cells in the nervous system that can respond to electrode implantation by forming scar tissue, potentially degrading signal quality over time.

H

High-Frequency Oscillations: Brain rhythms above 30 Hz that often contain rich information about neural processing and can provide robust BCI control signals.

Hybrid BCI: A system that combines multiple input modalities (e.g., EEG with eye tracking) or multiple signal types (e.g., different EEG frequency bands) to improve performance and reliability.

Hyperparameter: Configuration settings for machine learning algorithms that must be tuned for optimal performance, such as learning rates, regularization parameters, or network architecture choices.

I

Impedance: The electrical resistance between an electrode and neural tissue, which affects signal quality. High impedance can indicate electrode problems or tissue reactions.

Implantable Pulse Generator (IPG): A battery-powered device that generates electrical stimulation patterns for therapeutic applications like deep brain stimulation or spinal cord stimulation.

Independent Component Analysis (ICA): A signal processing technique used to separate mixed neural signals into independent components, helping to remove artifacts and isolate signals of interest.

Informed Consent: The ethical and legal requirement that research participants understand the risks and benefits of experimental procedures before agreeing to participate in BCI studies.

Intracranial EEG (iEEG): Brain recording from electrodes placed inside the skull, providing higher signal quality than scalp EEG while being more invasive.

Invasive BCI: Brain-computer interfaces that require surgical implantation of electrodes or other devices within the skull, offering high signal quality but carrying surgical risks.

L

Local Field Potential (LFP): The electrical activity recorded from a population of neurons in a small brain region, representing the combined effect of many synaptic inputs. LFPs are commonly used in BCI applications.

Locked-In Syndrome: A condition where patients are conscious and cognitively intact but cannot move or speak due to brainstem damage. BCIs offer particular promise for communication in these patients.

M

Machine Learning: Algorithms that can learn patterns from data without being explicitly programmed, essential for decoding complex neural signals in modern BCIs.

Magnetoencephalography (MEG): A non-invasive technique that records magnetic fields produced by neural activity, offering better spatial resolution than EEG but requiring expensive specialized facilities.

Microelectrode Array: A device containing many small electrodes (typically 10-100 micrometers in diameter) that can record from individual neurons or small groups of neurons simultaneously.

Motor Cortex: The brain region responsible for planning and executing voluntary movements, frequently targeted in BCIs for controlling prosthetic devices or computers.

Motor Imagery: The mental rehearsal of movement without actual muscle activation, commonly used as a control strategy in non-invasive BCIs.

Multimodal Interface: A system that combines neural control with other input methods such as eye tracking, voice commands, or residual muscle activity to improve performance and user experience.

N

Near-Infrared Spectroscopy (NIRS): A non-invasive technique that measures brain activity through changes in blood oxygenation, offering a portable alternative to fMRI for some BCI applications.

Neuroplasticity: The brain's ability to reorganize and form new neural connections throughout life, which can help BCI users improve their control through practice and can complicate long-term BCI function.

Neurofeedback: A technique that provides real-time feedback about brain activity, allowing users to learn to control their neural signals voluntarily.

Non-Invasive BCI: Brain-computer interfaces that do not require surgery, typically using EEG, MEG, fMRI, or NIRS to record brain activity through the skull.

O

Optogenetics: A technique that uses light to control genetically modified neurons, offering precise spatial and temporal control of neural activity. Still experimental in humans but promising for future BCI applications.

Oscillations (Neural): Rhythmic patterns of electrical activity in the brain at various frequencies (alpha, beta, gamma, etc.), often used as control signals in BCIs.

P

P300: A positive voltage peak in EEG recordings that occurs about 300 milliseconds after a rare or unexpected stimulus, commonly used in BCI spelling systems and other applications.

Penetrating Electrode: A thin electrode inserted into brain tissue to record from neurons at specific depths, offering high signal quality but carrying higher risks than surface electrodes.

Population Vector Algorithm (PVA): A decoding method that combines the activity of multiple neurons to estimate intended movement direction, commonly used in motor BCIs.

Prosthetic Device: An artificial device designed to replace a missing or impaired body part, increasingly controlled through BCI technology for improved functionality.

Q

Quality of Life: A measure of well-being that considers physical health, psychological state, social relationships, and personal beliefs, often used to evaluate the success of BCI interventions.

R

Real-Time Processing: The ability of a BCI system to process neural signals and generate outputs with minimal delay (typically less than 100 milliseconds), essential for natural control of devices.

Rehabilitation: The process of helping patients recover function after injury or illness, increasingly incorporating BCI technology for motor and cognitive training.

Reinforcement Learning: A machine learning approach where algorithms learn through trial and error with reward feedback, useful for adaptive BCI systems that improve over time.

S

Semi-Invasive BCI: Brain-computer interfaces that place electrodes on the brain surface (ECoG) without penetrating deep into tissue, balancing signal quality with surgical risk.

Sensorimotor Rhythm (SMR): Brain oscillations in the 8-12 Hz range over motor cortex, which change with movement or motor imagery and are commonly used in BCI control.

Signal-to-Noise Ratio (SNR): A measure of how much useful signal is present compared to background noise, crucial for BCI performance. Higher SNR generally enables better decoding accuracy.

Spike: The action potential or firing of an individual neuron, represented as a brief voltage peak in neural recordings. Spike patterns contain rich information for BCI decoding.

Steady-State Visual Evoked Potential (SSVEP): Brain responses to flickering visual stimuli at specific frequencies, used in some BCI systems for device control through gaze direction.

Support Vector Machine (SVM): A machine learning algorithm commonly used for classifying neural signals in BCI applications, particularly effective with limited training data.

Synchronous BCI: A brain-computer interface that only accepts user input during specific time windows, often cued by external prompts. This provides more controlled conditions but less natural interaction.

T

Tetraplegia: Paralysis of all four limbs, typically resulting from spinal cord injury. BCI technology offers particular promise for restoring function to tetraplegic individuals.

Threshold: A signal level used to distinguish meaningful neural activity from background noise, crucial for detecting action potentials and other neural events.

Training (BCI): The process by which both the user and the system learn to work together effectively, involving practice sessions where users develop control skills while algorithms adapt to their neural patterns.

Transfer Learning: A machine learning technique where algorithms trained on one dataset or user can be adapted for new situations, potentially reducing training time for BCI users.

U

Unsupervised Learning: Machine learning algorithms that find patterns in data without labeled examples, useful for discovering neural signal structures and reducing artifacts.

Utah Array: A specific type of microelectrode array with 100 penetrating electrodes arranged in a 10x10 grid, commonly used in motor BCI research and clinical applications.

V

Visual Cortex: The brain region responsible for processing visual information, targeted by visual prosthetics and some BCI applications that provide artificial vision.

W

Wavelet Transform: A mathematical technique for analyzing signals that vary in frequency over time, useful for extracting features from neural signals for BCI decoding.

Wireless BCI: Neural interfaces that transmit data without physical connections, reducing infection risk and improving user mobility compared to wired systems.

Measurement Units in BCI Research

Microvolts (μV): Electrical potential measurements for neural signals (1 μV = 0.000001 volts)

Hertz (Hz): Frequency measurements for neural oscillations and sampling rates

Bits per second (bps): Information transfer rate in communication systems

Milliseconds (ms): Time measurements for neural response delays and system latency

Ohms (Ω): Electrical resistance/impedance measurements for electrode interfaces

---

This glossary provides fundamental terminology for understanding brain-computer interface technology. As the field rapidly evolves, new terms and concepts continue to emerge, requiring ongoing updates to technical vocabularies.

Appendix B: Timeline of BCI Development

Major Milestones from 1875 to Present

The Foundation Era (1875-1950)

1875

Luigi Galvani's Legacy Confirmed

- Richard Caton records first electrical activity from animal brains
- Demonstrates that brain tissue generates measurable electrical signals
- Lays scientific foundation for all future neural recording

1924

First Human Brain Recording

- Hans Berger records first human electroencephalogram (EEG)
- Documents alpha waves (8-12 Hz) from scalp electrodes
- **Publication**: "Über das Elektroenkephalogramm des Menschen" (*On the Human Electroencephalogram*)

1929

EEG Enters Medicine

- Berger publishes comprehensive EEG findings
- Establishes different brain wave patterns (alpha, beta, theta, delta)
- Medical community begins recognizing clinical potential

1935

First Clinical EEG Applications

- EEG used to diagnose epilepsy and brain tumors
- Frederic Gibbs and Hallowell Davis advance clinical applications
- EEG becomes standard neurological diagnostic tool

1943

Computational Neuroscience Born

- Warren McCulloch and Walter Pitts publish "A Logical Calculus of Ideas Immanent in Nervous Activity"
- Creates theoretical framework for artificial neural networks
- Establishes mathematical models of neural computation

The Exploration Era (1950-1970)

1950

First Neural Stimulation Experiments

- Wilder Penfield maps human brain cortex during surgery
- Demonstrates that electrical stimulation can evoke specific sensations and movements
- **Discovery:** Motor and sensory cortex organization in conscious patients

1957

Computer-Brain Interface Conceived

- Grey Walter demonstrates EEG control of simple devices

- Patients control slide projector using brain waves
- **Milestone**: First true brain-computer interface demonstration

1963

The Bull Experiment

- José Delgado stops charging bull with remote brain stimulation
- Demonstrates wireless control of animal behavior through neural implants
- **Publication**: "Physical Control of the Mind" sparks ethical debates
- **Impact**: Proves feasibility of implanted neural control systems

1964

First Cochlear Implant

- William House implants first cochlear device in human patient
- Single-channel system provides basic sound perception
- **Significance**: First successful neural prosthetic device

1969

Military Interest Begins

- DARPA funds early brain-computer interface research
- Focus on augmented soldier capabilities and prosthetic limbs
- Establishes pattern of military investment in neural technology

---

The Innovation Era (1970-1990)

1973

Term "Brain-Computer Interface" Coined

- Jacques Vidal publishes first paper using "brain-computer interface"
- **Publication**: "Toward Direct Brain-Computer Communication"
- Establishes BCI as distinct research field

1978

Multi-Channel Cochlear Implants

- Graeme Clark develops multi-electrode cochlear system
- Provides speech understanding for deaf patients
- **FDA Approval**: First commercially successful neural prosthetic

1980s

EEG-Based Communication Systems

- Farwell and Donchin develop P300-based spelling system
- Patients spell words by focusing attention on letters
- **Innovation**: Non-invasive brain-controlled communication

1988

Real-Time EEG Control

- Gert Pfurtscheller demonstrates motor imagery BCI
- Users control computer cursors through imagined movements
- **Breakthrough**: Self-paced, asynchronous brain control

1989

First Invasive Motor BCI

- Richard Andersen records from monkey motor cortex
- Demonstrates neural population vectors encode movement intention
- **Foundation**: Modern invasive motor BCI approaches

The Acceleration Era (1990-2010)

1998

First Human Invasive BCI

- Roy Bakay implants electrode in paralyzed patient Johnny Ray
- Patient learns to control computer cursor with neural signals
- **Significance**: Proves feasibility of chronic human neural implants

1999-2000

Monkey Cursor Control

- Duke University team (Nicolelis lab) demonstrates monkey cursor control
- Real-time decoding of movement intentions from 100+ neurons
- **Publication**: Multiple Nature and Science papers establish field credibility

2002

BrainGate Founded

- Cyberkinetics launches first major BCI clinical trial
- Utah Array implants in paralyzed patients
- **Goal**: Restore computer and prosthetic control

2004-2006

First Human Motor BCI Success

- Matthew Nagle (BrainGate) controls computer cursor and robotic arm
- **Achievement**: Tetraplegic patient plays computer games, controls TV
- **Media Impact**: Worldwide coverage brings BCIs to public attention

2008

Monkey Controls Robotic Arm

- Pittsburgh team demonstrates monkey feeding itself via robotic arm
- Neural control of complex, coordinated movements
- **Advancement**: Proves feasibility of natural prosthetic control

2009

FDA Approves BCI Clinical Trials

- Multiple BCI systems receive FDA Investigational Device Exemptions
- **Companies**: Cyberkinetics, Neural Dust, Blackrock Neurotech
- Regulatory pathway established for neural implants

The Translation Era (2010-2020)

2012

Jan Scheuermann Breakthrough

- Paralyzed woman controls robotic arm to feed herself chocolate
- **Innovation:** 7 degrees of freedom control with natural dexterity
- **Significance:** Demonstrates practical applications beyond cursor control

2014

First Paralyzed Person Walks

- Brazilian man uses BCI-controlled exoskeleton at World Cup
- EEG-based system provides crude walking control
- **Symbol:** BCIs gaining mainstream recognition

2015

Sensory Feedback Integration

- First BCI systems providing tactile feedback to users
- **Advancement:** Bidirectional brain-machine communication
- Users can "feel" through prosthetic limbs

2016

Memory Enhancement Trials

- Theodore Berger's team demonstrates memory prosthetic in monkeys
- **Application:** Hippocampal implants improve memory formation
- **Potential:** Treatment for Alzheimer's and traumatic brain injury

2017

Neuralink Founded

- Elon Musk establishes Neuralink Corporation
- **Mission:** Develop high-bandwidth brain-machine interfaces
- **Impact:** Massive media attention and venture capital investment

2018

Speech BCI Breakthroughs

- Multiple teams demonstrate direct neural speech decoding
- **Achievement:** Paralyzed patients "speak" through neural interfaces
- **Companies:** Facebook (Meta) launches major speech BCI program

2019

High-Bandwidth Demonstrations

- Neuralink shows monkey playing Pong with brain implant
- **Technical Advance:** 1,000+ electrode recording systems
- Wireless, high-resolution neural interfaces proven feasible

---

The Commercial Era (2020-Present)

2020

COVID-19 Accelerates Remote Healthcare

- Telemedicine adoption boosts interest in neural monitoring
- **Development:** Home-based BCI systems for rehabilitation
- Remote neural interfaces become research priority

2021

Major Venture Capital Investment

- Over $500 million invested in BCI companies
- **Key Players:** Kernel, Paradromics, Synchron receive major funding
- **Trend:** Commercial applications beyond medical use

2022

First Commercial Neural Implant Approvals

- Synchron receives FDA approval for Stentrode system
- **Innovation:** Minimally invasive neural interface via blood vessels
- **Significance:** First FDA-approved implantable BCI for ALS patients

2023

Neuralink Human Trials Begin

- FDA approves first human clinical trial for Neuralink device
- **PRIME Study:** Paralyzed patients controlling computers
- **Milestone:** High-profile entry into human testing phase

2024

Multi-Modal Integration

- BCI systems combine with AI assistants and VR/AR platforms
- **Development:** Brain-controlled metaverse interactions
- **Advancement:** Natural language processing from neural signals

2025

Regulatory Frameworks Established

- FDA publishes comprehensive BCI device guidelines

- **International**: EU and other regions develop neural technology regulations
- **Ethics:** International neuroethics standards proposed

---

www.ingramcontent.com/pod-product-compliance
Lightning Source LLC
LaVergne TN
LVHW052030200926
848481LV00005B/1630